The ESSENTIAL LAW DICTIONARY

es·sen·tial ADJ. Of the utmost importance.

Amy Hackney Blackwell

SPHINX® PUBLISHING
AN IMPRINT OF SOURCEBOOKS, INC.®
NAPERVILLE, ILLINOIS
www.SphinxLegal.com

First Edition: 2008

Published by: **Sphinx® Publishing, An imprint of Sourcebooks, Inc.®**

Naperville Office
P.O. Box 4410
Naperville, Illinois 60567-4410
(630) 961-3900
Fax: (620) 961-2168
www.sourcebooks.com
www.SphinxLegal.com

This publication is designed to provide accurate and authoritative information in regard to the subject matter covered. It is sold with the understanding that the publisher is not engaged in rendering legal, accounting, or other professional service. If legal advice or other expert assistance is required, the services of a competent professional person should be sought.
From a Declaration of Principles Jointly Adopted by a Committee of the American Bar Association and a Committee of Publishers and Associations

This product is not a substitute for legal advice.
Disclaimer required by Texas statutes.

Library of Congress Cataloging-in-Publication Data
Hackney Blackwell, Amy.
  The dictionary of essential legal terms / by Amy Hackney Blackwell. – 1st ed.
    p. cm.
  ISBN 978-1-57248-650-8 (pbk. : alk. paper) 1. Law–United States–Dictionaries. I. Title.
KF156.H33 2008
349.7303–dc22

                            2008008866

Printed and bound in Canada.
TR 10 9 8 7 6 5 4 3 2 1

CONTENTS

DEFINITIONS

1L. N. A first-year law student.

2L. N. A second-year law student.

3L. N. A third-year law student.

401(k) plan. N. A retirement savings plan run by a company for its employees that allows employees to save or invest part of their salary tax-free and often includes contributions by the employer.

419 scam. N. A common scam named for a section of the Nigerian criminal code in which scammers persuade victims to send them large sums of money in order to receive promised large payoffs that never arrive.

A

ABA. ABBRV. American Bar Association.

abandon. V. To intentionally give up a right or property without any plan of reclaiming it in the future; to desert a spouse or child. N. *abandonment*.

abatable nuisance. N. A nuisance that can be reduced.

abate. V. To decrease, reduce, or diminish; to end, dismiss, or temporarily suspend a lawsuit. N. *abatement*. ADJ. *abatable*.

abatement of a legacy. N. A reduction in the amount of a legacy after the payment of debts owed by the person who granted the legacy.

abatement of taxes. N. A reduction in the amount owed by the taxee.

abdicate. V. To renounce a responsibility or position; generally used to describe the act of a sovereign giving up a throne or an official renouncing the privileges and duties of his or her office; also used to describe a government or official failing to fulfill responsibilities or duties. N. *abdication*.

abduct. V. (1) To take or carry away a person illegally by force or persuasion. (2) To take away or detain unlawfully a female, intending to force her into marriage, concubinage, or prostitution. (3) For a woman to entice a husband to abandon his wife for her. N. *abduction*. See also *kidnap, alienation of affections*.

abet. V. To help or encourage someone else to commit a crime.

abettor. N. A person who abets or instigates a crime; an abettor shares criminal intent with the person who in fact commits the crime. See also *aid and abet, accessory, accomplice*.

abeyance. N. A state of temporary disuse or suspension; an unsettled state; the condition of an estate in fee or freehold during a lapse in succession with no current titleholder or owner.

ab initio. ADJ. *(Latin)* From the beginning; used to describe contracts, marriages, deeds, etc., that are either valid or void from their inception.

ABM. ABBRV. Anti-ballistic missile.

abode. N. A home or place of residence; a domicile.

abolish. V. To end or do away with; generally used to describe formally ending an institution, system, or custom, such as slavery or a tax. N. *abolition*.

aboriginal. ADJ. Indigenous, native to a place from earliest times.

aboriginal title. N. The exclusive rights of American Indians to lands and waters they occupied before the United States claimed them.

abortion. N. The premature ending of a pregnancy; in legal context, generally refers to a deliberate termination, though the term can also apply to spontaneous natural expulsion of a fetus before it becomes viable. V. *abort*.

abortionist. N. Someone who performs abortions.

about. ADV. Approximately; near in time, degree, or quality.

abridge. V. To shorten or condense while retaining the sense of the original document. N. *abridgement*.

abrogate. V. To repeal, revoke, or end; particularly applies to laws, rights, orders, or formal agreements. N. *abrogation*.

abscond. V. To depart quickly and secretly in order to avoid arrest or a lawsuit, particularly after committing some crime such as theft; to leave the jurisdiction of local courts or to hide from them.

abstain. V. To refrain from doing something, such as voting. N. *abstention*.

abstention doctrine. N. A policy that allows federal courts to relinquish jurisdiction over a matter and allow a state court to decide a federal constitutional question or a matter of state law.

abstract. ADJ. Existing only in thought or theory and not in reality N. (1) A summary, abridgement, or condensation of a longer document. (2) That which is abstract or theoretical, often used in the phrase "in the abstract." V. (1) To summarize or abridge. (2) To remove something from something else, as in abstracting money from a bank. N. *abstraction*.

abstract of record. N. A short summary of the history of a case taken from the trial court record to show an appellate court what issues were considered at trial.

abstract of title. N. A short history of a piece of land tracing title through all conveyances, transfers, and liens or encumbrances; used to prove an owner's right to the property.

absurd. ADJ. Illogical, incongruous, and obviously untrue. N. *absurdity*.

abuse. V. To misuse; to wrong or mistreat a person or animal physically, mentally, or sexually. N. Improper use; corrupt acts; cruel treatment of another; violence or sexual assault toward another.

abuse, child. N. Cruel treatment of a child.

abuse of discretion. N. A decision or judgment made by a trial court that is inappropriate, inconsistent with the facts of the matter, and not according to precedent or established law.

abuse of process. N. Using the courts and legal process for some improper purpose, such as initiating a lawsuit for revenge or intimidation.

abut. V. To share a boundary; to touch; to adjoin.

accelerate. V. To go faster; to increase; to shorten the time in which a future event will occur, particularly used to discuss the vesting of property rights. N. *acceleration*.

accelerated cost recovery system. N. An accounting method that writes off the cost of a fixed asset over a period of time. See also *cash method*. ABBRV. *ACRS*.

acceleration clause. N. A clause in a contract or mortgage that causes the entire payment to become due if a specific event occurs; common in installment contracts, in which the entire debt becomes due if the buyer fails to make payments on time.

accept. V. To receive willingly; to agree voluntarily; implies the right to refuse.

acceptance. N. In contract law, voluntarily consenting to an offer, which then creates a binding contract.

acceptance, conditional. N. Agreeing to accept an offer if a certain condition is fulfilled.

acceptance, implied. N. An agreement that is implied from a person's words and deeds rather than from explicit acceptance of the offer.

access. N. An opportunity to do or use something; a means of approach or communication; an opportunity for sexual intercourse; a property owner's right to go to and from his or her land.

accession. N. (1) An addition; something added to an existing body of property; the right to ownership of one's property even after its form has been altered (e.g., if A cuts down B's tree and makes it into a chair, B can still claim ownership of the chair by accession). (2) The attainment of a rank or title, as in a monarch's accession to a throne. (3) Accepting or joining a treaty or association. V. *accede*.

accessory. N. (1) Something added to another object as a decoration or to make it more useful. (2) Someone who helps another person commit a crime.

accessory after the fact. N. A person who aids a felon, knowing that he or she has committed a felony and intending to help him or her escape punishment. See also *accomplice, aid and abet, conspiracy*.

accessory before the fact. N. Someone who encourages or helps another plan to commit a felony but who is not present during the commission of the crime.

accident. N. A chance occurrence or incident; an unforeseen and unintended event; often used to describe unfortunate occurrences, such as injury or mishap. ADJ. *accidental*.

accident, unavoidable. N. An accident that occurs despite the exercise of due care and common sense; an accident that could not have been prevented.

accommodate. V. To meet someone's wishes or demands; to adapt to; to do something as a favor, without consideration. N. *accommodation*.

accommodation loan. N. A loan given without any consideration or security out of friendship or the lender's desire to aid the borrower.

accommodation note. N. A note signed by an accommodation maker. Also called accommodation paper.

accommodation party (maker). N. A person who signs his or her name to a note or commercial paper to lend credit to another signer, the accommodated party, without consideration and thereby assuming liability for the debt; a cosigner or surety.

accomplice. N. Someone who knowingly and willingly helps another commit a crime. See also *aid and abet, accessory*.

accord. V. To give or grant; to agree. N. An agreement; a treaty; an agreement between two parties that settles a dispute and provides satisfaction to the wronged party.

accord and satisfaction. N. A means of ending a dispute by forming an agreement (the accord) that one party will pay the other some consideration (the satisfaction, often less than the amount originally agreed to) and that this will discharge any remaining obligation.

account. N. (1) A statement of financial events, debits, and credits. (2) A body of funds held by one institution or individual on behalf of another. (3) A description of an event.

accountability. N. Responsibility; the state of being answerable for something.

accountant. A person trained in accounting, bookkeeping, and taxes.

accountant, certified public. N. An accountant who has passed an official examination and fulfilled other requirements and has thus been licensed as an accountant by his or her state. ABBRV. *CPA*.

account for. V. To provide a satisfactory explanation for something.

accounting. N. (1) A system of keeping financial records. (2) An action in equity to settle the finances of a partnership.

accounting method. N. The method used by a business to calculate its income and expenditures for tax purposes. See also *accrual method, cash method.*

account payable. N. Debts owed by a business.

account receivable. N. Money owed to a business.

accredit. V. To recognize officially or authorize; to attribute; to send someone to another place (often internationally) as an official envoy.

accrete. V. To grow or increase by accumulation.

accretion. N. (1) Growing or adding on to something; typically used to describe natural growth such as the accumulation of sediment at the mouth of a river. (2) Income to a trust that comes from some unusual source. (3) The right of heirs and legatees to claim the property of any other heir or legatee who refuses to accept it or dies before inheriting.

accrual method. N. An accounting method that records incurred expenses and income earned during a period even if all money has not been paid or received; businesses that maintain inventory must use this method.

accrue. V. (1) To accumulate or increase; to receive at regular intervals; to become due. (2) To come into existence as a cause of action. N. *accrual.*

accrued interest. N. Interest due on the principal.

accumulate. v. To gradually acquire or gather an increasing amount of something. N. *accumulation*.

accusatory. ADJ. Accusing someone of a crime.

accusatory body. N. A group such as a grand jury that hears evidence and decides that someone should be accused of a crime.

accusatory instrument. N. A document that sets forth an accusation.

accusatory stage. N. The stage of criminal procedure after the accused has been arrested and is being interrogated.

accuse. v. To charge someone with a crime; to institute legal proceedings against a suspected criminal. N. *accusation*.

accused. N. Someone charged with a crime.

ACLU. ABBRV. American Civil Liberties Union.

acknowledge. v. To admit or confirm; to accept responsibility. N. *acknowledgement*.

acquiesce. v. To accept without protest; to give implied consent by silence. N. *acquiescence*. See also *laches*.

acquiescence, estoppel by. N. Estoppel that arises if a party has the opportunity to object to something but gives implied consent by inaction.

acquire. v. To gain or obtain; to become the owner of something.

acquisition. N. The process of acquiring; something acquired.

acquit. v. To set free or release; to absolve of criminal liability. N. *acquittal*.

acre. N. A unit of land with an area of 43,560 square feet (4,840 square yards).

ACRS. ABBRV. Accelerated Cost Recovery System.

act. V. To do something, usually voluntarily. N. (1) An action or deed. (2) A law or written ordinance passed by Congress or another legislative body; when done by Congress, this is called an act of Congress.

acting. ADJ. Temporarily performing the duties of a position or office without officially holding that position or office.

action. N. *(Latin)* (1) A proceeding or an action; the right to pursue a lawsuit. (2) A court proceeding; a lawsuit; a formal complaint brought by one party to prosecute another or demand rights within a court of law. See also *case.*

actionable. ADJ. Forming the legal basis of a cause of action.

action at equity. N. An action brought in a court of equity.

action at law. N. An action brought in a court of law.

actio non. N. *(Latin)* No action; a pleading of nonperformance; a nonsuit.

active. ADJ. Doing purposefully; currently in action; the opposite of passive.

active concealment. N. Intentional and purposeful concealment.

active duty. N. The state of serving full-time in the military; see *reserve.*

active negligence. N. Negligence that occurs through some positive act as opposed to passive inaction.

active participant. N. Someone who engages in some conduct that is part of the commission of a crime.

activism, judicial. N. The practice of making legal decisions based on beliefs about individual rights and attitudes rather than precedent and statute.

activist judge. N. A judge who uses his or her position on the bench to make decisions that reflect personal attitudes and beliefs instead of applying the letter of the law or following precedent.

act of God. N. Something that happens as a result of natural forces that cannot be controlled by humans, such as storms, earthquakes, or floods. Also called act of providence.

act of sale. N. An official document certifying that a sale has occurred, signed by the parties and verified by witnesses and a notary.

actor. N. A person who acts; one who performs an action.

actual. ADJ. Real; existing in fact.

actual damages. N. Damages awarded for real injuries as opposed to nominal or punitive damages.

actual residence. N. The place where someone actually lives, as opposed to a legal residence. See also *constructive*.

actual value. N. A value awarded in condemnation proceedings based on the price that a property would probably fetch from a willing buyer to a willing seller.

actuarial tables. N. Statistical tables that predict the likely ages that people will reach; used for such purposes as calculating the value of annuities or damages stemming from premature deaths; also called *life tables*.

actuary. N. Someone who uses statistics to calculate insurance rates. ADJ. *actuarial*.

actus reus. N. *(Latin)* The guilty act; a criminal action. See also *mens rea*.

ADA. ABBRV. Americans with Disabilities Act.

add. V. To join together; unite; attach.

ad damnum. N. *(Latin)* To the damage; the clause in a complaint in which a plaintiff specifies the damages he or she seeks.

addendum. N. Something that is added on; usually written material added to the end of a document.

addict. N. Someone who uses, does, or consumes something habitually and who is dependent on that substance or activity; usually applies to those who are dependent on drugs or alcohol and cannot control their consumption thereof.

addition. N. Something added to something else; a new structure added to an existing building.

additur. N. *(Latin)* A trial court's increase in the amount of damages awarded to a plaintiff by a jury; this can be done with the defendant's consent if the court rules that the jury's award is inadequate, and on the condition that the plaintiff's motion for a new trial will be denied.

ADEA. ABBRV. Age Discrimination in Employment Act.

adeem. V. To remove, revoke, or take away; to take away a legacy or future bequest in advance.

ademption. N. Revocation of a legacy by a testator before the testator's death, sometimes by giving the recipient the property mentioned in the will before death, and sometimes by disposing of the property in such a way that it is impossible to carry out the will.

adequate. ADJ. Sufficient, satisfactory.

adequate care. N. Care appropriate to the risk in question.

adequate compensation. N. Under eminent domain, the market value of property when taken.

adequate remedy at law. N. A remedy that provides complete and appropriate relief.

adhesion. N. Joining; clinging to; sticking together; allegiance. V. *adhere*.

adhesion contract. N. A contract offered to one party by another on a take-it-or-leave-it basis, in which the offering party creates all the details of the contract and the receiving party has no opportunity to bargain or modify the contract. This is common with standard form contracts. Often there is doubt as to whether an adhesion contract is valid because one party has so little bargaining power. See also *unconscionable*.

ad hoc. ADJ. *(Latin)* For this; arranged for one particular purpose. ADV. *ad hoc*.

ad hominem. ADJ. *(Latin)* To the person; appealing to the emotions instead of to logic and reason. ADV. *ad hominem*.

ad infinitum. ADV. *(Latin)* To infinity; repeatedly; forever.

adjacent. ADJ. Next to; near; neighboring.

adjective law. N. Rules of procedure; the rules that administer substantive law.

adjoining. ADJ. Joined with; touching; in contact with.

adjourn. v. To postpone; to suspend; to stop with the intent of resuming later.

adjudicate. v. To judge; to formally issue a final judgment in a court proceeding. Synonymous with adjudge. N. *adjudication*.

adjudge. v. To decide; to pass judgment; to sentence.

adjust. v. To alter; to make satisfactory; to remove discrepancies; to settle.

adjusted basis. N. Basis plus additions to capital minus depreciation.

adjusted gross income. N. Gross income minus expenses and capital loss deduction.

adjuster. N. A person who settles things, especially insurance matters; one who determines the amount of a claim against an insurer and then agrees on a settlement with the insured.

ad litem. ADJ. *(Latin)* For the lawsuit; for the purposes of the lawsuit being prosecuted.

ad litem, guardian. N. Someone appointed to act in a lawsuit on behalf of a child or incapacitated party.

administer. v. To manage; to run (a business or other operation); to make someone take an oath; to enforce a decree.

administration. N. The process of managing or running something; the people who manage something.

administrative agency. N. A governmental organization that implements a particular piece of legislation, such as workers' compensation or tax law.

administrative law. N. The body of laws that governs administrative agencies.

administrative law judge. N. The officer who presides over administrative hearings. This officer is not a judge of law; he or she may administer oaths, hear testimony, make determinations of fact, and recommend or make decisions.

Administrative Procedure Act. N. A federal law that governs the proceedings of federal administrative agencies.

administrator. N. A person appointed by a court to handle the estate of someone who dies intestate, i.e., without a will. FEM. *administratrix*. See also *executor*.

admiralty and maritime jurisdiction. N. Jurisdiction over events happening on the seas, oceans, and navigable waters.

admiralty court. N. A court that hears disputes related to admiralty and maritime matters.

admissible. ADJ. Acceptable; valid; able to be admitted.

admissible evidence. N. Evidence that is proper to admit at trial because it is relevant to the matter at hand. See also *admit*, *evidence*.

admit. V. (1) To allow in; to accept as evidence (2) To acknowledge that something is true; to confess to a crime. N. *admission*.

adopt. V. (1) To make one's own; to accept; to choose. (2) To create a legal parent-child relationship between people unrelated by blood. N. *adoption*.

adult. N. A fully grown person; one who has reached the age of majority.

adult entertainment. N. Entertainment not suitable for children, typically erotic or sexual acts or movies; pornography.

adulterate. V. To corrupt; to mix into a pure or good substance something of poorer quality. N. *adulteration*.

adultery. N. Voluntary sexual congress between a married person and someone who is not his or her spouse. ADJ. *adulterous*.

ad valorem. ADJ. *(Latin)* According to the value; in proportion to value.

ad valorem tax. N. A tax assessed on the value of property.

advance. V. To move forward or make progress; to approach; to pay money or some other payment before it is due, as when an author receives an advance before a book is written. N. Money paid before it is due; money or other objects given on credit, with some future repayment anticipated.

advance directive. N. A document such as a living will or durable power of attorney that describes the kind of medical care a person wishes to receive if he or she becomes incapacitated.

advancement. N. A portion of an anticipated inheritance paid before the death of the testator (usually a parent to a child) that is then deducted from the recipient's share of the estate after the testator's death.

advance sheets. N. Recent judicial opinions published in pamphlet or loose-leaf form that are later compiled into bound volumes of regional reporters; hardbound collections of court opinions.

adventure. N. A hazardous and risky enterprise or activity; often used in marine insurance policies as a synonym for "peril."

adversary. N. Opponent; opposing counsel.

adversary proceeding. N. A hearing or trial with opposing parties, one seeking relief from the other, and that ends with one party receiving a favorable outcome at the expense of the other. See also *case*.

adverse. ADJ. Against; opposed; contrary; hostile.

adverse possession. N. A method of acquiring property without buying it; if a person uses land not belonging to him or her in a manner that is open (so that the owner knows about it or should know), but without permission of the owner, continuously, actually, and exclusively for a period of time prescribed by statute (usually a number of years), then a court will find that the person has earned title to the land.

advertise. V. To describe publicly in order to promote sales or solicit applications; to announce; to call to public attention.

advertisement. N. A public notice promoting a product or service or soliciting applications.

advertising. N. The practice of creating advertisements.

advice. N. Guidance; suggestions; recommendations intended to help someone; the opinions and recommendations given to clients by lawyers.

advise. V. To counsel; to recommend a course of action; to offer helpful suggestions. ADJ. ***advisory***.

advisory opinion. N. An opinion rendered by a judge or court that indicates how the court would rule on a question without actually ruling on some adversary proceeding; an advisory opinion is only informative and is not binding.

advocacy. N. Pleading or arguing for a cause.

advocacy, trial. N. Arguing for a cause in court as part of a trial.

advocate. N. Someone who supports a cause or argues for something; someone who defends another; a legal counselor or representative. V. To argue in support or defense of; to recommend.

adware. N. A computer program that automatically displays advertisements on a computer, often bundled with another program that users buy for actual use. See also *bundling*.

aesthetic value. N. The value of something due to its beauty or artistic worth rather than its practical use.

affect. V. To have an effect on; to influence; to change.

affiant. N. Someone who makes and swears to an affidavit.

affidavit. N. A written statement of facts whose truth is confirmed by oath of the party making it, used as evidence in court.

affiliate. V. To associate with; to join officially. N. A person or organization allied with or officially joined to a larger body.

affiliation. N. The condition of being affiliated.

affinity. N. (1) A relationship; fondness or liking. (2) The degree of relationship between people who are related by marriage. See also *consanguinity*.

affirm. V. To confirm; state as fact; ratify; to declare that a previous judgment is correct.

affirmation. N. The act of confirming that something is true. It can be used as a substitute for an oath in the case of religious or ethical objections to swearing.

affirmative action. N. Deliberate and positive efforts to help victims of discrimination by remedying effects of past discrimination and preventing future discrimination.

affirmative defense. N. In pleading, a response to a complaint that constitutes a defense and justification for the defendant's actions instead of attacking the truth of the plaintiff's allegations; affirmative defenses include self-defense, assumption of risk, estoppel, and insanity.

affirmative misconduct. N. A deliberate act done by someone who knows it is wrong; deliberately misrepresenting a fact or concealing a fact.

affirmative relief. N. Relief or compensation granted to a defendant in a lawsuit.

affix. V. To attach; fasten to something.

AFL-CIO. ABBRV. American Federation of Labor and Congress of Industrial Organizations.

aforesaid. ADJ. Said earlier; previously mentioned.

aforethought. ADJ. Premeditated; planned in advance.

a fortiori. ADJ. *(Latin)* With a stronger reason; used in argument to describe a proposition that must be true because it is a subcategory of something that is true. ADV. *a fortiori.*

after-acquired. ADJ. Acquired subsequent to a particular time or event.

after-acquired property. N. (1) Property a debtor acquires after concluding an agreement putting up other property as security for a loan. (2) Property acquired by a bankrupt after filing for bankruptcy.

after-acquired title. N. A doctrine providing that if someone sells property he or she does not own but then acquires the title to it, the buyer receives the good title.

after the fact. ADJ. Subsequent to a particular event. See also *accessory*.

against. PREP. Opposed to; contrary.

against interest. ADJ. Describes a statement or admission that is disadvantageous to the person making it.

against the law. ADJ. Illegal; also describes a court decision made despite insufficient evidence or material issues.

against the (manifest) weight of the evidence. ADJ. Not supported by the evidence presented at trial, or based on false evidence; the evidence clearly leading to the opposite conclusion.

against the will. ADJ. Describes the state of mind of a victim of robbery or rape.

age discrimination. N. Unfair treatment in the workplace and in hiring based on age; prohibited by the federal Age Discrimination in Employment Act of 1967.

Age Discrimination in Employment Act. N. A federal law that prohibits discrimination against people on the basis of age. ABBRV. *ADEA*.

agency. N. (1) A relationship in which one person, the agent, is authorized to act on behalf of the other, the principal. (2) A department or group that performs a specific task for the government. (3) A business that provides a specific service, often arranging transactions between customers.

agent. N. A person authorized to act for another person, the principal, in specific or unlimited ways.

agent, insurance. N. Someone authorized to sell insurance policies on behalf of an insurance company.

agent, real estate. N. Someone authorized to sell or rent property on behalf of other people.

age of consent. N. (1) The age at which a person may marry without his or her parents' permission. (2) The age at which a person may consent to have sexual intercourse without causing his or her sexual partner to be guilty of an offense such as statutory rape or sexual assault.

age of majority. N. The age at which a person becomes a legal adult, responsible for his or her own actions, and able to enter into contracts and vote.

age of reason. N. The age at which a child is deemed responsible for his or her own actions, usually 7 years of age.

aggravate. V. To make worse. N. *aggravation*. See also *simple*.

aggravated assault. N. Assault made worse than simple assault by the addition of aggravating circumstances, such as extreme indifference to human life or the use of a deadly weapon.

aggravating circumstances. N. Circumstances that increase the severity of a crime or tort.

aggregate. N. The sum of several parts; the entire amount of something. V. To combine several elements into one whole, as when several causes of action are joined into a single lawsuit or several people are combined to form a group for a class action. N. *aggregation*.

aggrieved. ADJ. Feeling anger at some injury or unfair treatment.

aggrieved party. N. Someone who has been injured, suffered a loss, or whose rights or property are at risk.

aging of accounts. N. Arranging accounts in chronological order of days outstanding.

agrarian. ADJ. Having to do with land and agriculture.

agree. V. To concur; to consent; to settle.

agreement. N. A mutual understanding between two or more parties; a meeting of minds. It often leads to a contract.

aid and abet. V. To knowingly help someone commit a crime. See also *accessory, accomplice.*

air rights. N. Rights to use the air above land; air rights accompany land ownership of land, with some limitations, e.g., a landowner has the right to recover damages from airlines that interfere with his or her use of the land, but is not allowed to pollute the air.

aka. ABBRV. Also known as. See also *alias.*

alderman. N. A city or town official or legislator; a councilman.

aleatory. ADJ. Random, uncertain, depending on chance.

aleatory contract. N. A contract whose performance depends on some random event, such as an insurance contract.

alias. N. A fake or alternate identity. ADV. Used to indicate the use of a false name, e.g., "Samuel Clemens, alias Mark Twain."

alibi. N. A defense in which the defendant claims to have been someplace other than the scene of a crime when the crime was committed and produces evidence to prove it, thus proving that it was physically impossible for him or her to have committed the crime in question.

alien. N. A foreigner; someone born in another country who has not become a citizen of his or her country of residence. ADJ. (1) Foreign. (2) Strange, unfamiliar. See also *resident alien*.

alienable. ADJ. Able to be transferred.

alienate. V. To transfer property from one person to another. N. *alienation*.

alienation of affections. N. The tort of maliciously interfering with a marriage, resulting in damage to the marital relationship.

alimony. N. An allowance ordered by the court that one spouse pays to the other after a divorce or separation for the support and maintenance of the recipient.

allege. V. To claim; to assert; to state in a pleading what one intends to prove at trial. N. *allegation*.

allen charge. N. A charge by the court to a deadlocked jury admonishing them to work together to reach a verdict, and especially encouraging the holders of a minority opinion to listen to the arguments of the majority and to let themselves be convinced if possible. This is prohibited in some states.

allocate. V. To distribute for a particular purpose; to assign; to allot. In taxation, to allot portions of income to different purposes. N. *allocation*. ADJ. *allocable*.

allocution. N. A speech by a trial judge to a criminal defendant asking the defendant if he or she would like to make a statement on his or her own behalf, or asking if the defendant has any legal reason why he or she should not be sentenced if the jury's verdict is to convict.

allot. v. To apportion; to distribute portions of something to several individuals; to allocate something to someone.

allotment. N. The amount of something allocated to someone; a portion or share.

allow. v. To permit; to acquiesce; to accept as true.

allowance. N. (1) The amount that is permitted. (2) A sum of money paid to someone regularly.

alluvion. N. Land formed by the accumulation of silt on the banks or at the mouth of a stream or river. See also *accrete*.

also known as. ADJ. See *alias*.

alter. v. To change or modify. N. *alteration*.

alteration, material. N. A change in the language of a contract that affects the rights defined by the contract.

alter ego. N. *(Latin)* Other self; an alternative personality. In corporate law, a doctrine that allows the court to find an individual responsible for acts done in the name of a corporation.

alternative dispute resolution. N. Methods for settling disputes without recourse to litigation, including arbitration, mediation, and conciliation.

alternative pleading. N. A form of pleading in which the pleader sets forth two or more different and possibly inconsistent versions of his or her claim or defense.

ambiguity. N. Uncertainty of meaning; doubt. ADJ. *ambiguous*.

ambulance chaser. N. A derogatory term for a lawyer who represents plaintiffs in personal injury cases.

amend. V. To fix; to improve; to modify or revise a document. N. *amendment*.

amends. N. Reparations; something done to make up for a wrong done to someone else.

American Bar Association. N. A national association of lawyers and law students. ABBRV. *ABA*.

American Civil Liberties Union. N. A national organization dedicated to protecting constitutionally guaranteed civil rights and liberties. ABBRV. *ACLU*.

American Digest System. N. A digest of U.S. cases arranged chronologically and by subject, serving as a guide to American case law.

American Federation of Labor and Congress of Industrial Organizations. N. U.S. trade union organization made up of over fifty national and international trade unions representing over ten million workers. ABBRV. *AFL-CIO*.

Americans with Disabilities Act. N. A federal statute prohibiting discrimination against disabled people in jobs, transportation, and services. ABBRV. *ADA*.

amicus curiae. N. *(Latin)* Friend of the court; someone who is not a party to a lawsuit but who has a strong interest in the subject matter of a case and petitions the court for permission to file a brief providing information on the matter to aid the court in rendering its decision; such a brief is called an amicus curiae brief or amicus brief.

amnesty. N. An official pardon granted by a government to a group of people forgiving them for past crimes, usually political crimes such as treason or draft evasion.

amortize. V. To spread out the payment of a debt by periodically paying a portion of interest and capital; to pay off a debt such as a mortgage in installments; to write off the cost of an asset over time. N. *amortization*.

anarchist. N. A person who wishes to bring about a state of anarchy.

anarchy. N. A political system characterized by an absence of government and law-enforcement mechanisms and complete freedom for individuals; a state of lawlessness or disorder resulting from a lack of governing authority.

ancestor. N. A person from whom one is descended.

ancestry. N. A line of family descent.

ancient. ADJ. Old; having existed since the distant past.

ancient writings. N. In evidence law, old (twenty or thirty years old) documents kept in official custody, presumed to be genuine without express proof.

ancillary. ADJ. Supplementary; additional; supporting.

ancillary jurisdiction. N. Jurisdiction claimed by a federal district court to adjudicate matters raised as part of an existing controversy, even though the court would not ordinarily have jurisdiction over the matter. See also *supplemental jurisdiction*.

ancillary suit. N. A suit that grows out of an existing or prior suit in the same court.

animo. ADJ. *(Latin)* Intentionally.

animo, quo. ADJ. *(Latin)* With what intent.

animo testandi. ADJ. *(Latin)* Intending to make a will.

animus. N. *(Latin)* Will, intent.

animus donandi. N. *(Latin)* Intent to give.

annex. V. To add something to something else; to join; to unite. N. An addition to a building or document.

annexation. N. The act of adding or joining one thing to another.

annotate. V. To add notes to a text explaining it or commenting on it; often done to court cases and statutes. N. *annotation.* ADJ. *annotated.*

annual report. N. A yearly financial report prepared by a corporation for its stockholders, audited by an independent certified public accountant, and filed with the Securities and Exchange Commission on Form 10-K, including a balance sheet, income statement, and other information.

annuitant. N. One who receives an annuity.

annuity. N. A fixed sum paid to a person periodically for a set period of time, often for life.

annul. V. (1) To declare something invalid; to abolish; to make nonexistent. (2) To declare that a marriage was never legally valid and therefore never existed. N. *annulment.* See also *divorce.*

answer. N. (1) A response; a reaction. (2) A pleading submitted by a defendant in response to a plaintiff's complaint, containing denials of allegations, affirmative defenses, and counterclaims. V. To respond; to file an answer to a complaint with the court.

antenuptial. ADJ. Before marriage.

antenuptial agreement. N. An agreement entered into by prospective spouses before their marriage, to take effect upon marriage. It usually contains provisions about support and distribution of property in the event of divorce or separation. See also *prenuptial agreement*.

anti-ballistic missile. N. A defensive missile designed to meet and destroy a ballistic missile, i.e., a missile carrying some nuclear, chemical, biological, or other agent intended to inflict harm on its victims. ABBRV. *ABM*.

anticipate. V. (1) To do something before its proper time. (2) To expect, to predict. N. *anticipation*. ADJ. *anticipatory*.

anticipatory breach of contract. N. A breach of contract that occurs when one party announces before the time scheduled for performance that he or she will not perform according to the contract.

anticipatory offense. N. A crime whose purpose is to commit a crime, such as conspiracy.

Anticybersquatting Consumer Protection Act. N. A federal law enacted in 1999 that makes cybersquatting a wrongful act subject to civil liability.

anti-lapse statute. N. A law that provides for the heirs of a devisee to inherit the devisee's share of an inheritance if the devisee dies before the testator, instead of allowing the bequest to lapse as it would have under common law; e.g., if a mother dies before her father, her children can inherit her share of their grandfather's estate.

antitrust. ADJ. Intended to prevent monopolies and trusts and to promote competition in business. See also *Sherman Antitrust Act, Clayton Act*.

APEC. ABBRV. Asia-Pacific Economic Cooperation.

a posteriori. ADJ. (*Latin*) Relating to knowledge gained through recent observation or experience. See also *a priori*.

apparent. ADJ. Obvious; evident; true as far as one can see.

apparent authority. N. The authority an agent gains when a principal allows a third party to believe that the agent has such authority, whether or not it is part of the agent's actual authority.

apparent defect. N. A defect that can readily be seen on inspection.

appeal. V. To request a higher court to review a case that has been decided by a lower court and render a new decision, either a reversal or a new trial. N. *appeal*.

appeals court. N. A court that can hear appeals; also called a *court of appeals* or an *appellate court*.

appear. V. To come into court as a party to a lawsuit and submit to the court's jurisdiction. N. *appearance*.

appearance, general. N. An ordinary appearance in which the party is subject to the court's jurisdiction.

appearance, special. N. An appearance in which the party appears to attack the court's jurisdiction over him or her.

appellant. N. One who files an appeal.

appellate. ADJ. Having to do with appeals.

appellate court. N. A court that reviews decisions made by lower courts or administrative agencies and does not hear new cases.

appellee. ADJ. The party against whom an appeal is filed; the party who prevailed at trial in the lower court. See also *respondent*.

application. N. A computer program; software that performs a particular task, such as a word processor, a spreadsheet, or a Web browser.

appoint. V. To select, choose, or designate; to assign someone a job.

appointee. N. One who has been appointed.

appointment. N. (1) The designation of a person to do a job. (2) A person appointed to a position. See also *power of appointment*.

apportion. V. (1) To divide something and assign or allocate portions of it to different parties. (2) To distribute legislative seats among the parties to be represented. N. *apportionment*.

appraise. V. To assess the value of something; to evaluate. N. *appraisal*.

appreciate. V. (1) To grow in value. (2) To understand; to realize fully the implications of something.

appreciation. N. The increase in an item's market value over a period of time; the difference between an item's cost basis and fair market value.

appropriate. V. (1) To take something for one's own; often used to describe theft. (2) To allocate money or other items for a particular purpose. N. *appropriation*.

appurtenance. N. Something attached or appended to something else.

appurtenant. ADJ. Belonging to and necessary to the full use of a larger property.

a priori. ADJ. (*Latin*) From theoretical deduction. See also *a posteriori*.

arbiter. N. A referee; someone appointed by a court to settle a dispute by the rules of law or equity. See also *arbitrator*.

arbitrage. N. A financial transaction in which securities or goods are simultaneously bought in one market and sold in another; price differences in the different markets produce a profit.

arbitrary. ADJ. At whim or at random instead of according to logic or rules; capricious.

arbitrary and capricious. ADJ. Describes a decision made according to whim and without regard to facts or law.

arbitration. N. A form of dispute resolution in which a neutral third party renders a decision after both parties speak for themselves at a hearing. See also *arbitrator*.

arbitration clause. N. A clause in a contract that requires disputes under the contract to be submitted to arbitration; such clauses are designed to avoid the litigation of disputes.

arbitrator. N. A neutral person appointed or chosen to settle a dispute by hearing arguments from both parties and then rendering a decision at his or her own discretion, not bound by rules of law or equity. See also *arbiter*.

archive. N. A place where old records, articles, documents, or books are kept; a place on a website or computer where old articles are stored and can be accessed.

arg. ABBRV. Arguendo.

arguendo. ADV. (*Latin*) Arguing; for the sake of argument; hypothetically. ABBRV. *arg.*

argument. N. A set of reasons given in logical order intended to persuade hearers of a particular conclusion; a speech given by an attorney to the judge or jury in order to present a case and persuade the listeners to believe it.

ARM. ABBRV. Adjustable rate mortgage. See *mortgage, adjustable rate.*

arm's length. ADJ. Distant, not intimate; describes a good faith, fair market transaction by parties with relatively equal bargaining power, in which neither one forces the other to accept terms.

arraign. V. In criminal law, to bring a defendant into court, charge him or her with an offense, and allow him or her to plead.

arraignment. N. The first step in the criminal process, in which a defendant is called into court, charged with a crime, informed of his or her rights, and allowed to plead guilty, not guilty, or nolo contendere.

arrears. N. Overdue payments; money owed but not yet paid.

arrest. V. To use legal authority to deprive someone of liberty; in criminal law, to stop someone suspected of a crime and take him or her into custody. N. *arrest*.

arrest of judgment. N. A court's withholding of judgment in a case when there is some problem with the record that would make the judgment erroneous.

arrest record. N. The official record of times a person has been arrested.

arson. N. The crime of intentionally and maliciously setting property on fire.

article. N. One clause or paragraph of a legal document.

articles. N. A collection of several clauses or rules that comprise a statute, contract, or other legal document.

Articles of Confederation. N. The document that formalized the agreement between the original thirteen states of the Union. It was written in 1777, enacted in 1781, and replaced by the Constitution in 1789.

articles of impeachment. N. A document outlining reasons for removing a public official from office.

articles of incorporation. N. A document that creates a corporation; sometimes called articles of association.

artifice. N. A clever or cunning device, often used to commit fraud or some trickery.

asbestos. N. A silicate mineral that resists heat and can be woven into fire-resistant material.

asbestosis. N. A lung disease caused by inhaling asbestos particles.

Asia-Pacific Economic Cooperation. N. An international economic treaty organization of nations surrounding the Pacific Ocean. ABBRV. *APEC*.

as is. ADJ. In the present condition; goods sold "as is" are delivered in the condition in which they were when the buyer inspected them before purchase.

asportation. N. Moving goods or a person from one place to another, as in larceny or kidnapping.

assault. V. To attack physically; to threaten or attempt to cause injury to someone else. When contact occurs as well, the offense is often called assault and battery. N. ***assault***. See also *aggravate*, *battery*, *simple*.

assault weapon. N. A weapon used by soldiers in military operations; for the purpose of gun control laws, any automatic or semi-automatic weapon that meets certain criteria.

assembly. N. A group of people gathered together in the same place for the same purpose; the meeting together of a group of people for a common purpose.

assembly, right of. N. A constitutional right allowing citizens to gather for reasons connected with the government, including protests and political rallies.

assembly, unlawful. N. A gathering that results in undesirable behavior by the group, such as noise or obstruction of roads.

assent. V. To approve; to ratify; to agree. N. ***assent***.

assess. V. To evaluate; to determine a value or price for something; to set a value on property for tax purposes. N. ***assessment***.

assessor. N. One who assesses something.

asset. N. Something of value; real or personal property worth money.

assets, capital. N. All property held by a taxpayer.

asset, intangible. N. Assets that have no physical presence, such as trademarks or goodwill.

assign. V. (1) To transfer legal rights or property to someone else. (2) To select or designate. N. *assignment*.

assigned risk. N. In automobile insurance, a category of drivers that insurers would not choose to cover due to their poor driving records or other risk factors, but that the insurers are required by statute to insure.

assignee. N. A person who receives property from another.

assignment of error. N. A claim by an appellant that the trial judge made an error at trial.

assignment of income. N. Assigning income-generating property to someone else in an effort to avoid receiving the income and thus income taxes.

assignment of wages. N. Assigning the right to collect wages to a creditor of the wage-earner.

assignor. N. One who transfers property to another.

assigns. N. People who receive property from an assignor.

assize. N. A kind of court that formerly heard criminal and civil cases in England and Wales.

associate. V. To be connected with or work with someone. N. A colleague, often a subordinate one; in a law firm, associates are lawyers who are employees of the firm, as opposed to partners, who are owners.

association. N. A group of people joined together for a particular purpose; the act of joining together for a specific purpose.

assume. V. (1) To take on a responsibility or power; to receive. (2) To take on something deceitfully, such as a false name. (3) To suppose something to be the case without any proof. N. ***assumption***.

assumpsit. N. *(Latin)* He promised; a promise to do or pay something made by one person to another.

assumption of risk. N. An affirmative defense stating that a plaintiff voluntarily risked injury by exposing him- or herself to a known danger.

assurance. N. A declaration of certainty; also a British term for insurance.

assure. V. To confirm; to make certain; to make someone else sure of something.

asylum. N. Refuge or shelter from danger; a safe place for the poor and unfortunate to find help.

asylum, political. N. Protection granted by a nation to someone who has fled his or her homeland for political reasons.

ATF. ABBRV. Bureau of Alcohol, Tobacco, Firearms and Explosives.

atrocity. N. An act of extreme cruelty, brutality, and wickedness. ADJ. ***atrocious***.

attach. V. (1) To join or connect. (2) To seize a defendant's property before a judgment has been reached at trial as security for any judgment that the plaintiff might receive. N. ***attachment***.

attainder. N. Under common law, the forfeiting of all civil and property rights after being convicted of treason or a felony. See also *bill of attainder*.

attempt. N. The act of trying to do something, usually unsuccessfully; in criminal law, an intentional effort to commit a crime that failed but could have succeeded. V. *attempt*.

attendant circumstances. N. The facts and circumstances surrounding an event.

attest. V. To declare something to be true; to sign a document as a witness. N. *attestation*.

attorney. N. A lawyer; more generally, an agent appointed to act for another person.

attorney at law. N. A lawyer admitted by a court to practice law in a particular jurisdiction, including drafting legal documents and representing clients in court.

attorney-client privilege. N. In evidence law, the right of attorneys and their clients to withhold information about confidential communications made in the course of their professional relationship.

attorney general. N. An attorney who serves as the head of the Department of Justice and chief legal adviser to the president and who represents the United States in legal matters; each state also has its own attorney general who performs the same functions at the state level.

attorney's fees. N. The fees charged by a lawyer for services rendered to clients. See also *contingent*.

attractive nuisance. N. A doctrine in tort law that a person who keeps something on his or her property that is likely both to attract children and be a danger to them (such as a swimming pool) is under a duty to protect the children from the dangers (as by fencing in the pool).

auction. N. A public sale of goods or property to the highest bidder. V. *auction*.

auctioneer. N. A person licensed to conduct auctions, usually employed by the seller to act as the seller's agent.

audit. N. A systematic review of an organization's or an individual's accounts. V. *audit*.

auditor. N. A person who conducts an audit.

authenticate. V. To prove that something is genuine or true; to certify; to give something legal authority so as to allow it to be admitted as evidence. N. *authentication*.

authorities. N. Sources used in composing a legal document, such as statutes, cases, restatements, and articles.

authorities, table of. N. A list of citations to all the legal sources used in a brief or other legal document.

authority. N. (1) Power; the right to tell others how to act or to make others obey; rights or powers delegated by one person or body to another. (2) An expert.

authorize. V. To approve; to give permission; to give someone legal authority. N. *authorization*.

authorized stock issue. N. The number of shares of stock a corporation is allowed to sell under its charter.

automatic weapon. N. A gun that will continue to fire bullets as long as the trigger is held down and it still contains ammunition; a machine gun.

autopsy. N. The dissection and physical examination of a dead body to determine the cause of death.

aver. V. To assert or state; to declare.

averment. N. In a pleading, a positive assertion of fact.

avoid. V. (1) To escape or evade. (2) To nullify; to make void; to cancel; to destroy. N. *avoidance*.

avow. V. To acknowledge openly. N. *avowal*.

avulsion. N. The sudden removal of a large piece of land from one property and its deposit onto another, as when a river changes its course abruptly. See also *accretion*.

award. V. To grant something; to give something as a prize or compensation. N. Money or another object given as a grant or compensation; also the decision rendered by a nonjudicial decider such as an arbitrator.

B

back. V. (1) To support or be in favor of. (2) To support financially. (3) To endorse or countersign. ADJ. From the past; to the rear of.

background check. N. An investigation performed on a person's history and background that can include criminal records, bankruptcies, liens, civil court judgments, previous and current addresses, property ownership, and other information.

back pay. N. The difference between the wages received for a period of work and retroactive higher wages granted by a court.

back wages. N. Wages earned in the past but not yet paid.

bad check. N. A check written on a closed account or on an account with insufficient funds to pay it or on a closed account. See also *check kiting*.

bad debt. N. An uncollectible debt; a debt owed by an insolvent debtor.

bad debt reserve. N. An account used to estimate debts that ultimately will not be paid and will thus eventually be deducted for tax purposes.

bad faith. N. Deceit; intent to defraud; dishonesty in dealing with someone.

badges of fraud. N. A fact or circumstance that makes it appear as if a person intends to defraud someone else in a transaction and justifies an inference of fraud; examples include transferring funds in anticipation of a lawsuit, transferring all of a debtor's property to someone else, a confidential relationship between the parties, and fake consideration.

bad title. N. A title that does not convey any property to a purchaser.

bail. N. Money or other security given temporarily to the court to allow a prisoner to be released before trial and to ensure that he or she will return for trial; if the prisoner does not return for trial, he or she forfeits the bail. V. To furnish money or property to get someone released from prison.

bail bond. N. A contract between a prisoner, the state, and a third party known as a bail bondsman, in which the bail bondsman agrees to furnish bail for the prisoner in return for a fee and takes the risk that the prisoner will not return for trial. See also *bond*, *bondsman*.

bailee. N. A person who holds goods or property for someone else for a specific purpose, such as a mechanic keeping a car for repairs.

bailiff. N. (1) A court officer who keeps order and looks after jurors and prisoners. (2) An agent or steward who is responsible for property or goods.

bailiwick. N. A bailiff's jurisdiction.

bailment. N. The delivery of goods to a bailee to be held in trust for a specific purpose, such as repairs, often formalized with a contract.

bailment for hire. N. A bailment in which the owner of the goods agrees to compensate the bailee.

bailor. N. One who delivers personal property or goods to a bailee. See also *bailment*.

bailout. N. Financial assistance to an ailing business to save it from failure. V. ***bail out***.

bait and switch. N. A kind of deceptive advertising in which a merchant advertises a low-priced product to lure customers and then disparages that product or fails to have it in stock in order to persuade them to buy a more expensive item; generally prohibited by statute.

balance. v. (1) To compare the difference between debits and credits in an account. (2) To compare the value of one thing with another. (3) To distribute weights or values to create harmony or equality. N. *balance*.

balance sheet. N. A financial statement that includes debits, credits, assets, and liabilities.

balancing test. N. A test used by courts to weigh the rights of an individual against the rights of the state; common in cases involving freedom of speech or equal protection.

balloon mortgage. N. A mortgage in which the buyer makes regular payments at intervals and then must pay the rest of the balance at the end of the mortgage period.

balloon note. N. A promissory note in which the interest is paid in periodic installments and then the remainder of the principal is paid in one lump sum at the end of the term.

balloon payment. N. The large payment due at the end of the term of a balloon note.

ballot. N. (1) A piece of paper or other object used by a voter to cast a vote in an election. (2) The list of candidates or issues being voted on.

ballot, secret. N. A kind of voting in which a voter's choices cannot be identified as coming from him or her.

ballot box. N. A sealed box in which voters deposit ballots.

banc. N. *(French)* Bench; the place where a court sits; the full court with all judges. See also *en banc.*

bank. N. A financial institution that holds money for customers, invests it to earn interest, lends money at interest, issues promissory notes, handles trusts, deals in negotiable securities, and performs other financial services.

bank, commercial. N. The most common kind of bank, which provides a full range of banking services. See also *savings and loan association.*

bank account. N. A sum placed in a bank by a customer that is available to be withdrawn upon the customer's request.

bank draft. N. An order for payment of money drawn upon a bank by a bank officer, payable when the issuing bank accepts it.

bankrupt. ADJ. Insolvent and unable to pay debts as they come due.

bankruptcy. N. A process in which a court declares a person or business insolvent and orders the debtor's assets to be sold to pay off creditors, at which point the debtor is discharged from any further obligation and may begin anew.

bankruptcy, Chapter 7. N. Straight bankruptcy; a proceeding that liquidates property, pays off debts, and leaves the debtor discharged.

bankruptcy, Chapter 11. N. Business reorganization in which a court supervises an insolvent business while it continues to operate and comes up with a plan for reorganization.

bankruptcy, Chapter 12. N. A proceeding to allow for family farmers and fisherman to create a repayment plan to pay off debts over a specified period of time while being supervised by the court.

bankruptcy, Chapter 13. N. A proceeding that lets a borrower with enough income pay off bills over a specified period of time while being supervised by the court.

bankruptcy court. N. A federal court that handles only bankruptcy cases, presided over by a bankruptcy judge.

bankruptcy trustee. N. A person appointed by the court to handle a debtor's property during bankruptcy proceedings.

banner ad. N. A small advertisement that appears on a website, linking that website to the advertiser's own website; the advertiser pays the owner of the original website for every hit it receives through the banner ad.

bar. N. (1) The court; a particular place in the courtroom. (2) A body of attorneys; such bodies are organized at the local, state, or national level. See also *bench*. (3) An obstacle; something that prevents an issue from being litigated. V. To prevent or forbid.

bargain. N. An agreement between two parties to transfer goods or property or to perform some act or service in exchange for consideration. V. To negotiate the terms of a transaction or agreement.

bargain and sale. N. A contract commonly used in real estate to transfer title and use of property from buyer to seller; does not include warranties against liens or encumbrances.

bargaining unit. N. A group, such as a labor union, that represents employees during collective bargaining.

barratry. N. The offense of inciting lawsuits or quarrels.

barrister. N. In the United Kingdom, a lawyer who conducts trials. See also *solicitor*.

barter. V. To exchange goods and services for other goods and services without using money. N. *barter*.

base. N. Foundation; bottom; starting point.

basis. N. A taxpayer's cost in acquiring an asset.

basis, adjusted. N. Acquisition cost plus capital improvements minus depreciation.

basis, carryover. N. The basis of property acquired from a decedent, valued at the basis of the property just before the decedent's death.

basis, stepped-up. N. A basis that is increased to a certain level at a particular date, usually in property transferred through inheritance.

bastard. N. A child born to a mother and father not married to one another.

BATFE. ABBRV. Bureau of Alcohol, Tobacco, Firearms and Explosives.

battery. N. A wrongful and intentional physical touching that causes offense and possibly, though not necessarily, injury. See also *assault*.

bear. V. To carry.

bearer. N. One who possesses a document, instrument, or security.

bearer paper. N. Commercial paper, such as a check, payable to whoever has it; often written as "payable to bearer" or to "cash."

bed (and board). N. The right of a married couple to live together; *(Latin)* a mensa et thoro. See also *divorce*.

belief. N. A conviction that something is true; something that one thinks or supposes after examining evidence and information. V. *believe*.

bench. N. (1) A court; the seat a judge occupies in a courtroom; the office of judge. (2) The collective body of judges. See also *bar*.

bench trial. N. A trial conducted by a judge without a jury. See also *jury trial*.

bench warrant. N. An order issued by a court for the arrest of a person, often used to make that person appear in court.

beneficial. ADJ. Profitable; advantageous; often used to describe entitlements enjoyed by the beneficiary of a trust who does not hold legal title to a property but is allowed to use it.

beneficial interest. N. In trusts, the benefit or profit from the use of property enjoyed by a beneficiary who has an equitable interest in it, as opposed to the legal title held by a trustee.

beneficial owner. N. Someone who has equitable title of property but not legal title.

beneficial use. N. A right to use and enjoy property without holding legal title to it.

beneficiary. N. Someone who benefits from someone else's act, such as a person for whom property is held in trust, the recipient of the proceeds of an insurance policy, or someone named in a will as a recipient of property.

benefit. N. An advantage or profit.

benefit, fringe. N. Something given to an employee by an employer as part of compensation in addition to salary, such as health insurance; also called benefits.

benefit of the bargain. N. A rule that allows a defrauded purchaser to recover the difference between the real and represented values of the item purchased.

bequeath. V. To leave a gift of personal property to someone by a will. See also *bequest, devise.*

bequest. N. A gift of personal property made in a will; a legacy.

bequest, conditional. N. A bequest that takes place when specified conditions are met.

bequest, residuary. N. A bequest of all items remaining in an estate after specified legacies and debts are paid.

bequest, specific. N. A bequest of a specific item or items.

Berne Convention. N. An international agreement that establishes rules for copyrighting artistic works and regulating international copyright matters.

best evidence rule. N. A rule requiring that the best and most reliable evidence be presented at trial instead of less reliable evidence; thus, if the original version of a document or photograph is available, it should be presented instead of a copy.

bestiality. N. Sexual activity between a human and an animal.

Better Business Bureau. N. A private, nonprofit organization that assists consumers and businesses with marketplace issues such as advertising and selling practices.

beyond a reasonable doubt. ADJ. In a criminal case, proven by evidence to the point that a reasonable man or woman would be entirely convinced and morally certain that the defendant is guilty.

BFOQ. ABBRV. Bona fide occupational qualification.

bias. N. A preconceived opinion or prejudice; a condition that renders someone unable to judge a matter impartially. V. To influence in such a way as to render someone else's judgment prejudiced.

bid. N. An offer to buy or sell goods or services at a stated price, common at auctions or among builders or laborers seeking contracts. V. *bid*.

bid, best. N. The bid that best fits the needs of the one soliciting bids.

bidder. N. One who makes a bid.

bid, sealed. N. A bid submitted under seal, not to be opened until a stated time when all bids for the same thing are opened and compared simultaneously; common in construction.

bid shopping. N. A prime contractor's disclosure of current low bids to pressure subcontractors to submit even lower bids.

bigamy. N. Knowingly being married to more than one spouse at once.

bigot. N. A person who is prejudiced against people who live differently or who hold different beliefs from him or her.

bigotry. N. A sense of superiority over and intolerance of lifestyles and ideas that are different from a person's own.

bill. N. (1) A statement of goods purchased or services rendered and moneys owed for them. (2) A piece of paper currency. (3) A draft of a proposed law introduced into the legislature for debate and voting. (4) A pleading submitted by a plaintiff to an equity court stating grounds for a trial. V. To issue a statement requesting payment of moneys owed for goods or services.

billable. ADJ. Able to be billed; used to describe hours worked by attorneys on behalf of clients who pay their bills by the hour.

bill of attainder. N. A legislative act that inflicts capital punishment on someone who has been accused of a serious offense but has not been convicted at trial; prohibited by the U.S. Constitution.

bill of lading. N. A receipt given by a carrier to someone who entrusts goods to the carrier for shipment, serving as a contract between shipper and carrier and giving its holder title to the goods held by the carrier.

bill of lading order. N. A negotiable bill of lading that can be sold, and that causes title to the goods to vest in its holder, who can collect the goods by presenting the bill of lading to the carrier.

bill of particulars. N. In criminal law, a written statement by the prosecution describing in detail its allegations against the defendant and informing the court and the defendant what the prosecution's case will be.

bill of rights. N. A statement of fundamental rights of citizenship; the first ten amendments of the U.S. Constitution.

bill of sale. N. A written agreement that transfers ownership of personal property from one person to another.

bind. V. To obligate; to place legal duties upon someone. ADJ. *binding*.

binder. N. (1) A written agreement in which an insurer promises to cover a prospective insured between the time of application for a policy and when the policy is actually issued. (2) A written document summarizing the key terms of a preliminary contract.

bind over. V. To order a defendant to remain in custody or provide bail pending trial.

Biological Weapons Convention. N. An international treaty, effective in 1975, that requires its signatories to prohibit the creation and stockpiling of biological weapons such as disease-causing microbes.

bipartisan. ADJ. Containing representatives from both of two sides or parties.

blackacre. N. The name of a fictitious piece of property used as an example in teaching and discussing property law; sometimes the term "whiteacre" is used as well.

black letter law. N. An informal term for basic principles of law. See also *hornbook law*.

blacklist. N. A list of people to be shunned, usually due to nonconformity or untrustworthiness. V. *blacklist*.

blackmail. N. Demanding money in exchange for performing a duty or under threat of revealing injurious information or causing injury to one's person or property; extortion. V. *blackmail*.

blank endorsement. N. Endorsing a check or promissory note by signing it without writing in a recipient's name, leaving a space for insertion of a recipient's name.

blasphemy. N. Irreverent or profane speech or writing about religion or sacred things. V. *blaspheme*. ADJ. *blasphemous*.

blog. N. Web log; a website typically produced by an individual that contains entries on particular topics, links to other websites, and sometimes comments from readers.

BLS. ABBRV. Bureau of Labor Statistics.

Blue Book. See *Uniform System of Citation*.

blue sky laws. N. State statutes that regulate the issue and sale of securities.

board. N. A group of people who manage a business or public office.

board of directors. N. The governing body of a corporation that is elected by shareholders and that sets company policy and appoints officers.

board of education. N. A local or state agency that manages municipal or local schools.

board of health. N. A municipal or state committee dedicated to improving public health.

boilerplate. N. Standardized text used in legal documents; text always written identically in the same kind of document.

bona fide. ADJ. In good faith; genuine; not intending to deceive.

bona fide occupational qualification. N. A qualification that is truly necessary for performing a job, used to judge matters of employment discrimination. ABBRV. *BFOQ.*

bona fide purchaser. N. Someone who buys property in good faith for valuable consideration and has no reason to believe anyone else has rights to the property.

bond. N. Written evidence of a debt issued by a company or government in which the issuing body agrees to pay a fixed rate of interest during the period of the loan and to repay the principal at a specified date, called maturity.

bond, bearer. N. A negotiable instrument payable to its holder.

bond, coupon. N. A bond sold with a book of coupons that may be clipped when they come due and redeemed for interest.

bond, registered. N. A bond registered in the name of the holder in the issuing body's books.

bond, surety. N. A bond issued by a surety promising to perform an obligation if the person who is supposed to perform it defaults.

bond issue. N. Raising funds by offering bonds to investors; the bonds issued for that purpose.

bondsman. N. Someone who serves as surety for a bond. See also *bail bond.*

bonus stock. N. Common stock offered as an incentive with the purchase of another kind of securities, such as preferred stock or bonds.

book. N. A document containing the accounts or records of a business. V. To perform administrative tasks such as recording the name and alleged crime of someone who has been arrested and brought to the police station. N. ***booking***.

book value. N. An asset's official value, usually cost minus depreciation.

books, corporate. N. A corporation's written records of transactions.

boot. N. Taxable cash or property exchanged during an otherwise nontaxable exchange; cash or property given by one party to equal the value of items exchanged.

borrow. V. To take money or property from someone else and use it with the intent to return it. See also *loan.*

bound. ADJ. Obligated to by contract or moral constraint. N. The edge of a piece of property; the limit or boundary. See also *metes and bounds.*

boycott. V. To withdraw from commercial or social dealings with a person, business, or state as a way of showing displeasure with that party's actions. N. *boycott*.

brain death. N. The point at which the brain stops functioning irreversibly; this point is ambiguous, but some criteria for assessing it include lack of response to stimulation, absence of reflexes, cessation of breathing, and no brain activity for twenty-four hours.

breach. V. To break a promise; to fail to perform a duty or observe an agreement. N. *breach*.

breach, constructive. N. A breach occurring when one party does something to prevent his or her fulfilling contractual duties or announces beforehand that he or she will not fulfill contractual duties. See also *anticipatory breach of contract*.

breach, material. N. A serious breach of a contract that essentially destroys the value of the contract, excuses the nonbreaching party from further performance, and allows suit for breach of contract.

breach, partial. N. A failure to perform some of the duties of a contract, which gives the nonbreaching party the right to collect damages but does not excuse his or her performance of contractual duties.

breach of contract. N. Failure to perform acts promised in a contract.

breach of duty. N. Failure to perform legal or moral duties, or to use the care that a reasonable man or woman would use in given circumstances.

breach of trust. N. A trustee's failure to properly perform duties required by the trust.

breaking. N. Forcibly opening a door, window, or gaining other access to a building; the force required can be very slight, as in opening a closed and unlocked door.

breaking and entering. N. Forcibly opening a building and then entering it; two elements of the crime of burglary.

breathalyzer. N. A device used to check the level of alcohol in a person's breath; breathalyzer test results are admissible as evidence.

brethren. N. Plural of brother, i.e., brothers; when used in a will, also includes sisters; often used by Supreme Court justices to refer to their fellow justices.

bribe. V. To give someone money or a gift to induce or influence him or her to act in a particular way, usually an improper or illegal way. N. Money or a gift given to influence someone.

bribery. N. The act of offering a bribe.

brief. N. (1) A written document presented to the court and to the opposing counsel by a lawyer that describes the facts of a case, questions of law, and legal arguments in support of his or her client's position. (2) A summary or abstract of a case. V. (1) To write a summary of a case. (2) To inform someone of the details of something.

broker. N. A person who brings parties together to negotiate transactions between them in return for a commission or other compensation; a middleman. V. To negotiate a deal between parties.

broker, real estate. N. A person who negotiates transactions involving the buying and selling of land or property.

Brown v. Board of Education. N. A 1954 U.S. Supreme Court case that declared that "separate but equal" schools for black and white students were inherently unequal and thus violated the equal protection clause of the Fourteenth Amendment of the U.S. Constitution; this case overturned *Plessy v. Ferguson*.

browse. v. To move from website to website on the Internet by clicking from one to another; to surf the Web.

browser. N. A computer program that allows a user to view and use websites.

browse-wrap agreement. N. A contract stating that a user agrees to a website's terms and conditions. It is created when the user browses the website, without the user actively agreeing to the terms and conditions. See also *click-wrap agreement, shrink-wrap agreement*.

bug. N. A tiny hidden microphone used to secretly monitor conversations. v. To record conversations using a hidden microphone.

buggery. N. Anal intercourse; sometimes includes bestiality. See also *sodomy*.

bugging. N. Electronic surveillance by using bugs to eavesdrop on and record conversations, regulated by statute. See also *wiretapping*.

building code. N. The state and local laws and regulations governing the construction, maintenance, and operation of dwellings.

bulk sale. N. A transfer or sale of the majority of goods and supplies owned by a business in one transaction; often done as part of the liquidation of a business.

bulk sale acts. N. Statutes that require a business planning a bulk sale to first notify creditors, designed to protect creditors from secret bulk sales.

bulk transfer. N. A form of commercial fraud in which a business sells most of its stock and then fails to pay creditors.

bundling. N. The practice of combining two or more products and selling them as one item.

burden. N. (1) A duty; something oppressive. (2) A restriction on the use of land.

burden of persuasion. N. The requirement that the party with the burden of proof convince the judge or jury of the validity of his or her case.

burden of proof. N. A party's duty to furnish sufficient evidence to sustain an allegation.

bureaucracy. N. A form of government or organization with a hierarchical structure of officials, authority delegated from top to bottom, well-defined positions within the structures, inflexible rules, and usually a fairly complicated administrative system.

Bureau of Alcohol, Tobacco, Firearms and Explosives. N. A federal agency within the U.S. Department of Justice that handles gun licensing and the investigation of traffic and crimes involving alcohol, tobacco, firearms, ammunition, explosives, arson, and bombings. ABBRV. *ATF, BATFE.*

Bureau of Labor Statistics. N. An agency of the U.S. Department of Labor dedicated to assembling information and statistics about the U.S. workforce. ABBRV. *BLS.*

burglary. N. Under common law, breaking into and entering a dwelling at night intending to commit a felony once inside; under modern statutes, the definition has expanded to include all buildings, not just dwellings, and to require that the actor must merely enter the building instead of breaking into it, and must intend to commit any crime, not just a felony; the crime involved is usually theft.

business. N. An occupation or commercial activity done to earn money; making money by engaging in commerce.

business expense. N. An expense incurred in the process of running a business to generate income.

business gain or loss. N. Gain or loss resulting from sales or exchanges done in the course of business.

business judgment rule. N. A rule that exempts corporate executives from liability if there is reason to believe that they made the decision in question in good faith, with due care, and thought they were acting in the best interest of the corporation; their judgment may not be second-guessed.

business purpose. N. Something done specifically for business as opposed to personal reasons.

but for test. N. In tort law, a test used to decide whether an individual is responsible for something; the court asks whether the event would have occurred without, or "but for," the defendant's action; not commonly used today because of the difficulty in applying it.

buyer in ordinary course of business. N. An ordinary buyer; someone who buys something in good faith from someone in the business of selling that particular item and without any knowledge of a third party's interest in the goods.

bylaws. N. The internal rules and regulations made by a business or organization to govern its internal workings.

C

cabinet. N. The U.S. president's board of advisors, composed of the heads of the executive departments, the vice president, and occasionally other officials; in other countries, a group of senior officials who advise the king or chief executive, or who control the government themselves.

cafeteria plan. N. A fringe-benefit plan that allows employees to choose from a range of benefits, selecting them according to individual needs.

calendar. N. A chart describing the organization of days, months, and years.

calendar, court. N. The list of cases scheduled to be heard during a court session.

calendar call. N. A court session devoted to checking the status of pending cases and setting trial dates.

calendar year. N. January 1 through December 31.

call. N. (1) In property law, a natural object that marks a boundary and serves as a landmark in a deed. (2) A demand for payment. V. (1) To demand payment. (2) To redeem bonds before maturity.

callable. ADJ. Able to be paid off before maturity.

callable bond. N. A bond that may be called for payment before it matures.

call option. N. A contract giving its holder the right to purchase stock at a specific price by a specific date.

calumny. N. Slander or defamation; making false statements to harm someone's reputation; a slanderous statement.

campaign. N. (1) An organized effort to achieve some goal, usually election to political office or promotion of a political or social cause. (2) Military operations in a specific area or done for a particular reason. V. *campaign*.

campaign finance. N. Money raised to pay for politicians' election campaigns.

cancel. N. To annul; to revoke; to announce that something previously planned will not take place. N. *cancellation*.

canceled check. N. A check that has been paid and charged to the person who wrote it, and is marked in some way to indicate that fact.

canon. N. A rule or standard; a body of rules, particularly for governing the conduct of a kind of professional; a rule suggesting appropriate conduct for legal professionals.

canon law. N. Roman Catholic law, created by popes and cardinals.

CAN-SPAM Act. N. A law passed in 2003 that made certain commercial emails, often called "spam," illegal and empowered the Federal Trade Commission to take action to prevent spam.

capacity. N. Legal competence; having the age and mental capacity to understand the consequences of one's actions and to make rational decisions.

capacity, criminal. N. The age and mental ability necessary to intentionally commit a crime.

capacity, testamentary. N. The mental ability necessary to write a proper will.

capacity to contract. N. The age and mental acuity necessary to enter a binding contract.

capias. N. A writ issued by the court demanding that a named person be taken into custody.

capital. N. Wealth in the form of money and assets; all the assets owned by a business.

capital account. N. An account that records a business's capital assets, expenses, and liabilities.

capital expenditure. N. Money spent to acquire or improve a capital asset.

capital gain or loss. N. The profit or loss realized when a capital asset is sold.

capital intensive. ADJ. Requiring a large amount of equipment for production.

capitalization. N. All stock, bonds, and other securities issued by a corporation.

capitalize. V. To convert present or expected income into an asset; in business accounting, to record an expense (such as repairs to a building) as a capital asset because it will produce long-term benefits, thus allowing the expense to be written off over a period of time.

capital offense. N. An offense for which execution is a possible punishment; also called a capital crime.

capital punishment. N. The death penalty; punishment by death.

caption. N. The heading of a legal document such as a brief, motion, or pleading, containing the names of the parties, the court, the action, the docket number, and any other required information.

capture. v. To forcefully take possession of someone or something. N. *capture*.

carbon credit. N. A tradable permit giving its holder the right to emit a specified amount of carbon dioxide.

care. N. (1) Attention, concern, or caution. (2) Custody. (3) Duty of care; an obligation to conduct oneself in such a way as to avoid or prevent injury to another.

care, great. N. The care exercised by a reasonable person in very important matters, or the care used by an extremely prudent person in a similar situation.

care, ordinary. N. The care a reasonably careful person would use in a similar situation. See also *reasonable care, due care*.

care, slight. N. The care a reasonable person exercises in unimportant matters, or the care used by a careless person in a similar situation.

carnal knowledge. N. Sexual intercourse; penetration of a female's genitals by a male's.

carrier. N. A person or business that transports people or goods for a fee.

carrier, common. N. A carrier who makes transportation available to the public, and who will transport any person or the goods of any person who pays for the passage, as long as there is room available and no legal reason to refuse.

carrier, private. N. A carrier who transports people or goods by contract and only in particular cases.

carryback. N. In taxation, the process of applying a deduction or credit from one year to the tax liability of a previous year.

carryover. N. A deduction or credit from one year to the tax liability of a future year.

carry over. V. To extend past a stated deadline or boundary; in the case of health savings accounts, to transfer from one fiscal year into the next; in the case of taxes, it is the process of applying a deduction or credit from one year to the tax liability of a future year.

carte blanche. N. Complete freedom to act as one chooses; unlimited discretionary power.

cartel. N. A coalition of independent producers, usually industrial corporations, who band together to set prices and restrict competition. See also *monopoly*.

case. N. (1) A legal action or lawsuit to be decided in a court of law or equity. (2) The legal arguments and evidence used by one side of a lawsuit to support its position.

casebook. N. A textbook used in law school to teach a particular type of law, containing court opinions from cases in that subject and commentary by experts in the field.

case law. N. The body of law derived from examination of previously judged cases, including their treatment of a subject and interpretation of legislation. See also *common law, civil law*.

case system. N. A method of teaching law by having law students read and analyze cases.

cash. N. Ready money, i.e., coins and bank notes. Sometimes includes negotiable checks and bank accounts. See also *credit*.

cash flow. N. The total money generated; the cash remaining when all expenses are paid.

cash method. N. An accounting method that records only money that has been paid or received. See also *accelerated cost recovery system*.

cash value. N. Market value, the price an item would bring if sold on the open market.

castle doctrine. N. The principle that a person's home is meant to be safe from attack and that the person can therefore defend his or her home with a degree of force that would not be legal in any other setting. See also *duty to retreat*.

casualty. N. In insurance, an accident; something destroyed or badly damaged; a person killed. See *loss, accident*.

casus belli. N. *(Latin)*. Case of war; a reason to go to war.

causa. N. *(Latin)* Cause, reason.

causa mortis. N. *(Latin)* In anticipation of death.

causation. N. Causing something; a cause; the connection between cause and effect.

cause. V. To make something happen. N. (1) That which makes something happen. (2) A legal case; see also *cause of action*.

cause, direct. N. The action that sets in motion a sequence of events leading directly to a result, without any intervening actions to assist or interfere with the chain of events.

cause, intervening. N. Something that happens between the action that sets in motion a series of events and the ultimate result.

cause, proximate. N. A cause that directly produces a result, and without which the result would not have happened.

cause, superseding. N. An intervening cause that substantially affects the ultimate outcome of the series of events and breaks the chain of causation between the direct cause and the effect.

cause of action. N. A set of facts that creates a valid legal claim that can be grounds for a lawsuit.

cautionary instruction. N. A judge's instruction to the jury to consider specific pieces of evidence only for instructed purposes, not to allow extraneous information to influence their judgment, not to speak about the case to anyone outside the courtroom, and other matters.

caveat. N. *(Latin)* Let him beware; a warning.

caveat emptor. N. *(Latin)* Let the buyer beware; the principle that the buyer is responsible for examining merchandise and judging its quality before buying it.

CDA. ABBRV. Communications Decency Act.

CDC. ABBRV. Centers for Disease Control and Prevention.

cease and desist order. N. An order by a court, agency, or judicial body telling someone to stop doing a particular activity, usually because the activity in question is illegal.

censor. N. A person who examines published media, including print and film, in search of objectionable or offensive content. V. To examine published media looking for offensive content and suppressing it when found.

censorship. N. The practice of censoring.

censure. N. A formal reprimand or expression of disapproval. V. *censure*.

census. N. An official count of a population.

Centers for Disease Control and Prevention. N. An agency within the U.S. Department of Health and Human Services that works to promote public health. ABBRV. *CDC*.

certificate. N. An official document confirming a particular fact.

certificate, birth. N. A certificate stating the date and place of a person's birth.

certificate, death. N. A certificate stating the date and place of a person's death.

certificate, stock. N. A certificate issued by a corporation to a shareholder indicating that the shareholder owns a certain number of shares of the corporation's stock.

certificate of deposit. N. A document issued by a bank to a customer indicating that it has received a sum of money from the customer and will repay it with interest at a specific date.

certificate of incorporation. N. A document issued by a secretary of state approving a company's articles of incorporation and indicating that the corporation exists.

certificate of occupancy. N. A document issued by a local government confirming that a building complies with local building codes.

certified check. N. A check drawn on a bank account that has been certified in writing by a bank official, thereby making the bank responsible for it.

certify. V. To confirm formally; to authenticate in writing. N. *certification*.

certiorari. N. A writ issued by an appellate court to a lower court requesting the official record of a decision made by the lower court so that the appellate court can review it for errors.

cestui que. *(French)* The one who.

cestui que trust. N. The person who has a beneficial interest in a trust; the beneficiary.

cestui que use. N. The person who has a right to use property held by another.

cestui que vie. N. The person whose life determines the duration of a trust or insurance contract.

CFAA. ABBRV. Computer Fraud and Abuse Act.

chain of title. N. The history of ownership of a property, listed from the original owner to the present one.

challenge. V. To object; to dispute the truth of a statement. N. (1) An objection. (2) An objection by a lawyer to the inclusion on the jury of a juror proposed by opposing counsel.

challenge, peremptory. N. An objection to including a juror for no particular reason; each party is permitted a certain number of peremptory challenges.

challenge for cause. N. An objection to a juror based on a specific reason, which the judge must approve.

chamber. N. A hall or room in which a judicial or legislative body meets.

chambers. N. A judge's private office.

champerty. N. An illegal agreement between a party to a lawsuit and another person who agrees to pay the costs of pursuing the lawsuit in exchange for a share of the resulting proceeds.

chancellor. N. (1) A senior officer, especially at a university. (2) The judge of a court of chancery. (3) In some European countries, the head of the government.

chancery. N. Equity, or equitable jurisdiction. Court of chancery. A court of equity.

change. V. To alter or modify; to substitute one thing for another, often used in reference to money. N. *change*.

Chapter 7. See *bankruptcy, Chapter 7*.

Chapter 11. See *bankruptcy, Chapter 11*.

Chapter 12. See *bankruptcy, Chapter 12*.

Chapter 13. See *bankruptcy, Chapter 13*.

character. N. A person's moral qualities; reputation; disposition.

character evidence. N. Evidence about a person's reputation in society.

character witness. N. A witness who attests to a person's reputation and moral qualities.

charge. V. (1) To accuse someone of an offense. (2) To entrust someone with a duty. (3) To request money for something purchased or provided. (4) To issue instructions to a jury as to how they should analyze the facts and arguments presented at trial. N. *charge*.

charitable. ADJ. Done out of benevolence or a desire to help those in need.

charitable contribution. N. Donations of money or other valuable items to charitable organizations; often tax-deductible.

charitable organization. N. Under the Internal Revenue Code, a corporation or business devoted to specific charitable purposes and not operated for profit or political influence.

charitable trust. N. A trust whose property must be used for charitable purposes.

charity. N. (1) An organization whose focus is on charitable work and public benevolence. (2) The donation of money or help to those in need.

charity, public. N. A charity that receives most of its support from the public.

charter. N. A document granted by the state permitting the creation of a corporation, city, or university and defining its rights and privileges. See also *articles of incorporation*. V. To hire an airplane, boat, or other such vehicle for private use.

chattel. N. A possession; movable or personal property, as opposed to land or real property; something that can be owned.

chattel mortgage. N. A mortgage placed on personal property to secure a debt; chattel mortgages have been mostly replaced by the Uniform Commercial Code's security arrangements.

chattel paper. N. A document that records a debt and a security interest or lease of specific goods.

check. V. Examine; verify. N. A document indicating that the amount of money noted on it is to be drawn from the writer's bank account when it is presented to the bank.

check, cashier's. N. A check written for a bank customer on a bank's own account, guaranteeing that the bank will pay the amount of money recorded on the check.

check, personal. N. A check written on an account holder's personal account.

check, traveler's. N. A check purchased from a bank that functions as cash but is protected against loss or theft. See also *certified check.*

check kiting. N. A scam in which an individual deposits worthless checks in different banks and uses his or her good credit to withdraw funds before the checks clear, attempting to deposit the money into the account on which the check is drawn before the discrepancy is discovered. See also *bad check.*

Chemical Weapons Convention. N. An international agreement effective in 1997 that prohibits its signatories from creating and stockpiling chemical weapons such as nerve gases.

chief. ADJ. Most important; highest ranking. N. Leader or head.

chief justice. N. The judge who presides over a court with more than one judge.

child. N. (1) Offspring, a son or daughter. (2) A person under the age of majority; a minor. PL. ***children***.

child abuse. N. Physical, sexual, or mental mistreatment of a child.

child labor laws. N. Laws regulating the hours, conditions, and nature of work that may be performed by children.

Children's Internet Protection Act. N. A federal law enacted in 2000 that requires schools and libraries that receive federal funding to implement safeguards to prevent minors from viewing inappropriate content on the Internet. ABBRV. *CIPA.*

child support. N. Financial contributions that a parent must make toward the upbringing of a child, usually paid by the parent who does not keep custody of the child after a divorce.

chill. V. To inhibit; to discourage.

chilling effect. N. Limits on constitutional rights, such as free speech, created by fear of repercussions rather than outright government prohibition.

Chinese wall. N. A policy used by securities firms that prevents all departments from accessing nonpublic information in order to prevent insider trading and self-dealing.

choate. ADJ. Completed. See also *inchoate.*

choate lien. N. A lien that has been perfected and can be enforced.

chose. N. *(French)* A thing; a personal possession.

chose in action. N. A claim that can be brought as a lawsuit.

chose in possession. N. Something that is owned or can be owned.

churning. N. Excessive and unnecessary trades of stock by a broker in order to increase his or her commission.

C.I.F. ABBRV. Cost, insurance, and freight. Also called C.F.I.

CIPA. ABBRV. Children's Internet Protection Act.

circuit. N. A judicial division of a state or the country, usually covering several counties or districts.

circuit court. N. A court that hears cases from within a judicial circuit, so-called because its judges traveled a circuit within the region, hearing cases in different places. See also *district court.*

circumstantial evidence. N. Evidence drawn from inference or deduction; secondary evidence. See also *direct evidence, indirect evidence.*

citation. N. (1) A reference in a legal document or argument to a legal authority such as a precedent or statute. (2) A summons issued by a court ordering its recipient to appear in court at a specified date and time. V. *cite.*

citizen. N. A legally recognized member of a nation or state, who owes allegiance to the government and in return receives the government's protection.

citizenship. N. The status of a citizen. See also *naturalize.*

civil. ADJ. Having to do with the concerns of citizens and the state; the branch of law that handles private matters as opposed to criminal ones.

civil action. N. A lawsuit brought by a private citizen to protect a private or civil right or to seek a civil remedy; a noncriminal action.

civil court. N. A court handling civil actions, i.e., noncriminal matters.

civil disobedience. N. Deliberately refusing to obey a law as a way of protesting its unfairness.

civilian. N. A person not in the military; a private citizen.

civil law. N. (1) Law concerned with citizens and private matters. (2) The body of jurisprudence created by a nation or state, as opposed to natural law or international law. (3) A system of jurisprudence practiced in Europe and in Louisiana, based on the codes of ancient Roman law as opposed to the precedents that form the authority of common law.

civil liberties. N. Personal rights and immunities from government oppression established and guaranteed by the Constitution, including freedom of speech and freedom of association; natural liberties that cannot be limited by the government. See also *civil rights*.

civil procedure. N. The laws governing procedure and practice used in civil litigation.

civil rights. N. The rights of all citizens to personal liberties, freedom, and equality; rights specifically granted through laws enacted by communities, as opposed to civil liberties, which are rights that the government is not allowed to restrict.

Civil Rights Acts. N. Federal laws enacted to protect personal rights guaranteed by the Constitution, particularly freedom from discrimination.

civil service. N. The professional staff and workers of a government.

Civil Service Commission. N. A commission that exists to ensure that civil service jobs are awarded on the basis of merit rather than favoritism.

claim. V. (1) To state the truth of something; to assert. (2) To assert ownership of or right to money or property and demand it. N. (1) A demand for something that one considers one's own. (2) An application for compensation filed with an insurer. (3) A cause of action, including a right enforceable by the court, an injury, and damages.

claimant. N. One who makes a claim.

claim of right. N. (1) In property, the claim that someone in adverse possession of land intends to claim the land as his or her own. (2) In taxation, the requirement that a taxpayer report all income for the year, even if some of it might have to be repaid in a later year.

Claims Court, U.S. See *United States Court of Federal Claims*.

class. N. A group of people or things sharing common characteristics.

class action. N. A lawsuit brought by one or a few members of a group on behalf of all the members, specially certified by the court to confirm that all the members share a concern and meet other requirements.

classified stock. N. Common stock divided into classes.

classify. V. To put into groups on the basis of similarities and shared characteristics. N. *classification*.

clause. N. A paragraph, stipulation, or article in a legal document such as a contract or pleading.

Clayton Act. N. A federal statute that amends the Sherman Antitrust Act by prohibiting price discrimination and regulating mergers and contracts that might inhibit competition.

Clean Air Acts. N. Federal and state statutes that regulate air pollution.

clean hands doctrine. N. A doctrine holding that in order for someone to receive equitable relief for a wrong, he or she must be blameless in the transaction, and must have performed his or her duties in good faith without wrongdoing. See also *unclean hands*.

clear. ADJ. Obvious or evident; easy to understand; without a doubt.

clear and convincing. ADJ. Highly probable, establishing a firm belief that something is true; an evidentiary standard between a preponderance of the evidence and beyond a reasonable doubt.

clear and present danger. N. A constitutional doctrine that allows the government to restrict freedom of speech in cases where free speech would create an obvious and immediate danger that the government has a duty to prevent.

clearinghouse. N. A banking establishment where member banks exchange checks and bills all at once, paying only the balances in cash so as to settle daily accounts conveniently.

clear title. N. A title free of encumbrances; good title.

clemency. N. Mercy, forgiveness, or leniency.

clergy. N. Religious professionals; those ordained for the ministry.

cleric. N. A member of the clergy.

clerical. ADJ. Having to do with bookkeeping, records, filing, correspondence, and similar duties.

clerical error. N. A mistake made while drafting or copying a document.

clerk. N. (1) A person who works in an office handling documents, records, and other administrative duties. (2) A person who works in a store, selling and organizing merchandise, usually an assistant. (3) A court officer who keeps court records, files pleadings and motions, issues process, and enters judgment. V. To work as a clerk, especially a law clerk.

clerk, law. N. A law student or recent law school graduate who assists an attorney or judge with research; writing of briefs, memoranda, and opinions; and, other tasks.

clerkship. N. The period spent working as a law clerk.

click-wrap agreement. N. A contract formed when a user clicks a box on a website agreeing to the website's terms and conditions; see also *browse-wrap agreement, shrink-wrap agreement.*

client. N. An individual or organization that employs a professional to provide that professional's services; someone who employs an attorney to represent him or her in court, to draft legal documents, to advise, or to provide other legal services.

close. V. (1) To complete or bring to an end. (2) To cover an opening. ADJ. (1) Near, nearby. (2) Closed or restricted. N. (1) An enclosed piece of land surrounded by a visible or invisible boundary; see also *inclosure.* (2) The end of a period of time or event.

closed shop. N. A business in which a collective bargaining agreement requires that all employees be members of a particular union. See also *open shop.*

closing. N. The conclusion of a sale of real estate in which the buyer pays the purchase price, the mortgage is secured, and the seller hands over the deed to the buyer.

closing argument. N. An attorney's final arguments to the judge and jury at the conclusion of his or her case, summing up the facts supporting the case and explaining why the opposing side's case is inadequate.

closing costs. N. Expenses that must be paid on closing, including fees for title searches and title insurance, deeds, appraisals, credit reports, and escrow.

closing statement. N. A document that records the details of the sale, including purchase price, deductions, tax adjustments, and credits, resulting in the net amount that the seller receives.

cloture. N. A vote by a legislature to end excessive debate on the matter at hand and vote on it. See also *filibuster*.

cloud on title. N. An encumbrance or claim on a title that could potentially impair the title but can be proven invalid by outside evidence, and can be removed by an action to quiet title.

COBRA. ABBRV. Consolidated Omnibus Budget Reconciliation Act of 1985.

code. N. A systematic collection of laws, regulations, or rules.

code, civil. N. The collection of laws based on the French Napoleonic Code that governs Louisiana jurisprudence. Also known as code civil.

code, penal. N. A collection of laws dealing with criminal acts and punishments. See also *United States Code*.

co-defendant. N. Someone who is a defendant together with someone else accused of the same crime or offense, or who is sued with another defendant in a single action.

code of military justice. N. The collection of laws that govern the administration of military justice for all the armed services of the United States.

code of professional responsibility. N. A compilation of guidelines for the professional conduct and ethical behavior of attorneys and legal professionals; has been replaced by the Model Rules of Professional Conduct.

codicil. N. An addendum to a will, modifying, adding to, revoking, or explaining portions of the original document.

codify. V. To arrange laws or rules systematically. N. *codification*.

coerce. v. To force someone to act against his or her wishes, through the use of verbal or physical threats or other forms of compulsion. N. *coercion*.

cognizable. ADJ. Within a court's jurisdiction.

cognizance. N. Jurisdiction or judicial notice.

cognovit judgment. N. A debtor's written confession of judgment in the event of nonpayment.

cognovit note. N. A promissory note written by a debtor authorizing an attorney to confess judgment against him or her if the debt described in the note is not paid when due.

cohabit. v. To live together; to share a dwelling as a married couple without being married. N. *cohabitation*.

co-heir. N. One of two or more heirs inheriting from the same estate.

coif. N. A headdress; a white piece of cloth worn by top English lawyers on top of their wigs.

Coif, Order of the. N. An honor society for law students in the top 10% of their class.

coinsurance. N. A form of insurance in which the insurer pays only a portion of a claim for damage, sharing the risk with the insured.

collate. v. (1) To collect information and arrange it in order. (2) When someone dies intestate, to estimate the value of all advances made by the deceased to his or her children before death so that these advances can be considered in dividing the estate according to law. N. *collation*.

collateral. N. Something pledged as security for a loan, to be forfeited if the debt is not paid. ADJ. Beside; parallel; additional. See also *lineal*.

collateral attack. N. An attempt to defeat a judgment through a separate action instead of an appeal or other direct attack.

collateral estoppel. N. A doctrine holding that a judgment on issues litigated by two parties is binding on them for those issues in all subsequent actions with different causes of action.

collateral source rule. N. A rule stating that if an injured person receives compensation from a source such as insurance, the damages the injured person can receive from the tortfeasor are not reduced by that amount.

collective bargaining. N. Negotiation and dispute resolution over employment matters between a representative group of employees and the employer. See also *union*.

colloquium. N. In an action for slander or libel, a declaration that words spoken or written by the defendant were about the plaintiff and intended by the defendant.

collude. V. (1) Conspire; to agree secretly to commit some fraudulent act. (2) In a divorce proceeding, for the husband and wife to agree that one of them will commit some act that can be grounds for divorce. N. ***collusion***.

collusive action. N. A lawsuit brought by people who do not actually have a grievance in order to see how the court will rule or to establish a precedent; courts will not hear collusive actions because they have no real controversy.

color. N. Appearance as opposed to reality; disguise; hiding facts behind a false legal theory.

colorable. ADJ. Presenting a deceptive appearance.

color of law. N. The appearance of legal authority without the substance; something that appears to have the authority of law but in fact does not.

color of title. N. An instrument that appears to be a valid title but in fact is not.

comity. N. (1) Courtesy toward others. (2) The judicial practice of one court recognizing the decisions of courts from other jurisdictions out of respect. See also *full faith and credit*.

comity of nations. N. Recognition by one nation within its own territory of the laws of another nation.

commence. V. To begin. N. *commencement*.

comment. N. An opinion or reaction to something; an observation. V. *comment*.

commerce. N. The exchange, buying, and selling of goods, services, and property; trade and transportation of goods. ADJ. *commercial*.

Commerce Clause. N. Article I, Section 8, Clause 3 of the U.S. Constitution, which gives Congress the power to regulate commerce with foreign nations, among the states, and with American Indian tribes.

commercial paper. N. A document in which the maker promises to pay the bearer a certain sum on deposit or at a particular time; a short-term unsecured loan issued by a company.

commercial speech. N. Speech that has a specific commercial purpose, such as advertising.

commercial unit. N. An item or collection of goods that cannot be divided without impairing its value, such as a machine, a suite of furniture, or a bale of cotton.

commingle. V. To mix; to blend together.

commingling of funds. N. A fiduciary's mingling of a client's or beneficiary's money with his or her own.

commission. N. (1) A fee paid to an agent, broker, etc., for handling a transaction, usually a percentage of the total transaction. (2) A warrant issued by the government or a court authorizing its recipient to perform specific duties. (3) A group of people authorized to perform some function. (4) The act of committing a crime.

commissioner. N. A member of a commission, or a person with a commission.

commit. V. (1) To do or perform a deed or act. (2) To entrust to the care of someone else; to send someone to prison or a mental institution. (3) To bind oneself to someone or something.

commitment. N. (1) The act of committing. (2) An obligation.

committee. N. (1) A group of people appointed to perform a specific duty. (2) Someone who has been committed to a mental institution. (3) Someone appointed to care for an incompetent person.

commodity. N. (1) Something that can be sold; a thing of value. (2) Raw materials or agricultural products that can be bought and sold.

common. ADJ. (1) Ordinary; frequently occurring. (2) Shared.

common law. N. A system of law based on judicial precedent and custom rather than statute and code; the system of jurisprudence used in England and most of the United States. See also *civil law*.

commons. N. Parks and other land set aside for public use.

Commons, House of. N. The British legislative house that represents the common people, all subjects except the nobility and royalty.

common stock. N. Shares of ownership of a company. See also *preferred stock.*

commonwealth. N. A political unit governed for the common good; a commonwealth can take many forms, such as a nation, state, republic, or union.

communicate. V. To exchange information. N. *communication.*

Communications Decency Act. N. A law passed as part of the Telecommunications Act of 1996 that attempted to regulate obscenity on the Internet and was effectively ruled unconstitutional by the U.S. Supreme Court in the late 1990s and early 2000s. ABBRV. *CDA.*

community. N. (1) A locality or the people who live in it. (2) A group of people who share a religion, profession, or other characteristic. (3) A group of states or nations with common interests. (4) The sense of fellowship that comes from sharing a home, interests, or characteristics.

community property. N. Property owned equally by husband and wife, with all earnings divided equally between spouses; the form of marital property distribution used by a minority of states. See also *equitable distribution, marital property.*

commute. V. To replace or change; to replace a criminal sentence with a lighter one. N. *commutation.*

compact. N. An agreement between two or more parties, especially states or governments, to work together on shared concerns.

Compact Clause. N. Article I, Section 10, Clause 3 of the U.S. Constitution, prohibiting states to enter into compacts with other states or with foreign nations (i.e., interstate compacts) without the consent of Congress.

company. N. A group or association of people with the purpose of running a business or commercial enterprise; a business.

company, joint stock. N. A company that raises capital by pooling the contributions of its members, which are then divided into shares that are distributed to members to represent their share of ownership of the company.

comparative negligence. N. A system under which negligence is computed in terms of percentage, and a party's damages will be reduced by the amount that his or her negligence contributed to them; contributory negligence has largely replaced the doctrine of comparative negligence.

compensate. V. (1) To give someone money to make up for an injury he or she has suffered. (2) To pay someone for work he or she has performed. N. *compensation*.

competency. N. Ability to stand trial or serve as a witness.

competent. ADJ. Able; capable; having the ability to do something; capable of understanding.

competent court. N. A court with proper jurisdiction.

competent evidence. N. Evidence that is admissible because it is material and relevant.

complainant. N. A party who brings a legal complaint against another.

complaint. N. (1) The pleading that begins a civil lawsuit, in which the plaintiff sets forth his or her causes of action and demands relief. (2) In criminal law, a charge made before a magistrate that a particular person has committed an offense, in an effort to begin the process of prosecution.

compliance. N. The practice within a business of ensuring that all personnel are following applicable laws, rules, and regulations.

comply. V. To follow orders or rules; to submit.

compos mentis. ADJ. *(Latin)* Of sound mind; sane and mentally competent. See also *non compos mentis*.

compound. V. (1) To combine. (2) To make worse.

compound a crime or felony. V. For an injured party to agree not to prosecute the person who has committed the crime against him or her in exchange for some payment.

compound interest. N. Interest paid both on principal and on any interest already accumulated.

Comprehensive Test Ban Treaty. N. An international treaty effective in 1997 that bans all nuclear explosions. ABBRV. *CTBT*.

compulsion. N. Force or duress; forcing someone to do something. V. *compel*.

compulsory. ADJ. Required; obligatory.

compulsory arbitration. N. Arbitration in which the parties are forced to agree.

compulsory insurance. N. Motor vehicle insurance that drivers are required by law to purchase.

compulsory process. N. A court's use of subpoena, arrest, or attachment to force a person to appear in court; a defendant's constitutional right to force witnesses to appear and testify at trial.

Computer Fraud and Abuse Act. N. A federal law passed in 1986 that made hacking into computer systems illegal. ABBRV. *CFAA.*

conceal. V. To hide.

concealed carry. N. The practice of carrying a concealed weapon; open carry. N. The practice of carrying a weapon in plain sight on one's person.

concealed weapon. A handgun or other firearm that is concealed on a person's body or is kept in close proximity to the person.

concealed weapon permit. N. A license that allows a private citizen to carry a concealed weapon.

concealment. N. Intentionally withholding information.

conception. N. (1) The beginning of pregnancy, when an egg is fertilized by a sperm; the action of conceiving a child. (2) A notion or idea; the beginning of an idea. V. *conceive.*

concerted action. N. An act that has been planned and performed by two or more people with a common purpose. See also *conspiracy, accomplice.*

conciliation. N. Amicable resolution of a dispute by the parties themselves, often done before trial. See also *arbitration, mediation.*

conclude. V. (1) To end; to sum up. (2) To reach a judgment through reasoning.

conclusion. N. (1) An ending. (2) A final opinion arrived at through examination of facts and logical reasoning.

conclusion of fact. N. A conclusion reached by examining only the facts and evidence, without applying any law.

conclusion of law. N. A court's legal conclusions about a case, arrived at by applying rules of law.

conclusive. ADJ. Proving something beyond doubt; decisive.

conclusive evidence. N. Incontrovertible evidence; evidence that establishes a proposition and that cannot be disproved.

concur. V. To agree.

concurrence. N. A concurring opinion; an opinion written by a judge or justice of an appellate court agreeing with the majority conclusion in a case but describing a different path of legal reasoning. See also *dissent*.

concurrent. ADJ. Simultaneous; at the same time.

condemn. V. (1) To find someone guilty of a crime; to sentence someone to death. (2) To disapprove of publicly. (3) To officially declare a building unfit for use. (4) To use eminent domain to take private property for public use. N. *condemnation*.

condition. N. Something that must happen or be the case before something else can happen; a prerequisite. ADJ. *conditional*.

condition precedent. N. A fact or state of affairs that must exist before a particular contractual duty must be performed.

condition subsequent. N. A future event that will end a contractual obligation.

condominium. N. A kind of dwelling arrangement in which individuals own separate units in a multi-unit complex and all owners share common facilities and areas. See also *cooperative*.

condonation. N. In marriage, the forgiveness of some behavior that would be grounds for divorce by resuming cohabitation on the condition that the behavior not happen again.

condone. V. To approve, albeit reluctantly; to allow undesirable behavior to continue.

confederate. ADJ. United by a treaty or common agreement. N. An accomplice.

confederation. N. An alliance or league of states, each of which retains full sovereignty and self-government, with a limited central government.

confess. V. To admit to having committed a crime or wrongful act. N. *confession*.

confession and avoidance. N. A pleading in which the party admits the truth of the allegations in the complaint but then presents new information that makes those allegations ineffectual. See also *affirmative defense*.

confession of judgment. N. Entry of judgment against a debtor without a legal proceeding, done if the debtor signs a cognovit note at the time of purchase.

confidence game. N. A swindle in which a swindler earns the trust of the victim and then takes advantage of it to cheat the victim out of money; informally called a con game or simply con.

confidential. ADJ. Secret; private. N. *confidentiality*.

confidential communication. N. Statements made in private, meant to be heard only by the person addressed. See also *privilege*.

confirm. V. (1) To show that a statement is correct; to state that a fact is true. (2) To formally install someone in office; to ratify.

confirmation. N. Formal approval; written ratification of something.

confiscate. V. To take someone's private property for public use; during wartime, to take an enemy's property; for the government to appropriate private property without compensation. N. ***confiscation***.

conflict of interest. N. An ethical dilemma in which a person is entrusted with two duties at odds with one another, in which attention to one duty will harm the other.

conflict of laws. N. The conflict that results when a controversy occurs in more than one jurisdiction, thus raising the question of which jurisdiction's law to apply to the matter; the branch of law that considers these questions, also called choice of law.

conform. V. To comply with stated rules or standards. ADJ. *conforming*. N. ***conformity***. See also *nonconformity*.

conformed copy. N. An exact copy of a document with handwritten notations of items that were written by hand on the original; often prepared and certified by a clerk of court.

confront. V. To face someone; to come face to face with a problem or an accusation. N. ***confrontation***.

Confrontation Clause. N. A provision of the Sixth Amendment of the U.S. Constitution guaranteeing the accused the right to confront his or her accuser and witnesses at trial, to hear his or her testimony, and cross-examine him or her.

confuse. v. To make blurry or perplexing; to intermingle things so that they cannot be distinguished from one another. N. *confusion*.

confusion of goods. N. Mixing the property of different owners so that they can no longer identify their own goods.

conglomerate. N. A corporate entity composed of several different corporations merged together. See also *merger*.

congress. N. (1) A country's national legislative body; in the United States, the body composed of the Senate and the House of Representatives, usually capitalized to "Congress." (2) A formal meeting, usually by political or professional groups. (3) A union or coming together, as in the phrase "sexual congress."

conjecture. N. A tentative conclusion or opinion based on limited information; a guess. V. *conjecture*.

conjugal. ADJ. Having to do with the marital relationship.

conjugal rights. N. Rights that each spouse can expect from the other, particularly sexual rights but also the rights to society, comfort, and affection.

conjugal visit. N. A visit to a convict by his or her spouse during which the couple is given the opportunity to have sexual intercourse.

conjunctive. ADJ. Connective; joining.

conjunctive denial. N. A single collective denial of several facts stated in a complaint.

con man. N. Slang for a swindler. See also *confidence game, flim-flam*.

consanguinity. N. Blood relationship; the relationship of people who share a common ancestor. ADJ. *consanguine*, *consanguineous*.

consanguinity, collateral. N. The relationship between those who share an ancestor but are not descended in the same line, such as the relationship between aunts and uncles, nieces and nephews, and cousins.

consanguinity, lineal. N. Kinship between people descended in a direct line from one another, such as the relationship between parent and child and grandchild.

conscience. N. A personal standard that guides a person's view of what is right and wrong; moral sense.

conscience of the court. N. An equity court's application of community standards of fairness and decency along with principles of equitable law and precedent to its resolution of a controversy.

conscientious objector. N. A person who refuses to serve in the armed forces due to ethical, moral, or religious objections to war. See also *pacifist*.

conscript. N. One who has been compulsorily enrolled in the military. V. *conscript*.

conscription. N. The draft; compulsory enlistment in the military.

consent. V. To agree voluntarily; to give permission. N. *consent*.

consent, implied. N. Consent that is expressed indirectly through behavior and actions that make it appear that consent has been given.

consent decree. N. A binding decree issued by a judge that expresses a consensual agreement between the parties to a lawsuit.

consent judgment. N. A judgment that the parties agree to.

consent search. N. A search made by police after the subject of the search has voluntarily consented to it freely, which absolves the police of the need for a search warrant.

consequence. N. A result; the result that naturally follows a cause.

conservator. N. A guardian; someone appointed by a court to manage an estate, a business, or the personal affairs of someone unable to manage alone.

consideration. N. The payment or reward essential to the formation of a contract and that persuades a person to enter the contract; something of value given in exchange for a performance or a promise.

consign. V. To entrust goods to someone else; to deliver goods to the custody of a carrier or agent, usually so that they can be sold.

consignee. N. The recipient of consigned goods; the person named as recipient in a bill of lading.

consignment. N. (1) The act of consigning. (2) A batch of goods consigned to someone.

consolidate. V. To put together several things into one coherent whole. N. *consolidation*.

consolidated appeal. N. A single appeal filed by more than one appellant whose interests are similar enough to make their combination feasible.

Consolidated Omnibus Budget Reconciliation Act of 1985. N. A federal law that allows some employees to maintain health coverage through an employer after leaving employment. ABBRV. *COBRA*.

consolidation of actions. N. Combining several related lawsuits into a single action.

consolidation of corporations. N. Combining two or more corporations by destroying them and creating a new corporation with the assets and liabilities of the now nonexistent ones. See also *merger*.

consortium. N. (1) A married person's right to fellowship, help, and affection from his or her spouse. (2) An association of several companies that join together to pursue a common object for a specified period of time, in which the members do not assume liability for one another's actions. PL. *consortia*.

consortium, loss of. N. A cause of action that can be brought by someone whose spouse has been killed or injured, based on loss of material services, companionship, and sex.

conspiracy. N. Two or more people who join together to plan and commit an unlawful act. V. *conspire*.

conspirator. N. A person who participates in a conspiracy.

constituent. N. One who authorizes someone else to act for him or her, usually used to name the members of a community that elect and are represented by a legislator or politician.

constitution. N. A collection of fundamental principles of law according to which a nation or organization is to be governed.

constitutional. ADJ. According to principles defined in the Constitution.

constitutional question. N. A legal question that must be answered by interpreting the Constitution, as opposed to being addressed by a statute. See also *unconstitutional*.

construct. N. An idea composed of various conceptual elements, usually one that is not empirically verifiable or testable.

construction. N. (1) The interpretation of a statute or legal authority, particularly of ambiguous portions of it. See also *construe*.

construction, liberal. N. Interpreting a statute expansively, looking for the spirit of the law.

construction, strict. N. Interpreting a statute solely on the basis of what is written, bringing in nothing that is not expressed and looking for the letter rather than the spirit of the law.

constructionist. N. A person who interprets a law, especially the Constitution, in a particular way. (2) Building houses and other structures.

constructive. N. Implied or inferred; inferred by construing facts in a particular way.

constructive contract. N. A contract not intentionally entered into by the parties that arises legally to prevent injustice. Synonymous with *quasi contract*.

constructive discharge. N. A situation in which an employee finds conditions at work so intolerable that he or she feels forced to resign, without actually being discharged by the employer. See also *harass, discrimination*.

constructive eviction. N. A situation in which a landlord lets living conditions get so bad that a tenant feels compelled to move out.

constructive notice. N. Notice implied by law, usually because it is in a public record.

constructive possession. N. The power to control an item without actual physical possession of it.

construe. V. To find the meaning in words or actions. See also *construction*.

consultant. N. An expert, often an independent contractor, paid by a company to give it advice on some matter but not employed by that company.

consumer. N. A person who buys goods and services and consumes or uses them.

consumer-driven health plan. N. A health plan that is meant to give consumers a higher degree of control over their own health care, typically by allowing consumers to save money and use it to pay for medical care as they choose. See also *health savings account, high deductible health plan*.

consumer goods. N. Goods bought for personal use by an individual, household, or family, and not intended for resale; a category of goods under the Uniform Commercial Code.

consumer protection laws. N. Federal and state laws regulating sales and credit practices, intended to protect consumers from deceptive advertising, poor quality, dishonest credit and debt practices, and other dangers facing retail consumers who cannot engage in arm's-length bargaining with retailers and manufacturers.

contempt. N. Disregard for authority; willful disobedience or disrespect.

contempt, civil. N. Refusing to perform a duty ordered by the court to benefit another party to the litigation, such as producing documents.

contempt, constructive. N. Disregard for court authority that occurs away from the court, such as refusing to obey an injunction.

contempt, criminal. N. An act that directly interferes with the court's operation or obstructs justice.

contempt, direct. N. Contempt committed in the court or near enough that it interferes with orderly proceedings.

contempt of court. N. Disobedience to a court and its officers; any act intended to interfere with the operation or dignity of the court.

contiguous. ADJ. Touching, next to, sharing a border.

Continental Congress. N. A congress held by the American colonies at the start of the American Revolution; Continental Congresses were held in 1774, 1775, and 1776, and resulted in the creation of the Continental Army.

contingency fee. N. A fee charged by an attorney that is contingent on a successful outcome of the case; often the attorney will take a percentage of the client's recovery if the client prevails, and will receive nothing if the client loses; commonly used by attorneys representing plaintiffs in personal injury lawsuits. Also called a contingent fee.

contingent. ADJ. Depending on something; occurring if some specified condition occurs; provisional. N. A delegation; a group of people that represents a larger group.

contingent beneficiary. N. Someone who will receive the proceeds of a trust or some other arrangement only if a specific event occurs.

contingent estate. N. An estate that will only vest if a specific event occurs.

contingent interest. N. An interest that will only vest if a specific event occurs.

contingent liability. N. Potential liability; liability that will accrue if some specific event occurs first.

contingent right. N. A right that will only vest if a specific event occurs.

continuance. N. Postponement or adjournment of a trial or other court proceeding to a later date.

contra. ADJ. *(Latin)* Against.

contraband. N. Illegal goods; goods that are illegal to possess, such as narcotics or counterfeit money.

contract. N. An agreement between two or more parties that is enforceable by law; a transaction between two or more people in which one or both promise to perform some duty in exchange for consideration, and if a party fails to do what he or she promised, the law allows the other party to seek a remedy. V. *contract*.

contract, bilateral. N. A contract between two parties in which each one promises something to the other.

contract, oral. N. A contract that is executed verbally and not put in writing. See also *statute of frauds*.

contract, unilateral. N. A contract in which one party promises to do something in exchange for performance by the other party.

contractor. N. A person who contracts to do work for someone else, on an independent basis, using his or her own materials and methods and not under the control of the customer with regard to the details of how the work is done. See also *independent contractor, subcontractor.*

contribute. V. To give; to donate something in order to help some cause; to help or assist in bringing something about.

contribution. N. A payment of a portion of a liability recovery by one who shares liability, especially among insurers; the doctrine that allows someone who has already paid a judgment to recover part of the amount from another party who is also liable. ADJ. *contributory.*

control. N. Power over someone or something; power to direct a person's actions, manage a machine, or influence events. V. *control.*

controlled substance. N. A drug regulated by law whose distribution is restricted or prohibited because of potential for abuse, including narcotics, stimulants, depressants, hallucinogens, and marijuana.

controlled substance acts. N. Federal and state laws that regulate distribution and use of controlled substances.

controversy. N. A dispute that can be litigated in court; a civil action or lawsuit.

contumacy. N. Willful disobedience of the court's authority.

contumely. N. Contemptuous insolence; rudeness or insulting language.

convention. N. (1) An agreement, usually among several nations, that is less formal than a treaty. (2) A meeting of members of a professional, political, or social organization.

conversion. N. The tort of wrongfully taking another person's property and assuming ownership of it or preventing the owner from using it. V. *convert*.

convertible securities. N. Bonds or preferred stock that can be exchanged for common stock or another lesser security, generally within the same company.

convey. V. To transfer property from one person to another. N. *conveyance*.

convict. V. For a court to find someone guilty of a crime. N. One who has been found by a court to be guilty of a crime.

conviction. N. The legal act of finding someone guilty of a crime; the end of the prosecution, including the judgment or sentence.

conviction, summary. N. Finding a person guilty of a crime after a trial without a jury.

cooperative. N. A business owned and run by its members for the purpose of mutual help, in which profits and costs are shared.

cooperative apartment. N. An apartment in a complex of apartments in which each owner has a share in the entire complex and a lease of his or her own apartment. See also *condominium*.

copay. N. A set fee a person pays for a medical service received as part of a health insurance plan.

copyright. N. The legal right to publish, perform, or display a work of literature, art, music, drama, recording, or film, protected both by common law and by statute, including the Copyright Act of 1976. See also *infringe*.

coroner. N. A public official who investigates sudden, violent, and suspicious deaths. See also *inquest*.

corporal punishment. N. Physical punishment, such as beating.

corporate opportunity. N. The opportunity available to someone closely related to a corporation to use corporate information or appropriate corporate business opportunities for his or her own personal gain; the corporate opportunity doctrine prohibits this kind of opportunism.

corporation. N. The legal entity created by law of an association of people who hold shares of a business, existing as an artificial person that can sue and be sued and whose liability is generally limited to corporate assets.

corporation, C. N. A corporation formed under Subchapter C of the Internal Revenue Code; also called a Subchapter C corporation.

corporation, close. N. A corporation whose shares are not publicly traded but instead are held by a small group or a single shareholder who also runs the corporation's business; also called a closely held corporation.

corporation, private. N. An ordinary corporation formed to do business and earn a profit.

corporation, public. N. A corporation formed by the government for a particular governmental purpose.

corporation, S. N. A small corporation that can have its taxable income taxed to its shareholders to avoid corporate income tax.

corporeal. ADJ. Having a physical body.

corpus. N. *(Latin)* Body; a collection or mass; the principal mass of a physical substance. In trust law, it is the principal or res of an estate.

corpus delicti. N. *(Latin)* The body of a crime; the person or object on which the crime is committed, or the prima facie showing that the person or object was the victim of a crime; a necessary element for conviction, including the occurrence of some injury and some criminal act.

corpus juris. N. *(Latin)* Body of law; a book that collects principles of law.

Corpus Juris Canonici. N. *(Latin)* A collection of canon law.

Corpus Juris Civilis. N. *(Latin)* A collection of civil law.

correctional institution. N. A jail, reformatory, prison, or other institution where those convicted of crimes are sent.

correctional system. N. The government system of correctional institutions and parole systems.

corroborate. V. To confirm or verify; to agree with or give support to. N. *corroboration*.

corroborating evidence. N. Evidence that agrees with or supports evidence that has already been presented.

corrupt. ADJ. Willing to act dishonestly in exchange for money or advantage; morally depraved. V. To spoil; to make someone turn bad.

corruption. N. Abuse of an official position for personal gain; dishonest behavior by someone who holds official power. See also *bribe*.

cosign. V. To sign a document along with someone else, either to guarantee the first signer's obligation or to verify the authenticity of the other signature.

cosigner. N. One who cosigns a document. See also *surety*.

cost. N. The price; the amount that must be paid for something.

cost, insurance, and freight. A term meaning that the cost of goods, insurance, and shipping are included in the contract price. ABBRV. *C.I.F.*, C.F.I.

cost, opportunity. N. A potential benefit lost because of a decision made.

cost basis. N. The amount a taxpayer paid for an asset.

cost of completion. N. In a breach of contract action, a measure of damages calculated by the amount it would cost to pay for a performance that would put the plaintiff where he or she would have been had the contract not been breached.

cost of living. N. The amount it costs to live from day to day, measured by the Consumer Price Index.

cost-plus contract. N. A kind of contract, common in construction projects, in which the contractor is paid for costs of material and labor plus a percentage of those costs as profit.

costs. N. The expenses involved in taking a case to trial, sometimes awarded to the victorious party; costs usually do not include attorney's fees.

cotenancy. N. A tenancy shared by two or more people at the same time, including joint tenancy and tenancy in common.

cotenant. N. Someone who shares a tenancy with someone else.

counsel. N. (1) An attorney, a lawyer; also called counselor. (2) Legal advice. V. To give legal advice.

count. N. A distinct statement of a cause of action or a claim in a plaintiff's pleading; an allegation of a specific offense or charge in an indictment.

counter. ADJ. Against. V. To oppose; to rebut.

counterclaim. N. A claim made by a defendant to oppose the claim brought by the plaintiff; a counterdemand.

counterclaim, compulsory. N. A claim arising out of the same subject matter as the plaintiff's original claim and involving largely the same people; it must be made when the defendant answers the complaint.

counterclaim, permissive. N. A claim not arising out of the occurrence that brought about the original complaint, and that can be brought at the defendant's choice.

counterfeit. ADJ. Fake; forged; copied with the intention of passing off as authentic. V. *counterfeit*.

counterfeiter. N. A person who makes fake copies of money or other objects and passes them off as genuine.

county. N. A locally governed territorial division of a state; called a parish in Louisiana.

coupon. N. A certificate attached to a loan instrument that can be separated from the instrument and presented after a specified time for the collection of interest.

coupon bond. N. A bond that has coupons attached to it for the collection of several installments of interest before the bond matures.

course of business. N. Normal business operations.

course of dealing. N. A series of previous acts and conduct between the parties to a transaction that establishes an understanding that subsequent actions and conduct related to the same or similar transactions will be interpreted the same way. See also *trade usage.*

course of employment. N. The normal duties and activities associated with a job; the activities that an employee performs as his or her customary services to the employer.

court. N. A tribunal in which a judge and/or jury hears and decides civil and/or criminal cases; the governmental entity that applies the state's laws to cases and controversies and administers justice; also called a court of law.

court, civil. N. A court that hears civil cases.

court, criminal. N. A court that hears criminal prosecutions.

court, out of. N. Occurring before a case reaches trial or outside the courtroom; usually used to describe a settlement.

court, trial. N. The level of court at which a civil or criminal case receives its first hearing.

court-martial. N. (1) A military court that hears cases involving members of the armed forces. (2) A trial or proceeding before a military court. V. To try someone in a court-martial. PL. *courts-martial* or *court-martials.*

court of appeals. N. A court that hears appeals of decisions made by trial courts. See also *appellate court.*

court of equity. N. A court that hears cases in equity, particularly cases that would not have a suitable remedy at law; most states no longer have courts of equity. See also *chancery.*

court of last resort. N. The highest court to which an appellant can hope to appeal, such as the Supreme Court for federal cases.

court reporter. N. A person trained and certified to record testimony at trial or at a deposition and produce an official transcript of it.

court stacking. N. The practice by the president of appointing to federal benches only judges who espouse a particular ideological viewpoint, in order to increase the likelihood that courts will rule in that direction.

covenant. N. A contract or formal agreement; often produced in writing and signed by all parties. V. To enter into an agreement.

covenant, affirmative. N. A covenant in which one party agrees to do something.

covenant, negative. N. A covenant in which one party promises not to do something.

covenantee. N. A person for whom a covenant is made.

covenant for further assurance. N. A covenant in which a seller of land agrees to do whatever is necessary to perfect the buyer's title.

covenant not to compete. N. An agreement made as part of a contract for employment in which the covenantor agrees not to compete with the covenantee in a particular area for a specified time.

covenantor. N. A person who makes a covenant.

covenant running with the land. N. A covenant that is attached to a piece of land and is binding on those who come into possession of it.

cover. v. (1) In insurance, to protect against loss or liability; to furnish money to pay for the financial consequences of an accident or misfortune. (2) In commercial law, after a seller breaches a promise to deliver goods, to find an alternative source of the same goods on the open market.

coverage. N. In insurance, the amount that the insurer is prepared to pay for a particular loss.

coverture. N. In common law, the legal state of a married woman, which was generally merged with that of her husband, leaving her without the right to own property or enter contracts on her own.

CPA. ABBRV. Certified public accountant.

Creative Commons. N. A nonprofit organization dedicated to making creative work more freely available by providing free licensing services to creators of literary works, enabling copyright holders to grant some of the rights to their work to the public.

credibility. N. The quality, especially in a witness, of being believable and likely to tell the truth.

credible. ADJ. Believable; trustworthy.

credible evidence. N. Evidence that is likely to be true because it is natural and probable in light of other circumstances already known.

credible witness. N. A trustworthy witness whose testimony is believable.

credit. N. (1) The ability of a person or business to obtain money, goods, or services because of the likelihood that he or she will pay back any debt on schedule, usually based on a past history of payment and likelihood of future success. (2) Money lent on credit. (3) In accounting, a sum received; the opposite of debt.

creditor. N. A person or business to whom a debt is owed. See also *debtor*.

creditor's bill (suit). N. A proceeding brought in equity by a creditor who has secured judgment against a debtor to enforce payment of the debt if the creditor cannot reach the debtor's property at law.

credit rating. N. A number calculated by examining a person's assets, liabilities, and financial history that tells a lender how likely that person is to pay back a loan.

crime. N. An act that violates criminal law.

crime, white-collar. N. A crime usually done by professionals and businesspeople, such as extortion, computer crime, wire fraud, and government contract fraud. See also *felony*, *misdemeanor*.

crime against humanity. N. An attack on or persecution of a group of people who are part of a widespread practice or governmental policy that results in serious attacks on human dignity or degradation of the victims, including widespread rape, murder, torture, or racial, political, or religious persecution.

crime against nature. N. Sexual intercourse that violates statutorily mandated standards of behavior. See also *buggery*, *sodomy*.

crime malum in se. N. A crime that is illegal because it is wrong in itself. See also *malum in se*.

crime malum prohibitum. N. A crime that is illegal because it is prohibited by statute. See also *malum prohibitum*.

crime of passion. N. A crime committed in the heat of sudden passion.

criminal. N. One who commits a crime; one who violates a criminal law. ADJ. Related to a crime; done with malice or intent to injure.

criminalize. V. To decide that some act is a crime; to pass a law stating that an act is a crime; see also *decriminalize*.

criminal justice system. N. The government's system of law enforcement that apprehends, prosecutes, and punishes criminals, including law enforcement officers, courts, and correctional institutions.

criminal law. N. The branch of law that deals with the prosecution and punishment of criminals; the body of law that determines what constitutes a crime and what constitutes suitable punishment.

criminal maintenance. N. Helping a party to a lawsuit prosecute or defend the case in such a way as to obstruct justice and promote needless litigation.

criminal mischief. N. The crime of maliciously injuring property.

criminal procedure. N. The body of law that governs actions in criminal courts, including investigation, prosecution, and punishment.

criminal record. N. An official history of a person's arrests, convictions, sentences, and paroles; also called a rap sheet.

cross-claim. N. A claim brought by a party to a lawsuit against a co-party, out of an occurrence that is part of the subject matter of the original action. See also *counterclaim*.

cross-examination. N. At trial or a deposition, the examination of a witness by the party opposed to the side that produced him or her, regarding testimony already raised on direct examination and matters of witness credibility.

cruel. ADJ. Callously causing pain or suffering. N. *cruelty*.

cruel and inhuman treatment. N. As a grounds for divorce, treatment by one spouse that causes the other spouse suffering and makes life together completely unbearable.

cruel and unusual punishment. N. Punishment that offends ordinary people due to its excessiveness or cruelty, or that is far out of proportion to the offense it punishes; forbidden by the Eighth Amendment of the Constitution.

CTBT. ABBRV. Comprehensive Test Ban Treaty.

culpa. N. *(Latin)* Fault, blame.

culpable. ADJ. Guilty; deserving blame or punishment. N. *culpability*.

culprit. N. A person who commits a crime or wrongful act; a person accused of a crime.

cumulative. ADJ. Increasing with new additions; piling up.

cumulative voting. N. A system of shareholder voting in which a shareholder is allowed to apply all of his or her votes to one candidate for a board of directors instead of having to cast separate votes for each office, allowing minority shareholders a chance for meaningful representation.

curative. ADJ. Able or intended to correct a legal error.

curative instruction. N. An instruction given by a judge to a jury intended to correct an erroneous instruction or to fix the jury's interpretation of improper evidence.

curative statute. N. A statute passed to correct a defect in a previously enacted law. See also *declaratory*.

currency. N. Coined money and banknotes in general circulation.

current. ADJ. Of the moment; in the present time.

current assets. N. Property of a business that could or will be converted into cash as part of normal operations in the immediate future, usually within the year.

current liabilities. N. Liabilities that are part of normal business operations and that will be repaid within a year.

curtesy. N. A common-law right of a husband to take a life estate in all of his wife's lands if she dies before him, usually only applicable if they had children together; curtesy has been abolished or modified in most states. See also *dower*.

curtilage. N. The land surrounding and attached to a house, often enclosed in some way.

custodian. N. One who cares for something, ranging from buildings to financial assets.

custody. N. (1) Responsibility or guardianship of a person or thing. (2) Imprisonment.

custody, joint. N. Custody in which both parents share responsibility for caring for and raising a child.

custody, temporary. N. Custody awarded to one parent for a brief period, pending a decision on permanent custody.

custody of children. N. The daily nurture and control of a child, usually awarded to one parent in a case of divorce or separation.

custom. N. The traditional, ordinary, and accepted way of doing things in a particular community.

custom and usage. N. A customary practice that has been done so long that it has acquired the force of law in its locality.

customary. ADJ. Ordinary; according to usual practices or custom; habitual.

customer. N. Someone who buys goods or services from a business.

customs. N. (1) The government agency that collects tariffs and taxes on imports; also the place at an airport, port, or border crossing where imported goods are inspected. (2) Tariffs or taxes on imported goods; also called customs duties.

cybercrime. N. A crime committed using computers, networks, or the Internet.

cyberlaw. N. The field of law that encompasses issues involving computers, networks, and information technology.

cyberspace. N. The nonphysical territory occupied by the Internet and computer networks.

cybersquatting. N. Registering a trademarked name as a domain name with the intention of selling it to an individual or company that actually owns the trademarked name.

cy-près. ADJ. *(French)* As near; as near as possible; the doctrine that if a bequest is illegal or impossible, the court will try to replace it with one as close to the testator's intentions as possible. ADV. *cy-près*.

damage. N. Physical harm; injury. V. *damage*.

damages. N. Money awarded as compensation for injury or loss.

damages, actual. N. Damages for actual losses and injuries sustained; also called compensatory damages or general damages.

damages, consequential. N. Damages for an injury that arises from the consequences of an act, for loss that arises from an injury but is not directly caused by the injury and would not necessarily occur; also called special damages.

damages, double or treble. N. Damages awarded in particular kinds of cases in which the court will award two or three times the amount awarded by the jury.

damages, incidental. N. Damages for expenses that arise out of an occurrence that gives rise to a claim for actual damages.

damages, liquidated. N. A sum that a party to a contract agrees to pay if he or she breaches it; meant to be a reasonable estimate of the loss that the breach would cause.

damages, punitive. N. Damages over and above compensation for actual injury, intended to punish the wrongdoer for malicious conduct; also called *exemplary damages*.

damnum absque injuria. N. *(Latin)* Harm without injury; a loss or injury that does not give rise to a legal action to recover damages.

damnum fatale. N. *(Latin)* Harm due to fate; an injury caused by an act of God or some force beyond human control. See also *act of God*.

dangerous. ADJ. Able to harm or injure; risky or hazardous.

dangerous instrumentality. N. An object that can endanger people by either careless or improper use.

dangerous weapon. N. A device that can inflict serious injury or death; see also *deadly weapon.*

day in court. N. The day on which a litigant is appointed to appear in court and be given the opportunity to seek relief from an injury or to defend him- or herself from charges.

d/b/a. ABBRV. Doing business as.

dead hand. N. The continuing control by the dead over the affairs of the living; see also *mortmain.*

deadly force. N. Force that could kill the person against whom it is used.

deadly weapon. N. A weapon or instrument that is capable of killing someone, whether because of its inherent nature (such as a gun) or the way it is used (such as a hammer). See also *weapon.*

deal. V. To conduct business; to buy and sell a particular commodity. N. (1) An arrangement between two or more parties that works to their mutual benefit. (2) A transaction that involves buying or selling something.

dealer. N. A person who buys and sells a particular commodity; one who buys something in order to resell it. See also *retail, broker.*

death. N. The moment at which life ceases; the condition of being dead; see also *brain death.*

death, natural. N. A death that results solely from natural causes.

death, violent. N. A death caused by human actions.

death benefit. N. An amount paid to a beneficiary when an insured person dies.

death certificate. N. An official document issued to certify that someone is dead, usually including cause and time of death.

death penalty. N. Capital punishment; punishing someone for a serious crime such as murder by killing him or her.

death records. N. Official records of deaths kept by a municipal authority.

death tax. N. Any tax imposed on property or its transfer after its owner dies.

debauch. V. To corrupt; to destroy one's morals or manners; to seduce.

debauchery. N. Overindulgence in pleasures of the senses; sexual immorality.

de bene esse. ADV. *(Latin)* Conditionally; in preparation for a possible future need; usually used to describe a legal proceeding that is done provisionally and let stand for the time being, but that can be challenged in the future.

de bene esse, deposition. N. A deposition of a witness done just in case the witness cannot appear at trial, so that the litigant will have the testimony regardless. Also called *examination de bene esse*.

de bene esse, evidence. N. Evidence admitted provisionally by the court on the understanding that its admissibility will be shown later.

debenture. N. An unsecured loan instrument issued by a company and backed by a promise to pay or general credit rather than a specific property; an unsecured bond, often issued by a large company with good credit ratings; holders of debentures are creditors of a corporation and if the corporation dissolves, they receive payment before stockholders. See also *indenture*.

debit. N. In accounting, a sum of money that is charged and due; the opposite of credit.

debt. N. Something, usually money, that is owed; an obligation to pay a certain amount; see also *bad debt*.

debt, bonded. N. Debt issued as bonds.

debt, floating. N. Current and short-term debt.

debt, secured. N. Debt tied to collateral, such as a mortgage.

debt consolidation. N. The practice of combining debts from various sources into one account.

debtor. N. (1) A person who owes a debt to someone else; see also *creditor*. (2) A person subject to bankruptcy proceedings.

debtor, judgment. N. Someone who is the subject of a judgment awarding a sum to a creditor.

decease. N. Death. V. To die.

deceased. N. Someone who has died; a dead person. ADJ. Dead.

decedent. N. Someone who has died.

deceit. N. A fraudulent misrepresentation used to cheat someone; the act of deceiving someone by lying or misrepresenting the truth. ADJ. *deceitful*.

deceive. V. To make someone believe something that is not true; to mislead.

decide. v. To come to a conclusion or resolution after deliberation and consideration; to determine something.

decision. N. A conclusion reached after considering facts and applicable law if necessary; a judicial determination or judgment. See also *opinion*.

declaration. N. (1) A formal announcement or statement. (2) At common law, the first pleading presented to the court by a plaintiff, similar to a complaint in structure and purpose. (3) In evidence, an unsworn statement made by a witness, a party to a lawsuit, or a person who subsequently died. (4) When entering a country, a statement of goods brought into the country by the person entering.

declaration, dying. N. A statement made by someone who thinks he or she is about to die about the circumstances of his or her death; dying declarations are sometimes admissible as evidence.

declaration against interest. N. A statement made out of court that is so disadvantageous to the person making it that it is presumed to be true; declarations against interest are admissible as an exception to the hearsay rule.

Declaration of Independence. N. A document written by Thomas Jefferson and adopted by the thirteen colonies on July 4, 1776, listing the colonies' grievances against England and declaring the colonies a separate nation free from allegiance to Great Britain.

declaration of war. N. A formal public announcement by the leadership of a nation that it is at war with another nation.

declaratory. ADJ. Explanatory; meant to clarify an ambiguity.

declaratory judgment. N. A judgment issued by a court in which it determines the legal rights of the parties or expresses an opinion on the law but does not award a remedy; also called declaratory relief. See also *advisory opinion*.

declaratory statute. N. A statute enacted to clarify the law on a particular matter, intended to end any doubts as to its meaning. See also *curative*.

declare. V. (1) To announce something formally, such as war; to make a pronouncement about the state of something, such as naming something a fire hazard. (2) In taxation, to admit to having received income; when going through customs upon entering a country, to admit to possessing goods on which duty is owed.

decree. N. The judicial decision of a court in equity made after hearing testimony and determining the rights of the parties, equivalent to a judgment by a court of law, though the term "judgment" may also be used in reference to courts of equity.

decree nisi. N. A conditional judgment that will be made permanent unless a party can show cause why it should not be; common in actions for divorce. See also *consent decree*.

decriminalize. V. To legalize an act that was formerly criminal.

dedicate. V. For a private owner to convey land or an easement to the public for public use. N. *dedication*.

deduct. V. To subtract something from a total; in taxation, to subtract the cost of items from total income to determine taxable income. N. *deduction*.

deductible. ADJ. Able to be deducted; items that may be deducted from gross income are described as tax-deductible. N. The amount of money that an insured party must pay for a loss before an insurer will pay a claim.

deduction, itemized. N. Expenses individually listed and deducted from gross income.

deduction, standard. N. A standard amount that a taxpayer may deduct from gross income instead of itemizing individual expenses.

deed. N. A written instrument, signed and delivered, by which one person conveys land to another.

deed of release. N. A deed that releases property from an encumbrance, such as a mortgage.

deed of trust. N. A deed that transfers the title of property to a trustee as a security; used instead of a mortgage in some states.

deed poll. N. A deed made by and binding a single party.

deep rock doctrine. N. In corporate bankruptcy, a principle that prevents controlling shareholders from presenting their claims before or with those of other creditors.

de facto. ADJ. *(Latin)* In fact, in reality; used to describe a situation that is for all practical purposes the case, though it might not be legal or official; see also *de jure*.

de facto authority. N. Authority that exists in reality.

de facto government. N. A government that sets itself up in place of the legal government, often by use of force.

de facto judge. N. Someone who performs the duties of a judge but who does not have legitimate judicial authority.

de facto marriage. N. A union of two parties who live together as husband and wife but in which the legality of the marriage is in some way defective.

defalcate. V. To embezzle funds that have been entrusted to the embezzler; to fail to pay over trust funds or other money held in a fiduciary capacity at the proper time. N. *defalcation*.

defamation. N. An intentional publication or public statement of false information that damages someone's reputation. V. *defame*. ADJ. *defamatory*. See also *libel, slander*.

default. N. Failure to perform a legal duty or meet an obligation.

default judgment. N. Judgment entered against a defendant who fails to defend himself or herself by responding to the plaintiff's complaint or appearing in court.

defeasance. N. The action of rendering something null and void; an instrument that negates or nullifies some other instrument, such as a will or deed.

defeasible. ADJ. Able to be revoked, nullified, or undone; usually applied to estates and land interests that are subject to a conditional limitation and are not absolute.

defect. N. An imperfection or a flaw; a lack or deficiency.

defect, design. N. A defect inherent in the design of a product, so that even when it is correctly made and used it poses a danger to consumers.

defect, fatal. N. A defect serious enough to void a contract.

defect, latent. N. A hidden defect; a flaw that is not apparent to reasonable observation.

defect, patent. N. A defect that is immediately obvious upon normal observation.

defective. ADJ. Flawed or insufficient; lacking something necessary to completion.

defective pleading. N. A pleading that is insufficient or inaccurate in substance or form.

defective title. N. Unmarketable title; a title obtained by fraud or not in fact entirely owned by the purported owner.

defend. V. To resist an attack; to shield or repel; to represent a defendant in a lawsuit. See also *defendant, defense*.

defendant. N. The party against whom a lawsuit is brought; in civil cases, the party who responds to the complaint; in criminal cases, the person against whom charges are brought.

defense. N. A response, reason, or allegation offered by a defendant to a lawsuit as to why the plaintiff has not established a claim and should not receive relief; a denial of the plaintiff's claims or an attack on the validity of the plaintiff's causes of action. See also *affirmative defense*.

defense attorney. N. An attorney who normally represents defendants in lawsuits.

defense firm. N. A law firm that specializes in representing defendants in lawsuits, often paid by the hour. See also *insurance defense, plaintiff's firm*.

defer. V. To put off to a later time; to postpone. N. ***deferment, deferral***.

deferral of taxes. N. Postponing the payment of taxes to a later year.

deferred compensation. N. Compensation that is taxed when it is received as opposed to when it is earned, such as contributions made by an employer to an employee's retirement plan that are not taxed until the retirement funds are distributed.

deferred payments. N. Payments that are spread out over time or entirely postponed.

deficiency. N. A lack; a shortcoming; in taxation, the amount of tax owed that has not been paid on time.

deficiency judgment. N. A judgment issued against someone who holds a mortgage, imposing personal liability on him or her if a foreclosure sale does not yield enough money to cover the mortgage debt.

deficit. N. A shortfall; an insufficiency; the condition brought about by spending more money than is earned; in accounting, the opposite of surplus.

defraud. V. To take money or property from someone through the use of fraud or deceit; to cheat someone; to misrepresent a fact intending for someone to rely on it and thereby harm him or her. See also *fraud.*

degree. N. (1) The amount, level, or extent of something. (2) A certificate awarded to those who finish a course of study at a university or college.

degree of crime. N. A classification of crime based on the level of guilt involved in committing it.

degree of negligence. N. A measurement of different kinds of negligence, used to determine whether someone is sufficiently negligent to be liable for an injury.

degree of proof. N. The level of proof needed to convince a court to render a verdict for a particular case; see also *preponderance of the evidence, clear and convincing, reasonable doubt.*

de jure. ADJ. *(Latin)* By law, by right; the condition of being in compliance with all applicable laws; legitimate and lawful. See also *de facto*.

delegable duty. N. A duty that can be performed by someone other than the one originally intended to do it.

delegate. V. To entrust someone with a task or responsibility; to transfer one's authority to another person. N. A person appointed to act for someone else; a person elected or appointed to represent others at a conference or assembly. ADJ. *delegable*.

delegation. N. (1) A group of representatives or delegates. (2) The transfer of power by one branch of the government to another.

deliberate. V. To consider; to ponder; to examine reasons for and against something in order to come to a decision. ADJ. Slow and careful; done with full awareness and intention.

deliberate speed. N. Immediately; as quickly as practical considerations of law, order, and the welfare of the people will allow; often used to describe the speed expected by those enacting state-mandated school desegregation.

deliberation. N. Careful consideration of a matter, weighing all arguments and evidence.

delict. N. A violation of the law; a tort, injury, or crime. *(Latin)* *delictum*.

delicto, ex. ADJ. *(Latin)* Arising out of a tort. ADV. *ex delicto*.

delinquency. N. Neglect of duty; the commission of minor crimes.

delinquent. ADJ. (1) Of a person, neglecting one's duty; failing to pay a debt; guilty of a crime or failure of duty. (2) Of a debt, due and unpaid.

delinquent child. N. A minor below a specified age who tends to commit crimes or otherwise engages in immoral or disobedient behavior and therefore needs treatment or supervision. See also *juvenile delinquent*.

delist. V. To remove something from a list; usually refers to removing a security from an exchange for failing to meet the minimum requirements for listing. N. *delisting*.

deliver. V. To hand something over to someone else; to voluntarily transfer title or possession of something to someone else's possession or control. N. *delivery*.

delude. V. To deceive someone or persuade him or her to believe something that is false.

delusion. N. An erroneous belief that is contrary to fact, inappropriate to the age, class, and education of the believer, and that cannot be shaken by evidence to the contrary, usually a result of some mental disorder; see also *insanity*. ADJ. *deluded*.

demand. N. An insistent request under a claim of right, requiring someone to do or relinquish something to the demander. V. To require or insist on something; to ask authoritatively.

demand note. A note or instrument that is payable on demand or on presentation. Also called a *demand instrument*.

demesne. N. *(French)* Domain; something owned. N. Ownership of land held in one's own right, not subject to the claims of a superior or occupied by tenants; the phrase "held in demesne" means occupied by the owner as opposed to tenants. ADJ. In pleading, own or original, i.e., "son assault demesne" means "his own assault."

demilitarized zone. N. An area where no military activity is permitted. ABBRV. *DMZ*.

de minimis. ADJ. *(Latin)* Insignificant or unimportant; not of a level to interest the law.

de minimis crime. N. A crime that is not important enough to justify judicial involvement.

de minimis non curat lex. *(Latin)* The law does not care about insignificant matters.

demise. V. To lease property; to convey property for life or for years; to bequeath. N. A lease or conveyance of property for a period of years or for life.

demonstrate. V. To show; to prove the truth of something by using logic and evidence; to use practical illustrations to show how something works or happens. N. *demonstration*.

demonstrative evidence. N. Evidence composed of real objects that appeal directly to the senses, such as maps, charts, illustrations, or the weapon used in committing a crime.

demur. V. To object to a point of law or fact alleged by the opposing party on the grounds that it does not advance the interests of the party making the statement; to present a demurrer.

demurrer. N. *(French)* To stop; in common law, a formal allegation by a defendant that the facts stated in the complaint are true but nevertheless are not legally sufficient to allow the case to proceed, and requesting judgment for the defendant and dismissal of the cause of action; the use of demurrer has mostly disappeared under the Federal Rules of Civil Procedure.

denial, conjunctive. N. A denial of all allegations as entirely false.

denial, general. N. A denial of all allegations.

denial, specific. N. A denial of one specific allegation.

denounce. To publicly declare someone or something to be morally wrong or evil; to inform against someone, usually in order to allow the authorities to arrest that person. N. *denunciation*.

de novo. ADJ. *(Latin)* Anew; starting again at the beginning; doing something a second time as if the first time had not occurred. ADV. *de novo*.

de novo trial. N. A second trial for a matter that has already been adjudicated; starting over as if the first trial had never happened.

deny. V. In a pleading, for the defendant to contradict the allegations made in the complaint, to state that the plaintiff's allegations are not in fact correct. N. *denial*.

Department of Homeland Security. N. A department of the U.S. Cabinet that is charged with protecting U.S. territory from natural and man-made hazards, including terrorist attacks. ABBRV. *DHS*.

Department of Labor. N. A federal department that dedicates itself to the U.S. workforce, monitoring working conditions, regulating wages and retirement benefits, and gathering information.

dependency. N. A territory or possession governed by another country and geographically separate from the governing country; e.g., Puerto Rico is a dependency of the United States.

dependent. ADJ. (1) Needing support from an outside source. (2) Contingent on some external fact or condition. N. Someone who is supported by someone else; in taxation, a dependent is usually someone related to the supporting taxpayer or someone who lives in the taxpayer's home.

dependent coverage. N. Insurance protection for dependents of the insured.

dependent intervening cause. N. In common law, something that happens in between a defendant's action and its result that occurs as a normal and predictable response to the defendant's action; usually a dependent intervening cause does not break the chain of causation and the defendant is still held liable for the result of his or her original action.

dependent promise. N. A promise in which the promisor does not have to perform until the other party has done some agreed-upon duty first.

dependent relative revocation. N. The principle that if a person revokes a will intending to replace it with another will, the first will is actually revoked only if the second will is valid; otherwise, the first will continue to be in effect.

deplete. V. To use up a supply or resource; to exhaust assets or natural resources.

depletion. N. In taxation, a principle that allows the owner of a natural resource such as oil or gas to recover the capital cost of the property as the resource is used up.

depletion allowance. N. The tax deduction allowed to owners of property containing natural resources as the resources are used up.

deponent. N. A witness who testifies at a deposition.

deport. V. To send a foreign national from one country to another because he or she has committed a crime or is of illegal immigration status. N. *deportation*. See also *extradite*.

depose. V. (1) To question a witness at a deposition. (2) To testify under oath.

deposition. N. A form of discovery before trial in which an attorney questions a witness under oath and a court reporter makes a transcript of the testimony, which can then be used as evidence at trial.

depreciate. V. To decrease in value over time.

depreciation. N. The process of spreading the cost of an asset over a period of years, deducting an allowance for wear and tear as the asset is used up or worn out.

depreciation, accelerated. N. A method of depreciation that provides larger deductions in the earlier years of an asset's life.

depreciation, reserve. N. In accounting, an account kept of the likely depreciation of assets in order to plan for the reduction in value of assets.

depreciation, straight-line. N. A method of depreciation in which the cost of an asset is deducted in equal amounts over its life. See also *accelerated cost recovery system*.

depredation. N. Attacking or plundering; robbing or pillaging.

deputy. N. An agent; a substitute; someone empowered by a superior to exercise the functions of the superior's office and to act on the superior's behalf. V. *deputize*.

deputy sheriff. N. An officer who has the authority to exercise the duties of the office of sheriff.

derelict. ADJ. In poor condition; neglected; abandoned. N. (1) A homeless person. (2) A boat abandoned on the sea whose master and crew are not expected to return.

derivative. ADJ. Coming from, influenced by, or originating in someone or something else. N. Something that comes from another person or source. V. *derive*.

derivative action. N. (1) A lawsuit brought on behalf of a corporation by a shareholder. (2) A cause of action founded on an injury to another person, such as an action for loss of consortium brought by a wife after her husband is injured.

derivative tort. N. (1) A civil action in tort based on an injury caused by criminal conduct by the defendant, in which the plaintiff seeks compensation for the injury, independent of a criminal action brought for the same offense. (2) Tort liability imposed on a principal for a wrong done by his or her agent.

derogation. N. The partial repeal or relaxation of a law.

descent. N. Family origin; heredity; the transmission of property and goods by inheritance.

descent, collateral. N. Descent among relatives who share a common ancestor but are not in a direct line, as between uncle and nephew or between cousins.

descent, lineal. N. Descent in a direct line, as from parent to child or grandparent to grandchild.

descent and distribution. N. The rules that determine transmission of a person's real property if he or she dies intestate, i.e., without a valid will.

desegregate. V. To end separation of people by races at school, in the workplace, or in public facilities. N. *desegregation*. See also *segregate*.

desert. V. To abandon; to leave willfully with the intention of never returning. N. *desertion*.

desist. V. To stop; to refrain from doing something. See also *cease and desist order*.

despot. N. A ruler with absolute power. See also *tyrant*.

despotism. N. A form of government in which one ruler has absolute power.

destroy. V. To damage something so badly it can no longer be used or repaired; to ruin something completely; to demolish or annihilate; to nullify or revoke. N. *destruction*. ADJ. *destructive*.

desuetude. N. A condition of disuse; the state of obsolete laws and practices that are no longer applied because their subject matter no longer exists, such as laws governing carriages drawn by horses.

detain. V. To hold in custody; to arrest; to keep or hold back. N. *detention*.

detainer. N. (1) Preventing a person from possessing property or goods that he or she owns rightfully. (2) A request filed by a criminal justice agency asking a correctional institution to hold a prisoner for the agency or to notify the agency when the prisoner is about to be released.

detainer, unlawful. N. Wrongfully keeping a person's property or goods and refusing to deliver them at the right time or on demand.

determinable. ADJ. (1) Able to be known or ascertained. (2) Terminable; able to be ended if a particular condition occurs.

determination. N. The decision made by a judge, court, or agency that ends a lawsuit or controversy; a final judgment.

detinue. N. A common law action brought to recover property that has been unlawfully taken; see also *replevin*.

devise. N. A testamentary gift of real property made in a will. V. *devise*; see also *bequest, bequeath*.

devisee. N. The person who receives real property through a devise.

devisor. N. The person who makes the gift of real property by will.

devolve. V. To pass from one person to another, often as a result of the operation of law and without any intentional act by either party; often used to describe the passing of an estate from a deceased person to an heir.

DHS. ABBRV. Department of Homeland Security.

dictum. N. A statement or observation made by a judge about a case that is not an official part of a judicial opinion, does not embody the court's decision, and is not binding. PL. *dicta*.

dictum, considered. N. A dictum that is so well-developed it has gained an air of authority as if it were part of an opinion.

digest. N. A compilation or summary of a number of books, articles, cases, or other type of information, often arranged by subject and indexed for ease of reference; a listing of reported cases arranged by subject and court.

Digital Millennium Copyright Act. N. A federal law passed in 1998 that criminalizes copyright infringement of digital content as well as attempts to get around digital copyright protection measures.

digital rights management. N. The practice of restricting access to digital materials and information by copyright holders and publishers. ABBRV. *DRM*.

dilatory. ADJ. Deliberately slow; intended to delay something.

dilatory plea. N. A plea by a defendant that does not address the factual merits of the complaint but instead raises procedural or jurisdictional points in an effort to defeat or at least delay the action; very uncommon in modern civil practice.

diligence. N. Persistence and care; attentiveness; hard work. ADJ. *diligent*.

diligence, due. N. Investigation of the management, operation, and facts surrounding an investment opportunity; steps that a person must take to satisfy the requirements in buying or selling something.

dilute. V. In corporate law, to lower the value of shares currently outstanding by issuing new shares. N. *dilution*.

dilution doctrine. N. In trademark law, a doctrine prohibiting the use of a trademark by a second user even if there is no possibility of confusion so that the uniqueness of the first user's mark will be preserved and not weakened by the presence of another use of the name.

diminished capacity. N. In criminal law, a mental state that is not sufficient to have the mens rea needed to commit a crime, brought on by mental disease or defect, trauma, or intoxication; also called *diminished responsibility*.

diminution. N. Decrease; a reduction in size or number.

diminution in value. N. A means of measuring damages in a breach of contract case in which the plaintiff may recover for a decrease in value to property caused by the breach.

direct attack. N. An attempt to have a judgment reversed or vacated by attacking it directly through some process designed to do that, such as an appeal; see also *collateral attack*.

directed verdict. N. Judgment granted for the defendant by a judge without letting the jury consider the matter in a case where the plaintiff does not meet the requirements for presenting a prima facie case.

direct evidence. N. Evidence that proves a fact directly, without inference or presumption; evidence provided by a witness who actually saw or experienced what happened. See also *circumstantial evidence, indirect evidence*.

director. N. A person who runs or manages a business, company, or corporation, often as a member of a board of directors, with a fiduciary duty to direct its affairs in the best interest of both the business and its shareholders.

disability. N. A physical or mental condition that prevents someone from performing certain acts; lack of legal capacity, caused by a condition such as infancy or insanity; see also *Americans with Disabilities Act; workers' compensation*.

disability, partial. N. The condition of being unable to resume one's job before injury but being able to perform some suitable gainful employment.

disability, permanent. N. Disability that prevents one from ever returning to one's former occupation.

disability, total. N. The condition of being rendered unable to perform any functions of one's occupation.

disarmament. N. The act of destroying, taking away, or getting rid of weapons.

disaster unemployment assistance. N. Financial assistance provided by the U.S. Department of Labor to those whose jobs or self-employment have been lost or disrupted by a major disaster declared by the U.S. president.

disbar. v. To expel a lawyer from the bar and rescind his or her license to practice law. N. ***disbarment***.

discharge. v. (1) To perform a duty; to satisfy a debt. (2) To dismiss or release someone. (3) To terminate someone's employment. N. ***discharge***.

discharge in bankruptcy. N. The release of a bankrupt person from his or her debts.

disclaimer. N. A denial of something, usually one's own responsibility; a denial of someone else's claim.

disclaimer, qualified. N. A written statement made by a taxpayer refusing to accept an interest in a particular property.

disclose. v. To reveal; to make known, especially hidden or secret information. N. ***disclosure***.

discontinuance. N. An end to a lawsuit brought about voluntarily by a plaintiff; a nonsuit or dismissal.

discontinue. v. To stop, to end.

discount. N. An amount subtracted from a larger sum; a deduction from a loan or advance made by a bank when it buys a negotiable instrument due at a future date at a price below its face value.

discount rate. N. (1) A rate used for discounting negotiable instruments purchased by banks in exchange for money or credit. (2) The minimum interest rate that Federal Reserve banks charge their members for loans.

discovery. N. The process of gaining information about an opponent's case before trial by reviewing documents, inspecting and examining property, and asking questions through interrogatories and depositions. V. *discover*. See also *Federal Rules of Civil Procedure*.

discredit. V. To hurt someone's credibility or reputation; to make an idea, a statement, an individual, or a piece of evidence appear unreliable.

discretion. N. (1) Independent judgment; freedom and authority to decide how to act; the power given to public officials to act independently in fulfilling their duties. (2) The ability to recognize the difference between right and wrong. (3) Prudence; cautiousness; circumspection. ADJ. *discreet*. See also *abuse of discretion*.

discretion, judicial. N. A judge's freedom to make decisions as he or she sees fit, bound by the principles of law.

discrimination. N. Unequal or unfair treatment of people based on categories such as sex, race, religion, or age, when by all rights they should be treated fairly. V. *discriminate*. See also *civil rights, Americans with Disabilities Act*.

dishonor. V. (1) To fail to show proper respect. (2) To shame, to disgrace. (3) To refuse to accept a negotiable instrument such as a check when presented for payment. N. Shame or disgrace.

disinherit. V. To take steps such as changing a will to prevent inheritance by someone who otherwise would inherit.

disjunctive allegation. N. A statement in a pleading or a criminal charge accusing a defendant of two mutually exclusive acts connected by the word "or," as in "the defendant murdered or caused to be murdered." See also *alternative pleading*.

dismiss. V. (1) To allow to leave or to send away. (2) To terminate someone's employment. (3) For a judge to refuse to consider a lawsuit further, thereby ending it before a trial is completed.

dismissal. N. A judge's order that terminates a lawsuit, motion, etc., without considering the issues involved in the matter.

dismissal and nonsuit. N. An end to a case caused by a plaintiff's wish to end the matter or a plaintiff's failure to pursue it.

dismissal with prejudice. N. A dismissal that prevents the plaintiff from ever suing on that cause of action again, considered a judgment of the case on its merits and thus res judicata.

dismissal without prejudice. N. A dismissal that does not preclude the plaintiff's attempting to sue on the same cause of action again.

disorder. N. Confusion, a lack of order; unlawful and riotous behavior.

disorderly. ADJ. Contrary to standards of law-abiding, peaceful behavior.

disorderly conduct. N. Unruly behavior that disturbs the peace or shocks public morals.

dispose of. V. (1) To transfer property to another's care. (2) To settle a matter finally.

disposition. N. (1) Giving up or relinquishing property, especially through a will. (2) The settlement of a matter; a judge's final ruling. (3) In a criminal case, the sentence. (4) Demeanor or personality.

dispossess. V. To evict or oust from a property, either legally or illegally; to deprive someone of property or land that he or she owns.

dispute. N. A disagreement or argument; a conflict. V. *dispute*.

disqualification. N. The act of disqualifying; the condition that disqualified someone.

disqualify. V. To pronounce a person ineligible to perform a particular task, usually due to some offense or failure to observe applicable rules.

disseisin. N. The act of evicting someone from his or her property and taking it over as one's own.

dissent. V. To hold a contrary opinion; to disagree with the majority or official view of a matter; used especially of judges presiding over the same case. N. A contrary opinion; an opinion written by a judge or justice explicitly disagreeing with the majority decision. ADJ. *dissenting*.

dissenter. N. One who dissents.

dissolution. N. The act of terminating something, such as a business, partnership, or contract; the termination of a corporation's legal existence; the ending of a marriage.

dissolve. V. To close, annul, or end; to end the legal existence of a corporation. See also *dissolution*.

distinguish. V. To tell one thing apart from another; to point out differences between things; to show how one case is significantly different from another.

distinguishable. ADJ. Able to be distinguished.

distinct. ADJ. Clearly different from something else.

distraint. N. The seizure of a tenant's personal property by a landlord; see also *distress*. V. *distrain*.

distress. N. (1) Anxiety, fear, pain; see also *emotional distress*. (2) A landlord's seizing of personal property without court approval to satisfy a claim, such as nonpayment of rent; see also *distraint*. V. To cause anxiety, pain, or fear.

distributable net income. N. The maximum amount of money received from distributions from a trust or estate on which beneficiaries may be taxed. ABBRV. *DNI*.

distribute. V. To deal out portions or shares of something. N. *distribution*.

distribution, corporate. N. A corporation's paying out money to shareholders, such as accumulated earnings in the form of dividends.

distribution, partnership. N. Payment of a partner by a partnership.

distribution, trust. N. Payment by a trust to its beneficiaries.

distribution in kind. N. A distribution of property as it is, instead of selling it and distributing the proceeds.

distributive. ADJ. Concerned with the sharing and distribution of shares of something among recipients.

distributive share. N. A share that an heir receives from an intestate estate, or that a partner receives from a dissolved partnership.

district. N. A territory or region of a state or country, defined for administrative, political, or judicial purposes; a division of a state under the jurisdiction of a particular federal district court.

district attorney. N. A public officer of a state or county whose duty is to prosecute those accused of crimes within the area; different states use different titles, including prosecuting attorney, county attorney, state's attorney, or solicitor. See also *United States Attorney*.

district court. N. (1) A federal court that has jurisdiction over a particular region of a state and hears cases arising from offenses against federal laws and cases involving litigants from different states; see also *diversity*. (2) In some states, an inferior court with general jurisdiction over minor matters.

disturb. V. To interfere with peaceful, normal conditions; to throw into disorder; to intrude or interrupt.

disturbance. N. An act that interrupts or annoys someone; interference with someone's rights or property; a disruption of law-abiding, peaceful conditions; a riot.

disturbance of the peace. N. Conduct that disrupts the quiet and order of a community by riotous behavior or loud noise.

diversity. N. Heterogeneity; the state of being composed of different types of people as opposed to being single-sex, single-race, or otherwise homogeneous.

diversity of citizenship. N. The condition that exists when the parties to a lawsuit come from different states, or when one is a citizen and one an alien, and that forms the basis of federal diversity jurisdiction.

divestiture. N. In antitrust law, a remedy in which the court orders a defendant to sell off assets and property. V. *divest*.

dividend. N. Corporate profits and earnings distributed to shareholders in proportion to the number of shares they own.

dividend, cumulative. N. A dividend on preferred stock that accumulates if not paid regularly and must be paid before common stock dividends.

dividend, preferred. N. A dividend paid on preferred stock.

dividend, stock. N. A dividend paid in stock instead of money.

dividend addition. N. A dividend added to the face value of an insurance policy.

divorce. N. The legal dissolution of a marriage. V. *divorce*. See also *alimony, annul, separate*.

divorce, no-fault. N. A divorce in which neither spouse must prove the other guilty of some marital misconduct as grounds for divorce; also called divorce by consent.

divorce a mensa et thoro. N. A legal separation in which parties are forbidden to live together, but that does not end the marriage; also called divorce from bed and board.

DMZ. ABBRV. Demilitarized zone.

DNA. ABBRV. Deoxyribonucleic acid.

DNA testing. N. Using evidence contained in DNA to identify or rule out criminal suspects or fathers in paternity suits.

DNI. ABBRV. Distributable net income.

DNS. ABBRV. Domain Name System.

DOB. ABBRV. Date of birth.

docket. N. (1) A list on a court calendar of cases scheduled to be tried. (2) On appeal, a formal record summarizing the proceedings of a lower court. V. *docket*.

document. N. A piece of written, recorded, printed, or photographed information or evidence; a physical object or instrument on which information is recorded in letters, numbers, symbols, or images, including maps, letters, photographs, prints, x-rays, contracts, deeds, receipts, accounts, etc.

documentary evidence. N. Evidence consisting of documents whose authenticity has been established.

document of title. N. A written document that supplies proof that a person is entitled to receive and hold particular goods; see also *bill of lading*.

document review. N. A component of discovery in which attorneys for one party examine documents produced by the other party to identify the ones relevant to the lawsuit.

doing business. ADJ. Carrying on or conducting business affairs; usually used to describe a company that is conducting affairs in a particular state; see also *long arm statute*.

doing business as. N. Phrase used to identify a trade name or the name of a business. ABBRV. *d/b/a*.

domain. N. (1) Total ownership of land; land that is owned completely. (2) The property owned by a nation or state; synonymous with *public domain*. (3) An area of expertise or influence.

domain name. N. A name composed of letters and/or numbers, such as "ebay.com," or the portion of an email address that follows the @ sign, linked to a numerical IP address that identifies the location of a particular website or computer. See also *Domain Name System, DNS, Uniform Resource Locator, URL*.

Domain Name System. N. The system used to identify information on the Internet by linking domain names with computer-readable addresses. ABBRV. *DNS*.

domestic. ADJ. (1) Having to do with the home and family relations. (2) Occurring within a country's or state's borders. N. A household servant.

domestic partner. N. A person who shares a sexual relationship and a home with another person but is not necessarily married to him or her.

domestic relations. N. The branch of law that handles family matters such as divorce, adoption, and custody.

domestic violence. N. Violent physical behavior committed by one family member against another.

domicile. N. A legal home; the country or state that a person considers his or her permanent residence, even if he or she is living elsewhere; the place where a corporation conducts its affairs. ADJ. *domiciliary*.

dominant estate. N. A piece of property that has the use of an easement or servitude on another piece of property, usually adjacent to it.

dominion. N. Ownership and control over how a piece of property is used; title and possession.

donation. N. Something given; a gift. *(Latin) donatio*. V. *donate*.

donee. N. One who receives something from someone else. See also *donor*.

donor. N. One who gives something to someone else; one who creates a trust, gives a gift, or confers a power. See also *donee*.

double jeopardy. N. A second prosecution for an offense after the defendant has already been tried for it and acquitted; prohibited by the Fifth Amendment of the Constitution.

doubt. N. Uncertainty. V. *doubt*. See also *reasonable doubt*.

dowager. N. A widow who holds the title or property that belonged to her dead husband.

dower. N. In common law, a widow's right to a life estate in her dead husband's property; no longer exists in most states; see also *curtesy*.

downsize. v. To reduce the size of a workforce in response to economic conditions or business needs. See also *layoff*.

dowry. N. Money and property brought into a marriage by a bride.

draft. N. (1) A document in which the writer directs someone, usually a bank, to pay a specific amount of money to a third party; see also *bank draft*. (2) A preliminary or preparatory version of a document. (3) Compulsory induction into the military; see also *conscription, Selective Service System*. v. (1) To write a rough or preliminary version of a document. (2) To select people for compulsory military service.

draft, sight. N. A draft of money payable when presented.

draft, time. N. A draft of money payable on a specific day.

dram shop act. N. A law that imposes strict liability on a seller of intoxicating beverages if the sale results in injury to a third party's person, property, or means of support due to the intoxication of the buyer.

draw. (1) To create a draft that orders someone to pay money to someone else. (2) To aim a firearm at a target. (3) To select the members of a jury.

drawee. N. The person or entity on which a draft is drawn, often the bank.

drawer. N. The one who writes a draft, i.e., the person who writes a check from his or her account and signs it.

Dred Scott v. Sandford. N. An 1857 U.S. Supreme Court decision that ruled that no black person could be a citizen of the United States, that all slaves were the property of their owners and not citizens who could bring lawsuits themselves, and that the government could not revoke a slave owner's right to own slaves based on where he or she lived, invalidating the Missouri Compromise, which had tried to ban slavery in part of the Louisiana territory.

dress code. N. A set of rules dictating how people should dress in a given setting, such as students at a school or employees at a workplace.

driving under the influence. N. Operating a motor vehicle while under the influence of alcohol or drugs; also called driving while intoxicated (DWI) or drunk driving. ABBRV. *DUI*.

DRM. ABBRV. Digital rights management.

droit. N. *(French)* Law; a right; the entire body of law.

drug abuse. N. Chronic, habitual, uncontrolled, or excessive use of a controlled substance.

drunkenness. N. Intoxication; the condition of mental impairment brought on by consuming too much alcohol.

dual citizenship. N. The condition of being a citizen of two nations simultaneously; also the condition of being a citizen of both the United States and a state.

due. ADJ. (1) Proper, adequate, rightful, just, appropriate for the circumstances. (2) Expected to be paid at a particular time; payable. N. Something owed to someone.

due care. N. The legal duty a person owes to others in order not to be negligent; care that is sufficient and proper for the circumstances. See also *care, ordinary*.

due process, procedural. N. The guarantee of a fair civil procedure that follows the rules, including the right to be notified about a complaint or charge and the right to be heard in court.

due process, substantive. N. A guarantee that all legislation that binds citizens will be fair and reasonable, not arbitrary and unreasonable.

due process of law. N. Fair judicial treatment guaranteed to every U.S. citizen by the Constitution in the Fifth and Fourteenth Amendments, which promise that no citizen will be deprived of life, liberty, or property without the opportunity to first defend him- or herself, including the rights to a fair trial, to be present at one's trial, to be allowed to present testimony, and to present evidence to counter the opposing side's case.

DUI. abbrv. Driving under the influence.

dummy. N. A sham, imitation, or straw man.

dummy corporation. N. A corporation with no legitimate business purpose formed to protect its founders from liability or to hide their activities.

dummy director. N. A director of a corporation who is in fact merely a figurehead and who has no real interest in the corporation.

dummy shareholder. N. Someone who holds shares of stock in his or her own name but for the benefit of the real owner.

dump. V. To sell goods in quantity at a price far below market value, often in a foreign market. N. *dumping*.

duplicity. N. (1) Double-dealing. (2) In common law, the error of combining two separate causes of action in one count of a pleading or a similar mistake in a criminal pleading or legislation; now permitted under the Federal Rules of Civil Procedure.

durable power of attorney. N. A document in which a person names a surrogate decision maker to consent to or refuse medical treatment if the person becomes incapacitated and unable to direct medical treatment him- or herself.

duress. N. Conduct intended to force someone to do something he or she does not want to do, such as threat of violence or coercion.

duty. N. (1) An obligation, often legally sanctioned; in negligence cases, a legally recognized requirement to observe a specific standard of conduct toward another person. (2) A tax on imported and exported goods.

duty free. ADJ. Not subject to tax on imports or exports; see also *customs*.

duty to act. N. An obligation to perform some act to prevent harm to someone else.

duty to mitigate. The obligation of the plaintiff in a breach of contract case to minimize damages resulting from the breach.

duty to retreat. N. The principle that a person being attacked should always retreat if possible instead of using force in self-defense; see also *castle doctrine*.

dwell. V. To live in a place.

dwelling. N. A residence; a house, building, or any enclosed space or structure used as a home; a house and all buildings attached to it; also called a dwelling house.

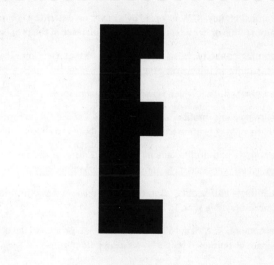

earn. V. To acquire money in return for work; to perform some task that makes one deserve some reward.

earner. N. A person who earns.

earnest. N. Something that one person gives another to mark a promise or bind a contract, such as a token, pledge, or partial payment. ADJ. Sincere; truthful.

earnest money. N. Money paid by a buyer on entering a contract as proof of his or her intention to pay the full price at the proper time.

earning capacity. N. The amount of money that a worker is capable of earning on the open market.

earnings. N. That which is earned, usually money.

earnings and profits. N. In tax, income earned by a corporation that would constitute a dividend if distributed to shareholders.

earnings and profits, accumulated. N. Earnings and profits from previous years that have not yet been distributed as dividends.

earnings and profits, current. N. Earnings and profits from the current taxable year.

easement. N. A right to use someone else's property (the servient estate or burdened property) for a specific purpose.

easement, affirmative. N. The right to do some positive act to or on the servient estate, such as using it as a right of way.

easement, appurtenant. N. An easement that is attached to a particular piece of property (the dominant estate or benefited property) and stays with it if it is transferred to another owner.

easement, implied. N. An easement that the law will find must have been intended by the parties to a transaction, even if they did not express it, i.e., easements that are necessary for both parties to continue to use their property.

easement, negative. N. An easement that prevents the property owner from doing specific things on or to the land, usually because it would impair use of the dominant estate.

easement, prescriptive. N. An easement that arises in a manner similar to adverse possession by long use of the servient estate.

easement, public. N. An easement that the entire community can use.

easement, reciprocal negative. N. An easement that automatically arises when an owner of two or more related properties sells one of them with a restriction on it, binding the other properties with the same restrictions.

easement in gross. N. An easement that belongs to a person, not to a piece of property.

easement of necessity. N. An easement that arises by operation of law if a dominant estate is completely cut off or otherwise rendered unusable without it.

eavesdrop. V. To secretly and unlawfully listen to a conversation, either by entering a private place to listen, installing a listening or recording device outside a private place, or intercepting communications over telephones or other devices. N. *eavesdropping*. See also *wiretapping*.

ecclesiastical. ADJ. Relating to the Christian church.

ecclesiastical court. N. A court with jurisdiction over religious and church matters.

ecclesiastical law. N. Law applying to religious matters.

e-commerce. Buying and selling goods and services electronically, particularly over the Internet.

EEOC. ABBRV. Equal Employment Opportunity Commission.

egalitarian. ADJ. Supporting equality and fair treatment for all people. N. *egalitarian*.

ejectment. N. A common law action brought by a property owner to eject a tenant who has refused to leave at the appointed time or someone claiming the land by adverse possession.

ejusdem generis. ADJ. *(Latin)* Of the same kind; a rule of interpreting statutes holding that if a statute lists a few examples of something, then it will be assumed that it only includes things similar to the examples; e.g., if for "dangerous weapon" it uses examples of guns, then the term refers only to firearms and not to other weapons such as knives.

elect. V. To choose or select; to select a public official; to choose one legal right from more than one option.

election. N. (1) The act of choosing. (2) The formal event in which public officials are chosen. ADJ. *elective*.

election by spouse. N. The right of a surviving spouse to choose how to inherit from the deceased spouse, whether from will, dower, or his or her share prescribed by statute (the elective share).

election of remedies. N. A choice between two or more remedies for an injury.

elector. N. (1) Someone who has the right to vote in elections. (2) A member of the electoral college.

electoral college. N. The group of representatives chosen from each state to cast their votes in a presidential election.

electronic. ADJ. Done on a computer or over a computer network.

Electronic Communications Privacy Act. N. A law enacted in 1986 that amended the Wiretap Act to restrict government surveillance of private electronic communications.

electronic publication. N. Publishing a work online or on a computer network.

electronic signature. N. An electronic symbol, sound, or process that can be used by a person to verify that he or she is taking the step of signing a record or document, such as by keying in a personal identification number or clicking a box to accept the terms and conditions of a website; also called a digital signature.

eleemosynary. ADJ. Charitable, related to charity.

element. N. A component of some abstract concept; one of the components of a criminal offense that the prosecution must prove.

elements. N. Forces of nature such as rain and snow.

eligible. ADJ. Able or qualified to do or receive something.

email. N. Electronic mail; correspondence by letter over the Internet or another computer network.

emancipate. N. (1) To free someone from the control of someone else; to liberate. (2) For a parent to relinquish parental rights and duties toward a child. N. *emancipation*.

Emancipation Proclamation. N. A proclamation issued by Abraham Lincoln in 1862 to free all black slaves in states at war against the Union.

embezzle. V. To misappropriate or steal funds entrusted to one's care. N. *embezzlement*.

embracery. N. The crime of trying to influence a juror with bribes, promises, etc.; see also *obstruction of justice*.

emergency doctrine. N. The principle that a person is not expected to exercise the same degree of care when faced with an emergency or sudden peril as he or she would under ordinary circumstances.

eminent domain. N. The government's right to take private property for public use in return for just compensation to the property owner.

emissions trading. N. The practice of assigning businesses a certain number of credits that permit them to emit specified amounts of pollution, which they can then trade with other businesses that need to emit more or less pollution than their credits allow; also called cap and trade.

emolument. N. The total compensation from a job, including salary, rank, benefits, and other privileges and advantages.

emotional distress. N. Severe mental and emotional suffering that results from another person's conduct.

employ. V. To hire someone to do a particular job in exchange for pay.

employee. N. One hired to do a job.

employee handbook. N. A manual given to all employees in a workplace that describes workplace policies on discipline and discrimination, defines positions and responsibilities, explains grievance procedures, and may require employees to sign a form stating that they have read and accept the terms of the handbook.

employee stock ownership plan. N. A kind of employee retirement benefit plan in which the employees own shares in the employer's company, often receiving contributions from the employer, and only recognize income from the shares upon collecting the proceeds at retirement. ABBRV. *ESOP*.

employer. N. One who employs someone else.

employer's liability acts. N. Statutes defining employer liability for injuries that happen to employees while working; see also *workers' compensation*.

employment. N. A job; the act of employing.

employment at will. A type of employment in which either employer or employee may end the working relationship at any time and for any reason.

Employment Retirement Income Security Act of 1974. N. An act of Congress that sets guidelines for employee benefit plans. ABBRV. *ERISA*.

enable. V. To make possible.

enabling clause. N. A clause in a statute that gives the proper officials the power to enforce it.

enabling statute. N. A statute that gives someone a new power.

enact. V. To make something happen; to create a law.

enacting clause. N. A clause at the beginning of a statute that identifies its purpose and the body that has created it.

en banc. ADJ. *(French)* On the bench; by the whole court; refers to occasions when all the judges of a court participate in a session, or when the panel of judges is expanded for a special case.

encroach. v. To intrude; to gradually advance into someone else's property or territory. N. *encroachment*.

encryption. N. The practice of converting information into code that can only be deciphered with a key.

encumber. v. To burden; to place a debt or mortgage on a property.

encumbrance. N. A mortgage, debt, or other burden on a piece of property.

Endangered Species Act. N. A federal law passed in 1973 that protects animal species and ecosystems that are threatened with extinction by human activity.

endorse. (1) To sign the back of a check or other negotiable instrument to make it payable to someone else. (2) To express approval of someone or something. N. *endorsement*. See also *indorse*.

endow. v. To bestow something on someone; to provide financial support by granting property or an income.

endowment. N. A fund granted to support something, usually an institution such as a university or charity.

end user license agreement. N. A contract presented by a software producer to the product's end user, i.e., the person who has acquired the software in order to use it, stating the terms and conditions associated with using the software. See also *browse-wrap agreement, click-wrap agreement, shrink-wrap agreement.* ABBRV. *EULA*.

enemy. N. An adversary; a hostile individual, group, nation, or military force.

enemy combatant. N. A member of the armed forces of an enemy state; during war with that state, a member of a force that commits a belligerent act against a state.

enfeoff. V. In feudal times, to give someone property in exchange for service; in modern usage, to give someone the title to property. N. *enfeoffment*.

enforce. V. To take action to ensure that a law is upheld.

enfranchise. V. To grant someone the right to vote. N. *enfranchisement*.

enjoin. V. To order or require someone to do something. See also *injunction*.

enjoyment. N. The ability to use and profit from the property one owns. See also *quiet enjoyment*.

enlargement. N. An extension of time, granted by a court, to do something that ordinarily must be completed by a specific deadline; also called enlargement of time.

enrollment period. N. A limited period of time in which individuals can sign up for benefits or health insurance plans, usually for the upcoming year.

enslave. V. To make someone a slave. See also *indenture, servitude*.

entail. V. (1) To bring along certain inevitable consequences. (2) To settle the inheritance of a property within a specific family line over generations, limiting it to particular descendants; to create a fee tail. N. An inheritance restricted to a particular family line; property that is settled in that way.

entailment. N. A restriction of the way a property will be inherited that is different from what the ordinary rules of inheritance would dictate.

enter. V. (1) To write down in a record; to file or deposit. (2) To go into a house or building; to go into a country or state. (3) To become a party to. N. *entry*.

entitlement. N. A right granted; a benefit or right guaranteed by law, such as Social Security.

entity. N. A being or abstraction, such as a corporation or estate, that can hold legal rights and obligations, owe and pay taxes, and sue or be sued.

entrap. V. To catch someone in a trap; particularly, to induce someone to commit a crime in order to arrest him or her. N. *entrapment*.

enumerated powers. N. Powers expressly granted by the Constitution to a branch of government.

en ventre sa mere. ADJ. *(French)* In the belly of one's mother; unborn but in gestation.

environmental impact statement. N. A document that a developer must prepare before receiving approval for a new project, predicting the project's likely effect on the surrounding environment.

Environmental Protection Agency. N. A federal agency that coordinates government actions to protect the environment and prevent pollution. ABBRV. *EPA*.

EPA. ABBRV. Environmental Protection Agency.

e pluribus unum. *(Latin)* One out of many; the motto of the United States.

equal. ADJ. The same; having the same value, size, degree, or quantity.

Equal Employment Opportunity Commission. N. A federal organization created by Title VII of the Civil Rights Act of 1964 whose purpose is to end discrimination in the workplace. ABBRV. *EEOC.*

equality. N. The condition of having the same opportunities, rights, privileges, and liabilities.

equal justice. N. Equal and impartial treatment of all people by the law and government.

equal opportunity. N. A policy of treating employees equally and not discriminating on the basis of race, sex, religion, national origin, age, etc.

equal protection (of the laws). N. The principal that every person is entitled to the same treatment under the law as other people in similar conditions.

equal protection clause. N. A clause in the Fourteenth Amendment to the Constitution that prohibits states from denying people within their jurisdictions equal protection of the laws.

Equal Rights Amendment. N. An amendment to the Constitution that was proposed but never ratified that would have prevented the states or nation from denying people equality based on sex. ABBRV. *ERA.*

equal time act. N. An act that requires a broadcaster who allows a political candidate to campaign on the air to provide equal time on the air to all other candidates for the office.

equitable. ADJ. (1) Fair, impartial, just. (2) Arising in equity instead of law.

equitable distribution. N. A method of distributing property fairly but not necessarily equally among interested parties, particularly between a husband and wife after a divorce.

equitable recoupment. N. A doctrine that allows a taxpayer who mistakenly pays taxes too soon and is later assessed taxes for the same taxable event to reduce the new tax by the amount already paid.

equity. N. (1) A branch of jurisprudence that arose in England as an alternative to the harsh common law in which courts tried to determine what would be fair in a given situation instead of strictly applying law and precedent, used in matters where the law was inadequate; today, equity and the law have merged for the most part, but equitable principles and remedies still exist. (2) Fairness, justice. (3) The value of a property minus any mortgages or liens on it. See also *chancery*.

equity, court of. N. A court that hears cases and makes judgments according to principles of equity; see also *chancery*.

equity jurisdiction. N. The body of cases and matters that are appropriate for hearing in equity.

ERA. ABBRV. Equal Rights Amendment.

ergo. CONJ. *(Latin)* Therefore. ADV. *ergo*.

Erie doctrine. N. A doctrine developed by the 1938 case *Erie v. Tompkins* stating that, except in matters governed by the Constitution of acts of Congress, in a federal case the court should apply the state law of the state in which the court is situated instead of applying federal common law.

ERISA. ABBRV. Employment Retirement Income Security Act of 1974.

erroneous. ADJ. Mistaken; in error.

erroneous judgment. N. A judgment rendered using a mistaken application of the law.

error. N. A mistake; an inaccurate conception of fact or law.

error, fundamental. N. An error committed by a trial court that harms the case enough to render the judgment void.

error, harmless. N. An error committed by a trial court that did not harm the rights of the party appealing the judgment and for which an appellate court will not reverse the trial court's judgment.

error, reversible. N. An error that justifies an appellate court's reversing a trial court's decision. See also *assignment of error*.

error of fact. N. A mistake made because an essential fact is not known or because something that was believed to be a fact was actually not true; also called error in fact.

error of law. N. A mistake made in applying the law to a case; also called error in law.

escalator clause. N. A clause in a contract that provides for an increase or decrease in price if a particular event happens.

escape clause. N. A clause in a contract that allows the parties to it to break the contract without penalty if a specified event happens or under specified circumstances.

escheat. N. The reversion of property to the state if it has no verifiable owner or anyone to inherit it. V. *escheat*.

escrow. N. A legal document, money, or property entrusted by the people making a contract to a third person, who holds it until the contract is finalized and then delivers it to the proper person.

escrow account. N. A bank account into which funds are held as security until the escrow condition is fulfilled.

ESOP. ABBRV. Employee stock ownership plan.

esquire. N. (1) The title added to the name of an attorney admitted to the bar. (2) Originally in England, a title used by men who owned land, or officers, barristers, or judges. ABBRV. *Esq*.

establishment clause. N. A clause in the First Amendment of the Constitution that prevents the government from passing laws establishing a religion; see also *free exercise clause*.

estate. N. (1) An interest in or ownership of land. (2) All the money, property, and goods that one person owns.

estate, equitable. N. An estate that can only be enforced in equity, particularly a trust held in beneficial interest for someone.

estate, future. N. An estate for which a person might receive title or interest some time in the future.

estate, legal. N. An estate recognized and enforceable by law.

estate, vested. N. An estate that is currently owned or held by the person to whom the property interest will go when a life estate or other current interest ends. See also *life estate*.

estate planning. N. The branch of law that deals with passing on a person's property and assets after death through wills, trusts, and insurance; also called trusts and estates.

estate tax. N. A tax on property transferred after the owner's death that is levied on the estate.

estoppel. N. A restraint or bar; a doctrine that prevents a person from doing or saying something that would contradict some earlier action or statement that another has relied on and the contradiction of which would hurt that other person. V. **estop**. See also *collateral estoppel*; *promissory estoppel*.

et. *(Latin, French)* And.

et al. ABBRV. *(Latin)* And others; used to indicate the presence of more people than are named in a category.

ethical. ADJ. Morally right.

ethics. N. Moral principles governing behavior.

et seq. ABBRV. *(Latin)* And what follows; used in page citations to instruct the reader to look at the identified page and the following ones; e.g., "p. 45 et seq." means "page 45 and following pages."

EU. ABBRV. European Union.

EULA. ABBRV. End user license agreement.

European Union. N. A union of European countries that exists to create uniform economic, judicial, and security policies throughout Europe. ABBRV. *EU*.

euthanasia. N. Mercy killing; painlessly killing someone who is suffering from a painful incurable disease or who is in a coma and has no hope of ever waking up.

euthanasia, active. N. Actively doing something to kill someone, such as administering poison.

euthanasia, passive. N. Withholding artificial support in order to let a person die naturally; see also *right to die, living will*.

evade. V. To avoid, elude, or escape. N. *evasion*. See also *tax evasion*.

evasive. ADJ. Elusive; trying to escape or avoid.

evasive answer. N. An answer that avoids a straightforward response, neither denying nor confirming something.

evict. V. (1) To recover something from someone through judicial action. (2) To expel a tenant from property he or she has leased. N. *eviction*.

eviction, actual. N. Physically expelling the tenant from the property.

eviction, retaliatory. N. Expelling the tenant from the property in retaliation for the tenant's valid complaints about the landlord. See also *constructive eviction*.

evidence. N. Anything used to prove the truth of an issue in court; includes testimony, documents, objects, and anything else that could persuade the jury.

evident. ADJ. Obvious; clear to see.

evidentiary. ADJ. Forming evidence.

evolution. N. The process by which something grows and changes; the scientific theory that explains how living organisms have developed throughout the history of the earth.

examine. V. To inspect; to investigate; to question or interrogate. N. *examination*.

exception. N. (1) Something excluded from a category to which it would ordinarily belong; something that does not follow the general rule. (2) An objection; an objection to a court's ruling or an error. (3) In insurance, a risk that is excluded from a policy. (4) In property, a piece of land that is not included in a transfer of an estate or interest. V. *except*.

excessive. ADJ. More than necessary; going beyond what is proper or fair. N. *excess*.

excessive bail. N. Bail set in an amount greater than that required to prevent the accused from fleeing, prohibited by the Eighth Amendment of the Constitution.

exchange. V. To give something to another person and receive something else in return; to barter. N. (1) The act of giving one thing and receiving something else in return. (2) An institution that facilitates the trading of a commodity such as stocks or bonds. (3) A transaction in which people living far away from each other settle accounts by transferring credits or drafts called bills of exchange.

exchequer. N. The national treasury of the British government.

excise. N. A tax on certain actions or occupations, the manufacture and sale of particular items, or the transfer of property; also called excise tax.

exclude. V. To deny access or entrance; to keep out; to remove.

exclusion. N. (1) Refusing admittance or removing. (2) In taxation, an item that is not included in gross income; see also *deduct*. (3) In insurance, something that is not covered by a policy.

exclusionary rule. N. A rule stating that evidence found during illegal searches and seizures cannot be used at trial.

exclusive. ADJ. Applying only to one subject, excluding all others.

exclusive contract. N. A contract in which a person promises to buy or sell from one source only.

exclusive control. N. Control over something exercised by only one person.

exclusive jurisdiction. N. Power over a kind of lawsuit or person that is held by only one court or tribunal, requiring that all actions of that sort be heard there.

exclusive license. N. A right granted by the owner of a patent to one person, allowing him or her to use, make, and sell the patented item.

exclusive use. N. In trademark law, the exclusive right to use a specific mark and other marks similar enough to be confusing.

exculpate. V. To show that someone is not guilty of a crime or wrongful act; to clear of blame or fault. ADJ. *exculpatory*.

exculpatory clause. N. A clause in a legal document that releases a party from liability for wrongdoing.

exculpatory evidence. N. Evidence that helps clear a defendant of guilt.

excusable neglect. N. Failure to perform the right action at the right time due to unexpected and unavoidable circumstances rather than through carelessness or disregard.

excuse. V. To forgive; to release from responsibility. N. A reason given to justify an action. ADJ. *excusable*.

ex-dividend. N. Without dividend; the condition of a stock sold without a recently declared dividend, which is retained by the seller.

execute. V. (1) To put into effect; to complete; to carry out an action; to sign a legal document and perform any other tasks needed to make it legally binding. (2) To put to death. N. *execution*.

executive. ADJ. Having the power to make things happen and carry out laws; the power held by the president of the United States.

executive agreement. N. An agreement similar to a treaty that the president of the United States can make with another country without Senate approval.

executive clemency. N. A chief executive's right to pardon criminals and commute criminal sentences.

executive order. N. An order issued by the president interpreting the Constitution or a law.

executive powers. The power to enforce and carry out laws held by the president and governors of the states.

executive privilege. N. An executive's freedom from the disclosure laws that bind other citizens when secrecy is necessary to fulfill the duties of the office.

executor. N. A person chosen by a testator to give away his or her property according to his or her will. FEMININE. *executrix* or *executress*.

executory. ADJ. Not yet complete; awaiting a future event for completion.

executory contract. N. A contract that will not be complete until some specific event happens.

executory interest. N. A future estate or interest in land.

executory trust. N. A trust that has a settlement or conveyance still to make in the future.

exemplar. N. Evidence other than testimony taken from a defendant and used to identify him or her, including fingerprints, voiceprints, blood samples, handwriting samples, etc.

exemplary damages. N. Damages awarded on top of actual damages if the wrong done to the plaintiff by the defendant was aggravated in some way.

exempt. ADJ. Not under an obligation that applies to others; free from liability or obligation. V. To release someone from an obligation or liability.

exemption. N. (1) Freedom from a normal obligation. (2) In taxation, a deduction given to a taxpayer for him- or herself and for dependents.

exhaustion of remedies. N. The state of having attempted and failed to get a remedy through administrative channels before bringing a matter to litigation, or through state court before bringing a matter before a federal court.

exhibit. V. To display something; to present something publicly. N. A piece of physical evidence or a document displayed in court or during a deposition or hearing to be made part of the case.

exigence. Urgent need; an emergency; also called exigency. ADJ. *exigent*.

exigent circumstances. N. An emergency situation in which immediate action is necessary, regardless of procedural requirements; generally applied to situations in which law enforcement officials conduct a search and seizure without a warrant.

exile. N. Banishment from a country; a person who has been expelled from a country. V. *exile*.

exit interview. N. An interview conducted between an employee and employer when the employee leaves his or her job with that employer, at which the parties discuss the employee's job satisfaction, performance, and other matters.

ex officio. ADJ. *(Latin)* Out of duty; by virtue of one's office or status; used to describe powers that are not explicitly defined in an officer's duties but that are implied because they are necessary to the performance of the office.

ex officio justice. N. A judge who serves in a particular capacity because it is part of his or her job description, not because he or she was chosen personally to perform that task.

ex officio member. N. Someone who is a member of a board or other group due to a title or office he or she holds.

exonerate. V. To absolve; to release from blame or obligation. N. *exoneration*.

ex parte. ADJ. *(Latin)* From a side; on behalf of one side of a case.

ex parte divorce. N. A divorce proceeding in which only one spouse attends or participates.

ex parte hearing. N. A judicial hearing held for the benefit of one party only, without notice to or attendance by an adverse party.

ex parte injunction. N. An injunction issued by a court after hearing only the party requesting it.

expectancy. N. Something that is expected or at least hoped for; in property, an interest or estate that is expected to occur when some specific event happens in the future. See also *life expectancy*.

expectant. ADJ. Hoping to receive something in the future.

expel. V. To force out; to eject; see also *expulsion*.

expense. N. Cost; the amount of money spent on something.

expense, business. N. An expense that is part of running a business.

expense, personal. N. Money spent on personal and family needs.

expenses. N. Costs incurred in performing a job; money that must be spent in the ordinary course of business or daily operations.

expenses, operating. N. The ordinary and regular costs involved in operating a business.

expert. N. Someone with great knowledge about a particular topic, such as science, medicine, art, or business. See also *lay witness*.

expert testimony. N. Opinions about a subject offered by an expert in the field in order to help the jury understand specialized evidence in a case.

expert witness. N. A witness who has training or experience in a field that gives him or her knowledge about it far beyond that of an ordinary person, whose testimony is provided to help the jury understand difficult technical information.

expiry. N. The end of something, such as a contract period or a period of time.

export. V. To transport goods from one country to another to sell them. N. Goods made in one country and sold in another. See also *import*.

exportation. N. The act of exporting goods.

ex post facto. N. *(Latin)* From the point of view of subsequent events; after the fact; retroactive.

ex post facto law. N. A law that is passed after an occurrence that changes the law at the time the act occurred; e.g., a law that creates criminal penalties for an act that was not a crime when it was committed; ex post facto laws are prohibited by the Constitution.

express. ADJ. Clear and explicit; directly stated; unambiguous. V. To state definitely.

expressio unius est exclusio alterius. *(Latin)* That which is expressed is included and that which is not is excluded; a rule of statutory interpretation that says that if something is mentioned as being included, then anything that is not mentioned is by implication meant not to be included.

expropriate. V. To take for the government under eminent domain. N. *expropriation*.

expulsion. N. Driving out; ejecting from a group, school, etc; depriving of membership; see also *expel*.

expunge. V. To erase; to destroy completely, especially information or documents.

expungement of records. N. Court-ordered destruction of criminal records after a certain period of time or if an accused is not convicted.

expurgate. V. To cleanse; to remove objectionable material from a document.

ex rights. N. Without rights; the condition of a stock sold without rights to purchase more stock from the issuing corporation.

extend. V. To make larger; to prolong; to push back the original boundary or deadline.

extension. N. (1) An allowance of additional time after a deadline has expired. (2) An addition that makes something bigger, such as a structure added to a building to make it larger.

extenuate. v. To mitigate; to make a crime or misdeed seem less wrong.

extenuating circumstances. N. Circumstances that make a crime appear less serious and make the one who committed it appear less blameworthy than would ordinarily be the case.

extinguish. v. To end; to cancel; to void a right; to quench or put out, as a fire.

extinguishment. N. The end of a right or contract by agreement between the parties or by operation of law.

extort. v. To get something from someone else through force, threats, or fear. N. *extortion*.

extortionate. ADJ. (1) Far more expensive than is appropriate. (2) Prone to extortion.

extradite. v. For a state or country to transfer a person accused of a crime to the country or state where the crime supposedly occurred. N. *extradition*.

extrajudicial. ADJ. Done outside of court; not legally authorized.

extramural. ADJ. Outside the walls, boundaries, or limits of an institution or business; in corporations, outside the limits of corporate power. See also *intramural*.

extraordinary. ADJ. Unusual, remarkable.

extraordinary circumstances. N. Circumstances and factors not usually associated with a particular time, place, or situation.

extraordinary risk. N. A risk not normally associated with a particular activity.

extrinsic. ADJ. Coming from the outside; not an inherent part of something.

eyewitness. N. Someone who sees an event firsthand.

FAA. ABBRV. Federal Aviation Administration.

fabricate. V. To invent; to create; to make up a story or manufacture an object, usually intending to deceive. N. *fabrication*.

fabricated evidence. N. Evidence created after the fact to disguise the truth.

face value. N. The value of a check, bond, note, insurance policy, or other negotiable instrument as stated on the instrument itself; see also *market price*.

facilitate. V. To assist; to make something possible or easier to accomplish; to make it easier for someone to commit a crime. N. *facilitation*. See also *aid and abet*.

facility. N. A building, a space, or the equipment used to provide some service or perform some function; an amenity. PL. *facilities*.

facsimile. N. An exact copy of something, usually a document.

fact. N. Something that is true; a thing that has happened or a situation that exists.

fact finder. N. The person or group of people whose job is to determine the facts in a case; also called the trier of fact. See also *jury*.

factor. N. (1) Something that influences an outcome. (2) An agent who buys and sells goods for a commission called a factorage.

factual. ADJ. Truthful; describing actual events or circumstances.

faculties. N. Physical and mental capabilities; the ability to do something.

fail. V. To be unsuccessful at something; to be deficient; to be unable to meet obligations; to lapse (a legacy). N. *failure*.

failure of consideration. N. A condition that occurs when a contract's consideration becomes worthless or no longer exists.

failure of issue. N. The condition of producing no children to inherit one's estate; dying childless.

failure of justice. N. Miscarriage of justice; a loss of rights or lack of reparation due to the absence of an adequate legal remedy.

failure of proof. N. Inability to prove a side of a case.

failure to state a claim (upon which relief may be granted). N. A plaintiff's failure to define and support a cause of action sufficient to support a case in court, resulting in dismissal of the case; see also *Federal Rules of Civil Procedure*.

fair. ADJ. Impartial and just; according to stated rules and standards.

fair and impartial jury. N. A jury composed of people who have no preconceptions about a case and who will form opinions based on a fair consideration of evidence and testimony.

fair and impartial trial. N. A trial or hearing before a court or jury that has no preconceived notions about the matter and that will hear testimony and examine evidence before making a decision.

fair comment. N. A defense in libel cases, used especially by the news media, that the published statements in question were meant to state facts that the writer or speaker believed were true.

fair hearing. N. An administrative hearing authorized in a case where a normal judicial proceeding would not satisfy the requirements of due process, such as a case in which no judicial remedy is available or in which the plaintiff would have to suffer much more harm to be eligible for one.

Fair Housing Act. N. A federal law passed as Title VIII of the Civil Rights Act of 1968 that prohibits discrimination in the rental, sale, and financing of housing based on race, sex, religion, national origin, handicap, and family status.

Fair Labor Standards Act. N. A federal statute passed in 1938 that set a minimum wage, a maximum work week, and established rules about work by teenagers for businesses engaged in interstate commerce.

fair use. N. The legal use of copyrighted materials without the owner's consent or payment of royalties; whether a use is a fair use or an infringement of copyright depends on factors such as who is using the material, the amount used, and whether or not the user acknowledges the copyright owner; see also *copyright, plagiarize.*

faith-based. Religious; based in religious beliefs.

faith-based initiative. N. A charitable project undertaken by a religious organization.

false. ADJ. Untrue; incorrect; deceitful or treacherous.

false advertising. N. The deliberate inclusion of false information in advertising, with the intention of misleading consumers in order to make them purchase the advertised product. See also *advertise.*

false arrest. N. Unlawfully arresting or detaining someone without legal authority or the detainee's consent.

falsehood. N. An untruth or lie.

false imprisonment. N. The tort of detaining someone intentionally and without justification.

false pretenses. N. Intentionally using fraud or misrepresentation to obtain property or money.

false representation. N. Intentionally misleading someone either by lying or by failing to disclose a fact when the fact should have been disclosed.

false statement. N. A statement made by someone who knows it is false or who makes it recklessly without honestly believing it to be true, intending it to deceive.

false swearing. N. When a person swears that something is true and he or she knows that it is not; also called a false oath.

family. N. A group of people related to one another by blood and marriage, often sharing a common ancestor; the unit consisting of parents and children; for insurance purposes, the people who live with and are dependent on an insured person.

family allowance. N. Money allocated to a surviving spouse and/or children to support them while the deceased spouse's estate goes through the probate process; see also *widow's allowance*.

Family and Medical Leave Act of 1993. N. A federal law that protects the jobs of and guarantees unpaid leave to certain workers who suffer medical problems or who must care for sick family members or new children. ABBRV. *FMLA*.

family automobile doctrine. N. A doctrine, also called a family purpose doctrine, that makes the owner of an automobile liable for negligent operation of it by a member of his or her family; this doctrine has been rejected by many states.

family court. N. A court with jurisdiction over matters related to families and children, including child abuse and neglect, support and custody, paternity, and juvenile delinquency.

FAQ. ABBRV. Frequently asked questions.

fatal. ADJ. Deadly; causing death; causing something to fail completely.

fatal error. N. An error at trial that hurts one party's case so badly as to be grounds for a new trial.

fatal injury. N. An injury that causes death to its victim.

fault. N. Blame; responsibility for a bad result; a wrongful act or mistake; negligence; breach of duty.

faulty. ADJ. Defective.

FBI. ABBRV. Federal Bureau of Investigation.

FCC. ABBRV. Federal Communications Commission.

FDA. ABBRV. Food and Drug Administration.

FDIC. ABBRV. Federal Deposit Insurance Corporation.

fealty. N. Sworn loyalty; in feudal times, allegiance to a feudal lord sworn by a tenant.

fear, uncertainty, and doubt. N. A marketing strategy in which the manufacturer of a product tries to make consumers worry that buying a competing product might result in bad consequences, typically by criticizing or spreading disinformation about the competing product. ABBRV. *FUD*.

featherbedding. N. A practice by employees of increasing or maintaining the number of workers required to perform a task or the time allotted to do a specific job in an effort to protect job security, especially against the threat of technology.

federal. ADJ. Relating to the central government of a union of states, such as the national government of the United States.

Federal Aviation Administration. N. The federal agency that handles civil aviation as part of the Department of Transportation. ABBRV. *FAA.*

Federal Bureau of Investigation. N. The federal agency that investigates violations of federal laws, including criminal, civil, and security matters as part of the Department of Justice. ABBRV. *FBI.*

federal common law. N. A body of case law composed of decisions made by federal courts, used in a very narrow range of cases; see also *Erie doctrine.*

Federal Communications Commission. N. The federal agency that regulates broadcasting by television, radio, telephone, satellite, etc. ABBRV. *FCC.*

federal courts. N. The courts of the United States, created by the Constitution or by acts of Congress and having jurisdiction created by statute, including federal district courts, federal courts of appeal, and the Supreme Court of the United States.

Federal Deposit Insurance Corporation. N. An agency within the executive branch of the U.S. government that insures deposits in banks and savings associations. ABBRV. *FDIC.*

Federal Emergency Management Agency. N. An agency of the U.S. Department of Homeland Security dedicated to coordinating national responses to major disasters such as hurricanes or earthquakes. ABBRV. *FEMA.*

Federal Firearms License. N. A license issued by the Bureau of Alcohol, Tobacco, Firearms and Explosives that allows an individual or business to manufacture or sell firearms and ammunition. ABBRV. *FFL.*

Federal Insurance Contribution Act. N. The act that regulates the Social Security system by taxing employers and employees and setting benefits. ABBRV. *FICA*.

federalism. N. The federal system of government, including a division of power between a central government and individual states, in which states handle local affairs and the central government handles matters that affect the entire nation.

federalist. N. Someone who supports federalism.

Federalist Papers. N. A collection of essays published by Alexander Hamilton, James Madison, and John Jay from October 1787 to August 1788, advocating that New York vote to ratify the Constitution that had already been adopted in Philadelphia in September 1787.

federal question jurisdiction. N. Original jurisdiction held by federal courts over cases in which interpretation of the Constitution, acts of Congress, or treaties of the United States are in dispute; federal question jurisdiction is granted to federal courts by Article III of the Constitution.

Federal Reserve System. N. A network of twelve central banks established by the Federal Reserve Act in 1913 to oversee a national system of banking, including monitoring the money supply by holding cash reserves and issuing currency for circulation, overseeing the credit system, and generally watching the nation's economy.

Federal Rules of Civil Procedure. N. A compilation of rules created by the Supreme Court in 1938 that govern the procedure used in civil cases in U.S. district courts, which have been used as a model for procedure by most state courts.

Federal Rules of Criminal Procedure. N. Procedural rules created by the Supreme Court in 1945 that govern proceedings in criminal cases before U.S. district courts and sometimes before U.S. magistrates.

Federal Rules of Evidence. N. Rules governing the admission of evidence before U.S. district courts, U.S. magistrates, and bankruptcy court, which have been used as a model for rules of evidence by many states.

Federal Trade Commission. N. A federal agency that promotes free trade and fair competition in interstate commerce by preventing price-fixing, advertising, and general unfair competition. ABBRV. *FTC*.

federation. N. A union of states that share a central government but also govern themselves independently.

fee. N. (1) Payment made to someone in exchange for services. (2) An estate of complete ownership of land; ownership of a piece of property.

fee, in. ADJ. Owning a property completely.

fee simple. N. Complete ownership of a property, with no time limit or restrictions on what can be done with it, that will pass to the owner's heirs if he or she dies intestate; also called fee simple absolute.

fee simple conditional. N. An interest in property that is given by a grantor to the owner that will become a fee simple if a particular condition is met, usually having to do with the estate passing to specific heirs of the owner, and if the condition is not met the estate goes back to the grantor when the owner dies.

fee simple defeasible. N. An estate that can end if a particular event does or does not happen; also called a fee simple determinable.

fee tail. N. A conveyance of property that establishes a specific line of succession, limiting the transfer of the property to a particular category of descendants of the recipient, and that goes back to the grantor if there are no suitable descendants; also called an estate tail.

fee tail male or female. N. An estate limited to male or female lines of descent.

fellow servant. N. A coworker; someone who works for the same employer.

fellow servant rule. A rule that absolved an employer from liability for injury done to one employee as a result of the negligence of another; now superseded by workers' compensation.

felon. N. One who has committed a felony.

felony. N. A serious crime; most felonies are defined by statute, and often include those that are punishable by death or by more than one year of imprisonment. ADJ. *felonious*. See also *misdemeanor*.

felony murder. N. A killing that occurs while committing a felony; whether the killing occurs accidentally or not, under the felony murder doctrine it could be prosecuted as first-degree murder; this doctrine varies from state to state.

FEMA. ABBRV. Federal Emergency Management Agency.

fence. N. (1) A structure made of wood, metal, or some other material that encloses or divides a piece of land. (2) Someone who receives and sells stolen property. V. To buy and sell stolen property.

fetus. N. An unborn mammal; an unborn human child after the first eight weeks of gestation. ADJ. *fetal*.

feudalism. N. A social, economic, and governmental system common in medieval Europe, under which nobles gave land to vassals who fought for them, and peasants farmed the land and gave much of their produce to their lords, who in return gave them protection. ADJ. *feudal*.

FFL. ABBRV. Federal Firearms License.

fiat. N. An arbitrary and authoritative command; a decree.

FICA. ABBRV. Federal Insurance Contribution Act.

fiduciary. ADJ. Involving trust, confidence, and good faith; describes the relationship of a trustee to a beneficiary or a guardian to a ward. N. Someone entrusted with a duty to act on behalf of and in the best interest of someone else, especially the management of someone else's property; a trustee.

fiduciary capacity. N. The condition of acting, transacting business, or handling money on behalf of someone else.

fiduciary duty. N. The duty of a person or institution entrusted with someone else's property to act in that person's best interest while putting aside personal interests; the highest duty imposed by law.

FIFO. ABBRV. First-in, first-out.

Fifth Amendment. N. An amendment added to the Constitution as part of the Bill of Rights that provides important protections from government actions, including a guarantee that no person will be required to answer for a capital crime unless first indicted by a grand jury; no one will suffer double jeopardy; no one must testify against him- or herself; no one will be deprived of life, liberty, or property without due process of law; and, no property will be taken for public use without just compensation.

fighting words. N. Words that in and of themselves cause injury or could provoke a violent response from listeners; fighting words are not protected under the First Amendment, and uttering them can constitute the tort of assault.

file. N. The documents that comprise a case, including pleadings, motions, briefs, affidavits, and other papers. V. To deposit a document with the court or other proper authority so that it becomes part of the official record.

file sharing. N. The practice of sharing computer files over a computer network such as the Internet.

filibuster. N. An excessively long speech intended to obstruct debate and voting on a piece of legislature, especially in the Senate. V. *filibuster*.

filing. N. A document that has been filed as part of a lawsuit. See also *file*.

final decision. N. A decision by the court that ends a dispute between parties and settles their respective rights, preventing further litigation of the matter unless it is reversed or set aside; also called a final judgment.

finance charge. N. A fee charged for the extension of credit and the deferral of payment of a loan.

financial institution. N. A business that deals in money, such as a bank or trust company, a thrift institution, a currency exchange, a securities trading company, a credit card company, an insurance company, etc.

financial intermediary. N. A person or company that brings together borrowers and lenders and specializes in transactions that change money from one form to another.

financial statement. N. A report of the financial condition of a person or institution, including a balance sheet, an income statement, and charges.

finder. N. A middleman who helps people find things such as jobs, business opportunities, or loans in return for payment of a finder's fee, and then lets the parties come to their own business arrangements.

finding. N. A court's or jury's conclusion about a matter of law or fact.

finding of fact. N. A court's or agency's determinations about the facts of a case after hearing testimony, examining evidence, and deliberating.

finding of law. N. A court's determination of how to apply law to the facts of a case.

fine. N. Money that a person must pay as a penalty for a crime or wrongful act. V. To punish someone by making him or her pay a fine.

fine print. N. Details of a contract, insurance policy, or other document that are printed in small type and placed where they will not be easily noticed or read, making it difficult for someone to learn about conditions that might be unfavorable.

fingerprint. N. The unique pattern of lines and whorls on the tip of a finger, used to identify individuals. V. To take someone's fingerprint.

fire. N. To end or terminate someone's employment.

firearm. N. A gun; a device that uses an explosive substance to propel a projectile from a barrel.

fire sale. N. A sale of merchandise at reduced prices, usually done after an emergency such as a fire or flood that destroys or damages the commercial premises.

firewall. N. A device or program that limits access to a computer network.

firm offer. N. An offer by a merchant to buy or sell goods made in writing and signed, assuring the other party that the offer will be held open for a specified period of time; regulated by the Uniform Commercial Code.

First Amendment. N. An amendment to the Constitution added with the Bill of Rights, guaranteeing freedom of speech, assembly, religion, press, and the right to petition the government for redress of grievances.

first-degree murder. N. Killing someone deliberately and intentionally, having planned it beforehand, with extreme cruelty, or while committing another felony.

first impression. N. The first consideration of something, particularly the first time a case appears before a court and presents an entirely new question of law that has never been considered before, and thus has no precedents to guide the decision.

first-in, first-out. N. An accounting method that assumes goods are sold in the order purchased; see also *last-in, first-out.* ABBRV. *FIFO.*

fiscal. ADJ. Concerning financial matters, particularly matters of government finance and the public treasury.

fiscal year. N. A twelve-month period used by a business as a tax and accounting period; the accounting year.

fit. ADJ. Of sufficient quality or ability to meet a specific purpose; adequate or suitable. N. *fitness*.

fit for a particular purpose. N. An item's condition of being suitable for the purpose for which it is intended, usually as promised by the seller. See also *warranty*.

fix. V. (1) To establish something permanently or for the long-term. (2) To decide or settle something; to set a price. ADJ. *fixed*.

fixed assets. N. The property that a business uses in its daily operations and will not convert into cash, such as equipment.

fixed capital. N. The money permanently invested in a company.

fixed income. N. Regular income that does not fluctuate over time; income from a retirement benefit or annuity. See also *price fixing*.

fixture. N. An object that is permanently attached to a building or property and is thus regarded as part of the property.

fixture, trade. N. An object used in business attached to a rented space by a tenant who runs a business there; trade fixtures remain the property of the tenant and do not become part of the property.

flee. V. To run away, usually to escape danger. See also *flight*.

flee from justice. V. For someone who has committed a crime to leave home or the jurisdiction where the crime was committed in order to avoid arrest.

flexible benefits. N. An employee benefits program that allows employees to choose from a range of possible benefits to create personalized benefits packages. See also *cafeteria plan*.

flexible spending account. N. A savings account in which an employee can save tax-free a portion of his or her earnings to meet a specific type of expense. ABBRV. *FSA*. See also *cafeteria plan, health savings account*.

flight. N. The act of running away or trying to escape something; fleeing. See also *flee*.

flight from prosecution. N. The act by someone who has committed an unlawful act of leaving the scene of the crime in an effort to avoid arrest.

flim-flam. N. A type of fraud or confidence game performed by two perpetrators, one of whom persuades the victim to give money to the other as part of a get-rich-quick scheme, whereupon both perpetrators disappear with the money.

float. N. The time between when a check is deposited and when the money it represents is deducted from the writer's account.

floating. ADJ. Not settled; fluctuating.

floating capital. N. Capital kept to meet current expenses, often kept in the form of current assets.

floating debt. N. Short-term debt held by a business or government.

floating interest rate. N. A variable interest rate that changes based on the money market.

FMLA. ABBRV. Family and Medical Leave Act of 1993.

FOB. ABBRV. Free on board.

FOIA. ABBRV. Freedom of Information Act.

Food and Drug Administration. N. A federal agency that regulates the safety of food, drugs, cosmetics, and other household products as part of the Department of Health and Human Services. ABBRV. *FDA*.

forbear. V. To resist an impulse to do something; to refrain from doing something. N. *forbearance*.

force. N. Compulsion; power exerted to make something happen. V. To make someone do something against his or her will.

force, deadly. N. Force likely to cause death or serious bodily injury.

force, unlawful. N. The use of force against someone who has not consented to its use.

forced heirs. N. People who cannot be disinherited by a testator's will, such as a spouse or children.

forced sale. N. A sale made by order of the court to enforce a judgment against the property owner.

force majeure. N. *(French)* Superior strength; unforeseeable and unavoidable circumstances outside the control of a party to a contract that render him or her incapable of carrying out contractual duties.

forcible. ADJ. Done by force, compulsion, or violence.

forcible detainer. N. (1) Using force to hold someone in custody. (2) A statutory remedy allowing someone who owns property to take possession of it from someone who refuses to relinquish it; see also *detainer*.

forcible entry. N. Using force or threat of force to illegally enter property that belongs to someone else against the owner's will.

forcible entry and detainer. N. A statutory proceeding that returns property to someone who has been wrongfully deprived of it.

foreclose. V. To end someone's right to a property; to take possession of mortgaged property as a result of the property owner's failure to make payments. N. *foreclosure*.

foreign. ADJ. From another country, state, or jurisdiction.

foreign corporation. N. A corporation that does business in one state but is incorporated in another.

foreign court. N. A court in another country or state.

foreign national. N. A person who is in one country but who is a legal permanent resident of another.

foreman. N. (1) A juror who leads jury proceedings and speaks to the court on the entire jury's behalf. (2) A worker in a leadership position over his or her coworkers. Also called a foreperson.

forensic. ADJ. Relating to law and courts.

forensic engineering. N. A branch of engineering that applies engineering principles to legal matters.

forensic medicine. N. A branch of medicine that applies medical principles to the investigation of legal matters, especially the investigation of crimes that result in death.

forensics. N. The application of scientific tests and techniques to the investigation of crimes.

foresee. V. To predict; to know in advance what is likely to occur in a given situation. ADJ. *foreseeable*. N. *foreseeability*.

foreseeable risk. N. The risk that a person of ordinary intelligence and prudence should reasonably expect to occur.

forfeit. V. To lose the right to something as a punishment; to be forced to give something up. N. A right or thing lost as a penalty; the act of forfeiting something. ADJ. Lost or given up as a penalty.

forfeitable. ADJ. Able to be given up or taken as a punishment.

forfeiture. N. The taking of property without compensation, usually as a punishment for breaking the law.

forge. V. To make a copy or imitation of something intending to pass it off as the genuine article; see also *counterfeit.*

forgery. N. The copying of a document, signature, work of art, or bank note with the intention of deceiving someone into thinking it is genuine.

form. N. (1) A model or frame of a legal document with blank spaces to be filled out with information that applies to an individual situation. (2) Customary procedure or formalities; the way something is expressed as opposed to what is expressed.

Form 1040. N. The form that most U.S. taxpayers must fill out to file their income tax returns.

forms of action. N. The categories of legal actions available under common law, such as trespass, debt, etc., and divided into actions at equity and actions at law; now all forms of action are gathered together under the Rules of Civil Procedure into the single heading "civil action."

fornication. N. Sexual relations between two unmarried people, or by an unmarried person (who commits fornication) and a married person (who commits adultery); definitions vary by jurisdiction. V. *fornicate.*

forthwith. ADV. Right away; immediately; at the first opportunity.

fortuitous. ADJ. Happening by chance rather than design. N. *fortuity*.

forum. N. A court or tribunal; a place where people can try to get a judicial or administrative remedy for some wrong.

forum non conveniens. N. *(Latin)* An inconvenient court; a court's discretionary power to refuse to hear a case that is within its jurisdiction if it would be more convenient for the parties or better serve the interests of justice for it to be heard elsewhere.

forum shopping. N. An attempt by a litigant to have the case tried in a specific jurisdiction that appears likely to rule in his or her favor.

found. V. (1) To establish something, usually an institution or charity, often by providing an endowment for it. (2) To serve as a basis for something.

foundation. N. (1) The lowest part of a building that supports the weight of the entire structure. (2) The establishment of an institution, hospital, charity, school, etc. (3) A fund that supports an institution, hospital, charity, school, etc. (4) Evidence and questions of a witness used to establish the relevance of other evidence, thus making it admissible.

founder. N. One who establishes a charity or institution by endowing it or supplying initial funds.

Founding Fathers. N. The men who created the U.S. Constitution in 1787.

four corners rule. N. A rule requiring that the meaning of a document and the intention of its creator be determined by considering it as a whole and not in isolated parts.

franchise. N. (1) The right to vote. (2) A privilege granted by the government or a company to a person or company, allowing it to engage in a specific activity not permitted to most citizens; a license from the owner of a trademark to sell products under that name, under which the franchisee agrees to follow certain rules and the franchisor promises assistance through advertising and other services. (3) A business owned by a franchisee.

franchisee. N. A person who owns a franchise of a business.

franchisor. N. A business or other entity that sells the right to engage in a particular activity or run a particular business.

fraternal. ADJ. Brotherly; having common interests.

fraternal benefit association. N. An organization whose members either belong to the same professional field or who are working toward the same goal that exists to promote a common cause and assist its members with benefits for death, injury, or illness; also called a fraternal benefits society.

fraud. N. Intentional misrepresentation of the truth done to cause someone else to rely on that misrepresentation and be deceived into surrendering a legal right or otherwise being injured. ADJ. *fraudulent*. V. *defraud*.

fraud, actual. N. A misrepresentation done specifically to cheat someone; also called fraud in fact.

fraud, constructive. N. An act or omission that might not be intended to deceive, but does anyway; also called fraud in law.

fraud, extrinsic. N. Fraud that prevents a party from knowing about and therefore defending or pursuing all legal rights available to him or her.

fraud, intrinsic. N. Fraudulent information, such as perjury, that is considered by the court in reaching a judgment.

fraud in the factum. N. Fraud that arises when a person signs a document that is not the document he or she believes is being signed.

fraud in the inducement. N. Fraud in which a person is misled about the details of a transaction or contract and enters into an agreement under a false impression about what is involved.

fraudulent concealment. N. Hiding a material fact that legally or morally should be disclosed.

fraudulent conveyance. N. A transfer of property done to hinder a creditor or place the property out of a creditor's reach.

fraudulent misrepresentation. N. A false statement about a material fact made by a speaker who knows it is false but intends the hearer to believe it and rely on it, and that injures the hearer if he or she does rely on it.

free and clear. ADJ. Of property, unencumbered by liens.

freedom. N. Liberty; absence of restrictions or restraints.

freedom of contract. N. The right to enter into contracts and agreements with others, guaranteed by Article I of the Constitution.

Freedom of Information Act. N. A federal law, 5 U.S.C.A. section 552, that attempts to prevent abuse of governmental power by requiring federal agencies to make documents and information about agency matters available to the general public, with a few exceptions. ABBRV. *FOIA.*

freedom of press. N. The right to publish views and opinions without interference by the government, guaranteed by the First Amendment of the Constitution.

freedom of religion. N. The right to choose and practice a religion without interference from the government or from established churches, guaranteed by the First Amendment of the Constitution.

freedom of speech. N. The right to express one's opinions verbally or in writing without interference or restriction from the government, guaranteed by the First Amendment of the Constitution.

free exercise clause. N. A clause in the First Amendment of the Constitution stating that Congress will pass no law prohibiting the free exercise of religion; see also *establishment clause*.

freehold. N. A piece of land held in fee or as a life estate; property that the owner holds at least for life and might also be able to pass on after death; see also *leasehold*.

free on board. ADJ. Describes a contractual agreement by a seller to deliver goods to a specified place without expense to the buyer, in which the seller assumes all delivery expenses and risks; such a contract is called an f.o.b. contract. ABBRV. *FOB*.

free trade agreement. An agreement between two or more nations, states, or other geographic units that requires each member to allow other members to sell specified goods freely within its territory, without imposing tariffs or duties. See also *North American Free Trade Association, NAFTA*.

freeware. N. Software made available by its copyright holder for use for an unlimited time free of charge. See also *public domain, shareware*.

freeze-out. N. A process in which a close corporation tries to force minority shareholders to sell their stock on terms favorable to the majority shareholders by preventing the minority shareholders from getting any profit from their investment. See also *squeeze-out*.

freight. N. (1) Goods transported by a carrier such as a truck, train, aircraft, or ship. (2) The cost of transporting goods by a carrier. V. To transport goods by a carrier.

freighter. N. (1) A ship or airplane used to transport cargo. (2) A person or company in the business of transporting goods.

freight forwarder. N. A business that consolidates small shipments of goods so they can all be sent as a single lot and assumes responsibility for their transport.

frequently asked questions. N. A list of questions frequently asked about a topic followed by their answers. ABBRV. *FAQ*.

fresh pursuit. N. Pursuit by police officers of a suspected felon fleeing the scene of the crime done immediately after the criminal act and without delay, which provides the officers with the common law right to cross state lines to make the arrest; also called hot pursuit.

friendly suit. N. A lawsuit brought by parties who agree on a particular settlement but need a judicial decision to make it binding; see also *declaratory judgment*.

fringe benefit. N. A benefit that supplements an employee's pay, such as health insurance, profit-sharing plans, or recreational facilities.

frisk. V. A quick physical search of a person to feel for concealed weapons done by running hands over the body over clothing.

frivolous. ADJ. Unimportant; not serious; lacking in substance; presenting no legitimate legal question.

frivolous appeal. N. An appeal that has no merit, presents no justiciable question, and has no hope of success.

frivolous claim. N. A cause of action that has no hope of success, brought primarily to annoy or embarrass the defendant.

fruit of the poisonous tree doctrine. N. The principle that evidence obtained for a criminal trial through an illegal search or illegal interrogation of a witness is tainted and therefore inadmissible against the defendant because it violates the guarantee of due process.

fruits of a crime. N. The items acquired by a criminal through crime.

frustration of purpose. N. A situation that arises when a condition that was part of a contract does not occur, through no fault of either party, but the condition was the reason for one party entering the contract in the first place; can be cause for terminating the contract.

FSA. ABBRV. Flexible spending account.

FTC. ABBRV. Federal Trade Commission.

FUD. N. Fear, uncertainty, and doubt.

fugitive. N. Someone who flees or hides in an attempt to evade capture.

fugitive from justice. N. A person who flees to another state or hides after committing a crime, hoping to avoid arrest.

full faith and credit. N. The constitutional requirement that all states must recognize the laws, judicial decisions, and public records of all other states and must give them the same degree of recognition that their own laws, judicial decisions, and public records receive.

fund. N. An amount of money saved or intended for a particular purpose. V. To supply money for a particular purpose.

fund, general. N. A fund that is not restricted to a specific purpose but can be used for general expenses. See also *mutual fund, sinking fund.*

funded debt. N. A debt that has a fund allocated for its payment.

fund in court. N. An amount of money deposited with the court either because the parties to a lawsuit both claim it, or to keep it in reserve to pay for potential liability.

fungible. ADJ. Interchangeable; describes goods that are essentially identical to one another and that can replace one another, e.g., oil, grain, or money.

future interest. N. An interest in real or personal property that will begin at some specified time in the future.

futures contract. N. An agreement to buy shares of a commodity at a fixed price but with delivery and payment occurring at an agreed-upon date in the future; if the price of the commodity rises during that period, the seller pays the buyer the difference between the agreed price and the current price, and if the price of the commodity drops, the buyer pays the seller the difference.

G

gag order. N. (1) An order issued by a judge prohibiting participants in a lawsuit from discussing the case publicly in order to protect the litigants' right to an impartial trial; gag orders may not usually be imposed on the press. (2) An order to restrain or silence a disruptive defendant in a criminal trial.

gain. N. Profit; growth of wealth, property, or value. V. *gain*. ADJ. *gainful*.

gainful employment. N. A job or an occupation that earns money or generates profit; employment for pay that is suited to the abilities of the worker; also called gainful occupation.

gamble. V. To bet; to play games of chance for money. N. A risky enterprise that could turn out as either a profit or a loss.

gambling. N. Betting; playing games of chance for money.

game. N. Wild animals that can be hunted.

game laws. N. Federal and state laws that regulate the hunting of animals for sport or food.

game of chance. N. A game in which the outcome is determined primarily by luck and chance rather than skill.

gaol. N. An archaic spelling of "jail."

garnish. V. To seize someone's money, property, or wages to settle a debt or claim.

garnishee. N. The third party who is ordered by the court to surrender money or property owed to a debtor so that it can be used to pay the debtor's debts.

garnishment. N. A court order that takes the property or money that a third party owes to a debtor (typically wages owed to the debtor by an employer) and gives it to a plaintiff creditor.

garnishor. N. A creditor plaintiff who brings a garnishment proceeding against a debtor.

GATT. ABBRV. General Agreement on Tariffs and Trade.

General Agreement on Tariffs and Trade. N. An international agreement that states guidelines and rules for international trade. ABBRV. *GATT*.

gender. N. The condition of being female or male, with emphasis on cultural implications of masculinity or femininity rather than biological and physical differences; the members of the female or male sex; see also *sex*.

general. ADJ. Not specialized; concerning an entire class or category as opposed to individuals. N. The highest-ranking kind of officer in the army.

general bequest. N. A bequest to be paid out of the general assets of an estate rather than a particular thing or money.

general election. N. An election taking place in an entire state to elect offices that come open regularly.

general exception. N. An objection to a pleading for lack of substance.

general jurisdiction. N. Jurisdiction covering all types of cases that can be brought before a court.

general law. N. A law that affects all people of a state or class.

general public license. N. A free software license used by software producers to ensure that all versions of software licensed by general public license will remain freely available. See also *open source*. ABBRV. *GPL*.

general reputation. N. The character of a witness as portrayed by testimony of people who know him or her.

general welfare. N. The health, peace, safety, and morality of the citizenry, promoted by Article I of the Constitution.

generation. N. (1) The period of time it takes a person to be born, grow up, and have children of his or her own, usually between twenty and thirty years. (2) A set of family members all born around the same time and at the same stage of descent from a common ancestor.

generation-skipping transfer. N. A transfer of wealth that passes over one generation to go down to a younger one, e.g., a transfer from grandparents straight to grandchildren.

generation-skipping trust. N. A trust created to facilitate a generation-skipping transfer.

generic. ADJ. General, not specific; covering a whole class of things.

generic drug laws. N. Laws that allow pharmacists to substitute generic drugs for equivalent brand-name drugs in order to save consumers money.

generic mark. N. A name of an item that is so general and commonly used as to lack the distinctiveness necessary to make it eligible for trademark protection.

Geneva Conventions. N. Four treaties created in Geneva, Switzerland, between 1863 and 1949 that set standards for how member nations should treat prisoners of war and civilians during wartime. See also *jus in bello*, *laws of war*.

genital mutilation. N. The practice of modifying genital organs by cutting off portions of them; usually done to young girls.

genocide. N. The practice of killing a race or ethnic group; systematic eradication of an ethnic or national group by murder, forced birth control, removal of children from the group, and a general program of persecution.

geopolitical. ADJ. Having to do with the combined effects of geography and politics.

gerrymander. V. To manipulate boundaries in dividing a state or territory into political divisions in order to secure an advantage for a certain party in elections. N. *gerrymander*.

gift. N. Something given to someone else willingly and without expectation of payment; a voluntary and intentional giving of property by a competent donor that is delivered to and accepted by the recipient without exchange of consideration.

gift, absolute. N. A gift given while the donor is still alive; also called a gift inter vivos.

gift in contemplation of death. N. A gift that is promised to someone by a donor who expects to die soon that will take effect if the donor does die as expected, but for which the donor retains the title while he or she is still living, and that becomes invalid if the donor recovers and does not die of the illness that he or she suffered from when the gift was made; also called a gift causa mortis.

gift over. N. A gift that occurs after an intermediate estate ends; e.g., if A gives B a life estate with a gift over to C, then C takes B's estate when B dies.

gift tax. N. A tax imposed on gifts.

going concern. N. A company or enterprise currently conducting its ordinary business.

going concern value. N. The value of a firm that is currently conducting business, which includes goodwill and other aspects that make it more valuable than its mere assets.

good cause. N. A good reason for doing or not doing something; a reason for one's behavior that is substantial enough to constitute a legal excuse, determined by the context of an individual case.

good faith. N. Sincerity, honesty, lack of deceit; a sincere intention to do what is promised.

good Samaritan. N. Someone who voluntarily aids a person who is in imminent danger or has been injured without expectation of compensation; a good Samaritan is not held liable for injury to the victim unless he or she fails to use reasonable care and the victim is injured further by the efforts at assistance.

good title. N. A title to property that is valid and can be sold without worry; a title free from doubts, encumbrances, and defects, and that is not the subject of litigation; also called merchantable title. Synonymous with *clear title, marketable title.*

goods. N. Personal property, chattels; all property that is not land or buildings, including animals and crops and all other movable items.

goods, durable. N. Items that are not consumed when used and thus last a long time, such as household appliances; also called hard goods.

goods, soft. N. Goods made of fabric, such as clothing or bedding, or textiles themselves; also called dry goods. See also *consumer goods.*

goodwill. N. An intangible business asset composed of a good reputation with customers, suppliers, and the community at large, good employee morale, the ability to attract customers and clients, good management, and other positive aspects that are difficult to value monetarily but that contribute to the success of a business.

govern. v. To control and regulate the affairs of an organization, institution, nation, state, or group of people.

governing body. n. A group or entity that controls the actions and policies of an institution, nation, state, group, or organization.

government. n. The body that controls, influences, and regulates the affairs of a nation, state, or community. ADJ. *governmental*.

governmental act. n. An act done by the government or its agents that uses legislative, judicial, or administrative powers for the public good.

governmental immunity. n. A doctrine limiting the federal government's power to tax states and the states' power to tax the federal government.

governor. n. The elected executive leader of a state.

GPL. ABBRV. General public license.

grace period. n. A period between an official due date and the time when an actual penalty will be imposed for failure to pay or perform; in insurance, the time between the due date of a premium and the time when insurance will actually be cut off if payment is not made.

graded offense. n. A crime that has different degrees and penalties depending on level of guilt; e.g. murder can come in first, second, or third degree. See also *degree of crime*.

graft. n. Corrupt practices used by public officials to unlawfully take public money; money obtained by corruption.

grandfather clause. N. A clause in a new statute that exempts those who are already engaged in the enterprise or activity it regulates from the new requirements.

grand jury. N. A group of people who are selected to investigate an alleged crime and indict suspected criminals. See also *petit jury*.

grant. V. To give; to bestow something on someone; to agree (to a request). N. (1) A legal conveyance of property. (2) A sum of money given by the government or an organization for a particular purpose.

grant, land. N. A donation of land by the government to a state or institution such as a university.

grantee. N. A person who receives a grant.

grantor. N. A person who grants something.

gratis. ADJ. Free; without charge.

gratuitous. ADJ. (1) Done for free; given without expectation of payment. (2) Unjustified; done without good reason.

gratuitous promise. N. A promise made without consideration, making it unenforceable as a legal contract.

gratuity. N. Money or other property given freely, usually in return for some service or favor.

gravamen. N. The essence or most serious part of a complaint, cause of action, charge, etc.

gray market. N. An unofficial trade in something, especially of unissued shares of stock, controlled or scarce goods, or goods manufactured abroad that use U.S. trademarks without permission of the trademark holders.

green card. N. A registration card that allows a permanent resident alien to live and work in the United States.

grievance. N. A complaint; an allegation that someone has committed some injury or injustice that deserves recompense; in labor law, a complaint about working conditions filed by a worker or a union in order to seek relief.

gross. ADJ. (1) Of income or profit, total, before deductions. (2) Extreme; blatant. Gross income. N. All income from all sources. See also *negligence*.

gross national product. N. The total value of goods and services produced by a country in one year plus net income from foreign exports and investments.

ground lease. N. A lease of vacant land with no buildings on it, usually rented in order to build structures such as office buildings or hotels on it; ground leases often run for many years and are renewable by the lessor.

ground rent. N. Rent paid for the use of land, usually to build on it.

growth stock. N. A security that is likely to increase in market value.

guarantee. N. (1) A promise or formal statement that specific conditions are the case or will be met. (2) A person who receives a guarantee. V. *guarantee*.

guarantee clause. N. (1) A clause in the Constitution in which the U.S. government guarantees each state a republican form of government and promises to protect each of the states against invasion and against domestic violence. (2) A clause in a contract in which one party promises to pay someone else's obligations if necessary.

guarantor. N. A person or organization that guarantees something; one who makes a guarantee.

guardian. N. A person who looks after the legal and financial affairs or takes care of someone who is unable to look after his or her own because of age or disability; see also *ad litem, ward*.

guardian by election. N. A guardian chosen by a child who lacks parents.

guardian, testamentary. N. A guardian appointed by the will of a child's father or mother.

guest. N. Someone who receives hospitality; someone invited into another person's home for entertainment or driven by another person in a car without paying for the ride.

guest statute. N. A statute that absolves a driver from liability injury to a passenger in the car if the injury was the result of ordinary negligence, requiring that the driver exhibit gross or willful negligence, reckless disregard, or some other higher level of carelessness to be liable; many states have repealed these statutes.

guilt. N. (1) The condition of having committed a crime or wrongful act. (2) A feeling of remorse after committing a wrongful act or failing in some obligation.

guilty. ADJ. (1) Having committed a crime; culpable; having been determined by a jury to have committed a specific crime. (2) Remorseful; see also *innocent*.

guilty plea. N. A voluntary admission of having committed a crime made to a court by a criminal defendant, punishable in the same way as a guilty verdict after trial.

Gun Control Act of 1968. N. A federal law that regulates interstate commerce in firearms by prohibiting certain categories of people from possessing firearms and by limiting trade in firearms to certain licensed dealers. See also *Federal Firearms License, FFL*.

gun control law. N. A law regulating the sale, possession, and use of guns and firearms.

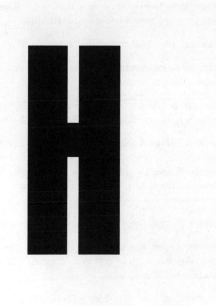

habeas corpus. N. *(Latin)* You have the body; a writ that institutes a court proceeding to determine whether a criminal defendant has been lawfully imprisoned, or to test the constitutionality of a conviction; also used in cases of child custody and deportation.

habitable. ADJ. Referring to a building or dwelling, of good enough quality to be lived in or occupied without serious inconvenience or danger to health and safety. N. *habitability*.

habitual. ADJ. Customary, usual, regular.

habitual drunkenness. N. The practice of frequently drinking to the point of intoxication.

habitual offender. N. A person who regularly commits crimes; also called a habitual criminal. Synonymous with *recidivist*.

hack. V. To break into a closed computer network by using software or clever programming. N. A quick fix to a computer programming problem; a modification to a program that allows the user to enter an area of the program or network that was previously closed to the user.

hale. V. To drag forcibly; to summon forcefully into court.

halfway house. N. A temporary residence for people who have left an institution, such as a prison or mental hospital, to help them readjust to life in society.

handwriting. N. Writing done by hand with a hand-held implement such as a pen or pencil; the unique writing produced by a particular person and identifiable as his or her production.

hanging. N. A form of capital punishment in which the convicted person has a rope placed around his or her neck and is then hung until dead. V. *hang*.

harass. v. (1) To pressure, intimidate, or attack repeatedly; to annoy; to insult or abuse verbally. (2) To bring a criminal prosecution against someone without a reasonable expectation of conviction. N. *harassment*. See also *harassment, sexual*.

harassment, hostile environment. N. Harassment that is determined by a pattern of sexual behavior by supervisors or fellow employees that creates an environment that the victim finds intolerable.

harassment, quid pro quo. N. Sexual harassment in which a superior demands sexual favors from an employee as a condition of his or her continued employment, threatening to fire the employee if the demands are not met.

harassment, sexual. N. Employment discrimination that involves sexual demands and acts, which can involve perpetrators and victims of either sex.

harbor. v. (1) To provide shelter to someone. (2) To hide or take in a criminal or alien, usually secretly. N. (1) A protected body of water for anchoring ships. (2) A safe place; a refuge.

hard case. N. A legal case in which the judicial decision accommodates the extreme hardship faced by one party by deviating from strict legal principles.

hardship. N. Suffering, privation, difficulty, oppression. See *unnecessary hardship*.

hardware. N. Computer equipment; the physical devices that make up a computer system. See also *software*.

harmless error. N. An error made by an appellate court during a trial that is usually trivial or academic, does not prejudice the rights of the party affected by it, and does not necessitate the reversal of the judgment.

hdhp. ABBRV. High deductible health plan.

headnote. N. A short summary of a case and its legal holdings placed at the beginning of the case report.

head of household. N. (1) A person who lives with and supports one or more people living in the same home, and generally manages household affairs. (2) An unmarried taxpayer who houses and supports one or more dependents.

healthcare. N. The prevention and treatment of diseases and injuries by medical professionals and institutions.

Health Insurance Portability and Accountability Act. N. A federal law enacted in 1996 that allows many workers to maintain health insurance coverage when they lose or change jobs and that protects the privacy of health data. ABBRV. *HIPAA*.

health maintenance organization. N. A form of health insurance consisting of a group of physicians, hospitals, and other health care providers that join together to provide health care services for people who pay a fee to the group. ABBRV. *HMO*.

health plan. N. A health insurance plan; a benefits plan that provides medical care through a predetermined network of doctors, clinics, and hospitals. See also *insurance*.

health savings account. N. A savings account available to people who participate in a high deductible health plan that allows them to save pretax earnings to pay for qualified medical expenses and carry over their savings from year to year. ABBRV. *HSA*.

hearing. N. A legal proceeding, usually less formal than a trial, in which the parties to a case are given an opportunity to present evidence and testimony to a judge or other official who determines the facts and makes a decision based on the evidence presented.

hearing, final. N. The last stage in a lawsuit, in which the case is determined on its merits.

hearing, preliminary. N. An initial hearing in a criminal case in which a magistrate or judge decides whether there is sufficient evidence to justify detaining a person accused of a crime.

hearing de novo. N. A hearing in which a matter that has already gone through trial is presented again as if for the first time, starting over from the beginning.

hearsay. N. A report made by a witness of something that another person said or communicated nonverbally, usually not admissible as evidence.

heat of passion. N. The mental and emotional state caused by sudden anger, hatred, terror, or extreme excitement that provokes someone to commit a crime.

hedge. V. To protect an investment by making a compensatory or counterbalancing transaction. N. *hedging*.

hedge fund. N. A mutual fund or partnership of investors that uses hedging techniques such as arbitrage, futures contracts, and selling short in an attempt to maximize profits.

heir. N. A person legally entitled to inherit an estate if its owner dies without a will.

heir, collateral. N. An heir who is not directly descended from a decedent but instead related collaterally, such as a cousin, niece, or nephew.

heir, lineal. N. An heir descended directly from the decedent, such as a child or grandchild.

heir apparent. N. A person who has a legal right to inherit an estate if he or she outlives its owner, and whose right to the property cannot be defeated.

heiress. N. A female heir.

heirloom. N. A valuable object that is passed down through generations of a family.

heir of the body. N. An heir who is the natural child or direct lineal descendant of the decedent.

heir presumptive. N. A person who would inherit a property if the owner were to die immediately, but whose right could be defeated if a nearer heir is born first.

heirs and assigns. N. A phrase used in conveying an estate in fee simple, used to define and limit the class of people who can inherit the estate.

hereditament. N. A thing that can be inherited.

hereditary. ADJ. Transmittable through or based on inheritance.

hereditary succession. N. Inheritance; the passing of estates through the laws of descent and distribution.

heretofore. ADV. Before the present time.

hereunder. ADV. Within or further on in the document.

hidden. ADJ. Concealed from view.

hidden asset. N. An asset recorded on a company's books at much less than its market value.

hidden defect. N. A defect in an object or property that is not immediately apparent on inspection and for which a buyer has the right to revoke an acceptance to purchase.

hidden tax. N. A tax built into the price of an item, usually incurred at some point in manufacturing or distribution.

high deductible health plan. N. A health insurance plan that attempts to reduce costs by imposing a high deductible on medical expenses, on the reasoning that if consumers must pay for most medical care themselves they will avoid unnecessary care and shop for the lowest prices when they do seek treatment. ABBRV. *hdhp*. See also *health savings account*.

hijack. V. To commandeer a vehicle such as an airplane, bus, or ship, while in transit, in order to take it to a different destination, to steal its cargo, or to take hostages. N. *hijacking*.

HIPAA. ABBRV. Health Insurance Portability and Accountability Act.

hire. V. To give someone a job; to take someone on as an employee. N. A person who has been given a job.

hit and run. ADJ. Describes an automobile accident in which the driver of one of the vehicles involved immediately leaves the scene without identifying himself or herself or providing statutorily required information to the police or other drivers and passengers.

HMO. ABBRV. Health maintenance organization.

hoard. V. To acquire and keep goods or money beyond what is needed, often done in times of scarcity. N. *hoarding*.

hobby. N. An activity engaged in for pleasure during leisure time, not done for profit.

hobby loss. N. A loss incurred from a hobby, usually not deductible.

holder. N. A person with legal possession of a document of title, promissory note, check, or other instrument, and who is entitled to receive payment on it.

holder in due course. N. A bona fide purchaser who acquires an instrument in good faith, for value, and without notice of any claim against the instrument.

hold harmless. V. To assume the liability for a situation, thereby absolving another party of any responsibility for it. See also *indemnify, save harmless*.

holding. N. (1) A court's ruling on an issue presented at trial; a legal principle produced by a court in deciding a case. (2) Property or stocks owned by someone.

holding company. N. A company that exists solely to own the stock of or manage the affairs of another company.

holding period. N. The period of time an asset must be held before its sale or exchange will result in a capital gain or loss.

holdup suit. N. A lawsuit without a legal basis instituted to delay or obstruct some occurrence.

holograph. N. A will written by hand by a testator, signed by the testator, and not witnessed; also called a holographic will.

home equity loan. N. A loan in which a lender gives money to a borrower in exchange for a lien on the borrower's house, using the borrower's equity in his or her house as collateral.

Homeland Security. N. The U.S. government's collective efforts to keep the territory of the United States free from hazards, including natural disasters such as hurricanes and man-made disasters such as terrorist attacks.

home port. N. The port where a ship or vessel is registered, or the port nearest to the residence of its owner or manager.

home port doctrine. N. A doctrine in maritime law holding that a vessel engaged in foreign and interstate commerce is subject to property tax only at its home port.

home rule. N. A means of apportioning power between state and local governments that allows local entities a certain degree of independent self-government, allowing them to pass laws without first getting permission from the state.

homestead. N. The residence of a family, including house, land, and outbuildings.

homestead, probate. N. A home taken from a probate estate by the court for the use of the surviving spouse and children of the deceased in order to guarantee them a place to live.

homestead exemption. N. A doctrine that allows a homeowner to designate his or her home as a homestead and thereby exempt it from claims by creditors.

homicide. N. The killing of one human being by another.

homicide, excusable. N. The killing of a person by accident or in self-defense.

homicide, justifiable. N. The intentional killing of a person without evil intent in circumstances that make the killing necessary, such as self-defense or the execution of a criminal sentenced to death.

homicide, negligent. N. The killing of a person through the killer's negligence.

homicide, vehicular. N. The killing of a person through the negligent or reckless operation of a motor vehicle such as an automobile, airplane, or boat.

honor. V. To accept a check, note, credit card, or other form of payment. V. A title of courtesy given to a judge, as in the phrase "Your Honor" or the adjective "Honorable."

honorable discharge. N. A declaration by the government that a soldier is leaving military service with a good record.

honorarium. N. A payment of money or a valuable item rendered to a professional in exchange for a service for which a fee is traditionally or legally not paid; a gift given instead of pay as consideration for services.

honorary. ADJ. Conferred as an honor or reward without the usual requirements or responsibilities.

hornbook. N. A short treatise that summarizes the fundamental principles of a branch of law; a primer.

hornbook law. N. General principles of law that are widely known and not questioned; see also *black letter law*.

hostage. N. A person held by a criminal or an enemy who threatens to kill or harm the hostage if demands are not met or promises are broken. See also *kidnap*.

hostile. ADJ. Antagonistic; acting like an enemy.

hostile possession. N. Occupying and claiming ownership of a property without permission of the owner.

hostile witness. N. A witness who is so obviously antagonistic to the party who has called him or her that the party is allowed to cross-examine him or her as if he or she had been called by the opposing party.

house. N. (1) A building or structure used as a dwelling. (2) A legislative body. V. To provide a home for someone.

House of Commons. N. The lower house of the British Parliament, consisting of representatives from all the common people of the realm.

House of Lords. N. The upper house of the British Parliament, consisting of representatives from the nobility.

house of prostitution. N. A building in which prostitutes work.

House of Representatives. N. The larger of the two legislative bodies that make up Congress, consisting of elected representatives from each state whose number is set by population; often called the House.

house of worship. N. A church or other building used for religious services.

HSA. ABBRV. Health savings account.

humanitarian. ADJ. Working to promote the welfare and preserve the dignity of human beings.

human resources. N. The management of personnel and issues surrounding employees, such as hiring, firing, pay, discipline, and benefits.

human rights. N. The basic rights to which all humans are generally considered to be entitled, which can include life, liberty, freedom of speech, freedom of religion, due process, equal rights, and dignity.

hung jury. N. A jury that cannot agree on a verdict.

husband-wife privilege. N. Privilege covering spouses, who are not required to reveal confidential communications between them while married.

hypnosis. N. A state of consciousness in which the subject loses the power to control his or her actions and becomes very sensitive to suggestion. V. *hypnotize*.

hypnotist. N. A person who hypnotizes others.

hypothecate. V. To pledge money or property for a particular purpose, often as security for a debt.

hypothesis. N. A supposition; a proposed explanation for an occurrence based on available evidence, serving as the beginning of further exploration of the question. See also *theory*.

hypothetical. ADJ. Based on assumptions but not necessarily true.

hypothetical question. N. A question in which the questioner asks someone to offer an opinion based on the assumption that certain conditions are true.

ibid. ABBRV. *(Latin)* Ibidem.

ibidem. *(Latin)* In the same place; used to cite a source that has already been cited in full in the preceding footnote. ABBRV. *ibid.*

ICANN. ABBRV. Internet Corporation for Assigned Names and Numbers.

ICC. ABBRV. Interstate Commerce Commission.

id. ABBRV. *(Latin)* Idem.

idem. *(Latin)* The same; used when citing a text that is part of the source that has just been cited in the immediately preceding reference. ABBRV. *id.*

ignorance. N. The state of being unaware of something; lack of knowledge. ADJ. *ignorant*.

illegal. ADJ. Forbidden by law or not according to law; unlawful.

illegal immigrant. N. A foreign national present in a country without legal permission to be there.

illegally obtained evidence. N. Evidence acquired by violating a person's constitutional protection against illegal searches and seizures; evidence obtained without a warrant or probable cause.

illegitimate. ADJ. (1) Not authorized by law; illegal. (2) Born to parents not married to one another at the time of conception.

illicit. ADJ. Illegal; against rules or custom.

illusory. ADJ. Not real; deceptive; having a false appearance.

illusory promise. N. A promise with such vague terms that it actually promises nothing because the person making it is allowed to choose whether or not to do the promised act and does not in fact agree to do anything.

immaterial. ADJ. Irrelevant; not essential; of no material importance. See also *material*.

immaterial evidence. N. Evidence that has no real bearing on the issue in question.

immigrant. N. A person who moves to a foreign country to live there.

immigrate. V. To move to a foreign country with the intention of living there permanently. N. ***immigration***.

Immigration and Naturalization Services. N. The federal agency that registers immigrants and oversees the process of making them into citizens. See also *naturalize*. ABBRV. *INS*.

immoral. ADJ. Against accepted moral standards; dissolute. N. ***immorality***.

immoral conduct. N. Conduct that is willful, flagrant, or shameless, and in disregard of the moral opinions of respectable members of the community.

immunity. N. Exemption or protection from something such as prosecution, duty, or penalty.

immunity, official. N. Personal immunity given to public officials, protecting them from liability for injury caused by acts they have done as part of their official duty. See also *sovereign immunity*.

impanel. V. To list or enroll the jurors who have been selected for a trial.

impartial. ADJ. Fair, unbiased; not favoring one side over another.

impeach. V. To accuse a public official of misconduct; to question the validity of something, such as a judgment, or the integrity of a witness.

impeachment. N. A criminal procedure in which a public official is charged with misconduct.

impertinent. ADJ. Not pertinent; irrelevant. N. *impertinence*.

implication. N. A conclusion that can be drawn from information but that is not expressly stated; a likely consequence.

implied. ADJ. Strongly suggested by circumstances and evidence but not directly stated; see also *express*.

implied authority. N. Power given to an agent by a principal that is not expressly stated but that can be assumed as a necessary part of the agent's job.

implied powers. N. Powers not expressly stated or enumerated but that can be implied as necessary to do a particular job, sometimes found by the Supreme Court in its interpretation of the Constitution.

imply. V. To suggest strongly that something is true without stating it directly. See also *infer*.

import. V. To bring goods into a country for sale. N. Goods brought from another country for sale. See also *export*.

importation. N. The act of importing goods.

importer. N. A person who imports goods. See also *customs*.

impossibility. N. A situation that makes it impossible to do something; circumstances that make it impossible to perform a contract, such as the destruction of something necessary to the performance or the death of one of the parties, which relieves a party of his or her duty to perform under the contract. ADJ. ***impossible***. See also *impracticable*.

impossibility, legal. N. A condition arising when a law makes it impossible for a person to do a particular act; e.g., a minor cannot make a valid will, so any will made by a minor is invalid because it is a legal impossibility.

imposter. N. Someone who pretends to be someone else with the intention of deceiving others, usually to gain some benefit.

impound. V. To seize and take legal custody of something, such as a vehicle; to capture animals and shut them in an enclosure.

impracticable. ADJ. So inconvenient or difficult as to be essentially impossible. N. ***impracticability***.

imprimatur. N. *(Latin)* Let it be printed; a license to print and publish a book.

imprison. V. To put in prison; to keep someone restricted to a place that essentially functions as a prison; to confine; to deprive of liberty.

imprisonment. N. See *incarcerate*.

improve. V. To make something better.

improvement. N. A change that makes something better; an addition or change to buildings or land that goes beyond mere repairs and enhances its value, utility, or attractiveness.

impute. V. To attribute; to assign someone responsibility for the act of another person over whom the first person exercises control.

imputed knowledge. N. Knowledge that is attributed to a person because he or she had a duty to know it and it was available.

in absentia. ADV. *(Latin)* In absence; not physically present at an event.

inadmissible. ADJ. Not able to be admitted under the rules of evidence.

inalienable. ADJ. Not able to be taken away or given up without consent of the possessor.

inalienable interest. N. A property interest that cannot be sold or transferred.

inalienable rights. N. Rights such as freedom of speech, equal protection of the laws, and due process that cannot be taken away from or given up by anyone without his or her consent.

in camera. ADV. *(Latin)* In chambers; done in a judge's private chambers.

incapacity. N. Inability to do or understand something; lack of physical, mental, or legal ability to do a particular task.

incarcerate. V. To put in jail or prison; to imprison. N. *incarceration*.

incendiary. ADJ. Able to start a fire. N. A person or device that starts fires.

incest. N. Sexual contact between people who are so closely related to one another by blood that they are prohibited by law from marrying.

in chief. ADJ. Main; primary; principal.

in chief, case. N. The initial case presented at trial by the party with the burden of proof, i.e., the party bringing the lawsuit, including testimony and evidence, after which the opposing party has an opportunity to rebut.

inchoate. ADJ. Not yet fully developed; incomplete. See also *choate*.

inchoate crime. N. A crime that could constitute the initial stages of another crime; e.g., assault could be an inchoate form of battery.

inchoate interest. N. A potential future interest in property.

incident. N. (1) An event. (2) Something that is inseparably connected with something else. ADJ. Attached to something in a subordinate way; dependent on something.

incidental. ADJ. Accompanying something else, usually in a subordinate way; occurring in connection with something else by chance or as a consequence.

incidental beneficiary. N. A person who is indirectly benefited by a contract formed between other people.

incidental powers. N. Powers that are a necessary accompaniment to powers expressly granted.

incident of ownership. N. Partial or complete ownership or control of a life insurance policy.

inclosure. N. A piece of land surrounded by a fence, wall, or other barrier; also called an enclosure.

income. N. Money received as compensation for work, through investments, or as profits from a business.

income, accrued. N. Income earned but not yet received.

income, adjusted gross. N. Gross income minus deductions.

income, deferred. N. Income received before it is actually earned.

income, earned. N. Income brought in through work or business, as opposed to income from investments.

income, gross. N. Total income from all sources.

income, imputed. N. Value acquired by a taxpayer through use of his or her own property, or by performing work services for himself or herself, and not included in gross income.

income, net. N. A business's income minus operating expenses and taxes.

income, unearned. N. Income received from investments.

income in respect of a decedent. N. Income earned by a taxpayer but received by his or her heirs or personal representatives after his or her death.

income statement. N. A statement of financial gains and losses over a twelve-month period; also called earnings report, operating statement, profit and loss statement.

income tax. N. Tax levied on a person's income by the federal government and some state governments.

incompetency. N. The state of being incompetent.

incompetent. ADJ. Lacking the skills or capability necessary to do something; not legally qualified to perform a particular duty. N. A person who lacks the ability or qualification to do something. N. *incompetence*.

inconsistent. ADJ. (1) Self-contradictory; not staying the same; adopting two or more mutually exclusive viewpoints simultaneously. (2) Not in keeping with one's own beliefs. See also *prior inconsistent statement*.

incorporate. V. (1) To combine something into something else as part of one whole. (2) To create a corporation. N. *incorporation*.

incorporeal. ADJ. Having no physical or material existence; intangible.

incorporeal property. N. Property that exists as a legal right without physical substance, such as a copyright.

incorrigible. ADJ. Unable to be reformed or corrected. N. A person who refuses to be reformed; an unmanageable person, especially a juvenile.

increment. N. An increase, usually part of a scale of regular increases.

incriminate. V. To suggest or charge that someone is guilty of a crime. N. *incrimination*. ADJ. *incriminating*.

incriminating evidence. N. Evidence that helps establish the guilt of an accused person. See also *self-incrimination*.

inculpate. V. Accuse; blame.

inculpatory. ADJ. Helping to establish guilt or incriminate a criminal defendant.

incumbent. N. A person who currently holds a particular office. ADJ. Necessary; required as part of duty or responsibility.

indecent. ADJ. Offensive, vulgar, against modesty or proper behavior, obscene or lewd. N. *indecency*.

indecent exposure. N. Lewdly exposing private parts of the body in a public place. See also *obscene*.

indefeasible. ADJ. Not able to be defeated, annulled, or revoked; usually describes an estate or a right that cannot be revoked.

indefinite. ADJ. Vague; not clearly expressed or defined; temporary.

indefinite failure of issue. N. A dead person's lack of living children or descendants that can occur at any time after the decedent's death, however far in the future; see also *failure of issue*.

indemnify. V. To pay or reimburse someone for a loss or injury; to take on legal responsibility for someone else's actions; to insure.

indemnity. N. Money given as compensation or reimbursement for a loss or injury; security against legal responsibility for one's own actions; the benefit provided by an insurance policy.

indemnity against liability. N. A promise to take on another person's liability or compensate him or her if and when that liability arises.

indemnity against loss. N. Compensation given to a person when he or she suffers a particular loss. See also *insure, subrogation*.

indenture. N. (1) A formal agreement conveying real estate from one party to another and binding both parties with obligations. (2) An agreement issuing corporate bonds and debentures, often between a corporation and an indenture trustee, who holds title to the trust property and carries out the terms of the agreement. (3) Historically, a legal contract made into several copies with the edges indented to mark them as authentic. (4) Historically, an agreement in which a person in the British colonies agreed to pay the transportation costs for someone who wanted to immigrate in exchange for the recipient's labor for a specified number of years; the recipient was called an indentured servant.

independent contractor. N. A person who does a job for another person independently, using his or her own methods and is not under the control of the employer in regard to how the work is accomplished.

independent counsel. N. A person or group of people appointed to investigate accusations of criminal conduct by a high-level public official.

index. N. (1) An alphabetical list of entries or topics in a book or series, including the pages on which they appear. (2) A statistical method of tracking fluctuations in the value of stocks, mortgages, inflation, the economy, etc., over time.

index fund. N. A mutual fund that chooses its stocks according to a stock market index number.

indexing. N. Tying wages, mortgages, or other financial issues to inflation in order to keep values relatively constant.

Indian. N. For the purposes of many U.S. laws and treaties, an indigenous American; a Native American or American Indian.

Indian Affairs, Bureau of. N. A federal agency in the Interior Department that oversees dealings between American Indians and the federal government.

Indian Claims Commission. N. A commission that hears claims brought against the federal government by Indian tribes or other groups of American Indians.

Indian reservation. N. Public land set aside for the use of American Indians, supervised by the federal government.

Indian title. N. A right granted to American Indian tribes by the federal government to use and occupy certain territories that they have occupied for a long time, though without any right of ownership.

Indian tribe. N. A distinct group of American Indians of the same or similar race, occupying a specific territory, and under the same leadership.

indicia. N. Indications, signs; circumstances indicating that something is probably true; synonymous with *circumstantial evidence*.

indicia of title. N. A document showing title to a piece of property.

indict. V. To formally charge someone with a crime.

indictable offense. N. A crime that can be prosecuted by indictment, usually a serious crime.

indictee. N. A person who has been indicted.

indictment. N. A formal, written accusation presented by a grand jury to the court charging someone with a specified crime.

indigenous. ADJ. Native, indigenous people. N. An ethnic group that was present in a nation before the current population was created by colonization from a foreign nation, which generally maintains a culture, language, and social organization distinct from that of the current surrounding population.

indigent. ADJ. Poor; poverty-stricken; destitute. N. A poor or needy person.

indigent defendant. N. A criminal defendant who lacks the financial resources to pay for a lawyer to defend him- or herself.

indignity. N. In divorce law, abusive or cruel treatment directed at the mind and emotions rather than the body, such as vulgarity, harsh criticism, ridicule, neglect, or abusive language.

indirect. ADJ. Circuitous or roundabout; not going straight from one point to another; not directly caused by something.

indirect evidence. N. Evidence that makes a hypothesis appear plausible but does not actually prove it. See also *circumstantial evidence, direct evidence*.

indispensable. ADJ. Necessary; essential.

indispensable evidence. N. Evidence that is absolutely necessary to prove a particular fact.

indispensable party. N. A party who has such an important interest in a lawsuit that the judgment cannot be issued without his or her presence; see also *joinder*.

individual retirement account. N. A tax-advantaged personal retirement account that an individual acquires and funds himself or herself, not through an employer. ABBRV. *IRA*.

indorse. V. To endorse; to sign the back of a check or negotiable instrument in order to transfer its payment to someone else. N. *indorsement*.

indorsee. N. The person to whom a check or instrument is transferred by indorsement.

indorsement, accommodation. N. An indorsement made without consideration for the benefit of the person holding the instrument, allowing that person to receive credit or a loan on the basis of the indorsement.

indorsement, blank. N. An indorsement that does not name a recipient, allowing any bearer to place his or her own name on the instrument and collect the funds it transfers.

indorsement, restrictive. N. Words placed on an instrument that limit the circumstances in which it can be paid out, e.g., "for deposit only."

indorsement, special. N. An indorsement that specifies the person to whom the instrument is payable.

indorser. N. The person who signs the check or instrument to transfer it to another.

induce. V. To cause; to bring about; to influence or persuade.

inducement. N. The benefit that persuades a party to enter a contract; the motive that causes someone to commit a crime.

industrial relations. N. Relations between workers and their employer on issues of compensation, safety, hiring, etc.

industry. N. Commercial activity conducted for profit; economic activity that uses a great deal of labor, capital, and raw materials for the manufacture of goods. ADJ. *industrial*.

inebriate. V. To make intoxicated or drunk.

inebriation. N. A person under the influence of too much alcohol.

ineligible. ADJ. Not legally allowed to hold a position or conduct an activity; disqualified. N. *ineligibility*.

in extremis. ADV. *(Latin)* At the outermost limits; at the point of death; in extreme difficulty.

infamous. ADJ. Well-known for some misdeed or bad reputation; notorious; wicked. N. *infamy*.

infamous crime. N. Historically, a crime that renders its perpetrator infamous; under the modern view, a crime punishable by death or imprisonment in a state penal institution for more than one year.

infamous punishment. N. Punishment by imprisonment or by hard labor.

infancy. N. Childhood; minority; the period before which a person reaches legal majority.

infant. N. A person below the age of legal majority, or before marriage. See also *emancipate*.

infanticide. N. Killing a baby soon after birth.

infer. V. To deduce or conclude through a process of reasoning based on facts and logic. N. *inference*. See also *imply*.

inferior court. N. A court whose decisions are subject to review by an appellate court; see also *trial court*.

infirm. ADJ. Weak; sickly.

infirmity. N. Weakness or disability, especially caused by age or disease; in insurance, a disease or illness that substantially impairs a person's health, and if revealed will discourage an insurer from issuing that person a life or health insurance policy.

informal. ADJ. Unofficial; not drafted or executed in the proper legal form. N. *informality*.

informal contract. N. A contract that is valid without being executed formally, such as an oral contract.

in forma pauperis. ADV. *(Latin)* In the form of a pauper; the right given an indigent person to sue without having to pay court fees or costs.

informal proceeding. N. (1) A trial or hearing less formal than a regular trial, such as a proceeding in a small claims court. (2) In probate court, a proceeding that admits a will to probate without first providing notice to all interested parties.

information. N. A written document filed with the court accusing someone of a crime that serves essentially the same function as an indictment but without a grand jury, informing the accused of the charge against him or her.

information and belief. N. A legal term used to describe testimony that is not based on a witness's firsthand knowledge but that the witness nevertheless sincerely believes to be true, and that is based on a reasonable, good faith effort to know the truth.

information technology. N. The field of study and work that concerns itself with computers, networks, and the electronic transmission of information. ABBRV. *IT*.

informed consent. N. Consent given after learning and understanding all relevant facts needed to make an intelligent decision, required in situations where someone is giving up rights, as when being arrested, or in potentially risky situations, such as surgery.

informer. N. A person who confidentially gives information about a crime to police officers; also called an informant.

informer's privilege. N. The government's right to keep the identity of an informer secret from the defendant about whom the informer has provided information.

infra. ADV. *(Latin)* Below; used to refer to information further on in a document. See also *supra*.

infraction. N. Violation of a law, agreement, or duty.

infringe. V. To encroach or trespass on something; to violate the terms of a contract, right, or law; to violate a copyright, patent, or trademark by using it without permission or payment to the owner. N. *infringement*.

ingress. N. Entrance; the act of entering or the right of entrance; opposite of egress.

inhabit. V. To live in a place; to dwell, to reside.

inhabitant. N. Someone who lives in a place.

inherent. ADJ. Existing as a permanent, essential, and intrinsic part of something.

inherent defect. N. A defect built into an object that exists regardless of how it is used.

inherent powers. N. Powers and authority that are an intrinsic part of an office or position and that exist without being expressly granted.

inherent right. N. A right that a person has simply by virtue of being a person and that is not granted from some outside source.

inherit. V. To receive property or money as an heir after the owner's death; technically refers to receiving property by the rules of descent and distribution when the owner dies without a will, but has also come to mean receiving property through a will. N. ***inheritance**.*

inheritance tax. N. Tax imposed on someone who receives property and money through inheritance.

inhuman. ADJ. Cruel, brutal, lacking normal human compassion.

inhuman treatment. N. Treatment that is so physically or mentally cruel or brutal as to endanger the health or life of its victim.

initial public offering. N. The first set of shares a new company sells on a public stock exchange, usually in an effort to raise money from investors in order to enlarge the company. ABBRV. *IPO*.

initiative. N. A process in which citizens file a petition proposing a new piece of legislation and submit it to a vote by the legislature or the electorate. See also *referendum*.

injunction. N. A court order prohibiting someone from doing a specified act in order to prevent future injury. ADJ. ***injunctive**.*

injunction, mandatory. N. An injunction that requires the defendant to do a particular act instead of prohibiting an act. See also *restraining order*.

injunction, permanent. N. An injunction actively sought by a party to a trial and issued at its conclusion.

injunction, temporary. N. An injunction issued as a preliminary preventive measure, pending trial.

injure. V. To harm or damage a person or property.

injury. N. Harm or damage; damage that comes from the violation of a legal right.

injury, irreparable. N. An injury for which damages cannot be assessed accurately, usually addressed by injunction.

injury, personal. N. An injury done to someone's body or personal rights, as opposed to reputation or property.

injustice. N. An absence of fairness; an unfair occurrence; a mistake made by a court that results in unfair and unjust treatment.

in kind. ADJ. Of the same kind, category, or type; used to describe the act of exchanging one thing for another thing of the same or similar type. ADV. ***in kind***.

in loco parentis. ADJ. *(Latin)* In the place of a parent; describes a situation in which someone (e.g., a teacher or camp counselor) supervising a minor temporarily assumes the legal obligations normally held by a parent or guardian. ADV. ***in loco parentis***.

inmate. N. A person confined to a prison, hospital, or other institution.

innocent. ADJ. Not guilty; in good faith; without intention of committing a wrong or knowledge that a wrong is being committed. N. ***innocence***.

innovate. V. To create something new. N. ***innovation***.

innuendo. N. A suggestive remark or hint; in a libel action, the part of the pleading in which the plaintiff explains the meaning of the allegedly libelous words.

in perpetuity. ADJ. Forever; perpetual. ADV. ***in perpetuity***.

in person. ADJ. Describes a situation in which a person actually attends a trial, hearing, or other event, and speaks for himself or herself, instead of allowing an attorney or other representative to appear and speak for him or her. ADV. *in person*.

in personam. ADJ. *(Latin)* Against a person; describes actions concerning the personal rights and liability of a person or jurisdiction over a particular person, as opposed to jurisdiction over property. See also *in rem*. ADV. *in personam*.

in personam jurisdiction. N. The jurisdiction a court holds over an individual defendant, as opposed to jurisdiction over his or her property.

inquest. N. A judicial investigation into the facts surrounding a death, conducted by a coroner or medical examiner; a court's inquiry into the facts surrounding an incident, often made by a jury; sometimes called an inquisition.

in re. PREP. *(Latin)* In the matter of; concerning; in regard to; used to entitle judicial proceedings that do not involve adversaries but instead concern themselves with disposing of some situation, such as the settling of an estate.

in rem. ADJ. *(Latin)* Against a thing; describes actions or proceedings concerning property rather than people, used in cases to determine title to or interests in property within the court's territorial jurisdiction and that are brought against the property itself, not against the people who own it. ADV. *in rem*.

in rem, quasi. ADJ. Describes proceedings brought against a defendant personally but that concern property, usually claims for money damages such as foreclosures or attachments. ADV. *quasi in rem*.

INS. ABBRV. Immigration and Naturalization Services.

insanity. N. Madness or mental illness; the condition of being mentally ill to the point that one's perceptions and behavior are seriously impaired and one is not responsible for one's actions. ADJ. *insane*.

insanity defense. N. A defense to criminal prosecution based on the claim that the defendant cannot be guilty because he or she lacked the ability to behave correctly and the capacity to understand that his or her act was criminal.

insider. N. In securities and corporations, someone who has access to information about a business that is not available to the general public, such as corporate directors, officers, and major stockholders; insiders are not allowed to buy and sell stocks in such a way as to take advantage of their privileged position and use it for personal gain.

insider information. N. Information about a corporation that is available only to insiders and not revealed to the general public.

insider trading. N. The illegal buying and selling of stock based on information available only to insiders.

insolvent. ADJ. Financially unable to pay debts. N. *insolvency*.

inspect. V. To examine closely, looking for defects and quality, often done to make sure the object meets some official standard; to scrutinize. N. *inspection*.

inspection of documents. N. A process done during discovery in which a party examines and copies documents held by the opposing party that are relevant to the lawsuit.

inspector. N. (1) An official charged with issuing permits and inspecting objects or places, such as buildings or restaurants, to ensure that they adhere to legal standards. (2) In some jurisdictions, a police officer.

Inspector General. N. A high-ranking administrative official in charge of monitoring operations and finding and eradicating fraud and waste.

installment. N. A sum of money that serves as partial payment of a debt, usually as part of a payment plan that divides payment up into several portions spread out over a period of time; partial satisfaction of an obligation.

installment contract. N. A contract that divides its obligation, such as delivery of goods or payment, into portions that are performed periodically over a specified period of time.

installment sale. N. A contract in which a consumer purchases an item and receives it at once but pays for it over a period of time in installments.

instant. ADJ. Current, present.

instant case. N. The case currently under consideration.

institute. V. To begin, establish, or inaugurate; to commence legal proceedings. N. (1) An organization with a particular purpose, often an authority in a particular field. (2) A commentary on legal principles.

institution. N. (1) The act of starting or establishing something; the act of beginning a legal action. (2) An organization with a professional, charitable, educational, or similar purpose. (3) An organization or place that houses people with special needs, such as mental patients or prisoners.

instruct. V. To teach; to provide information about something; to direct or command.

instructions. N. Directions given by a judge to a jury, telling them how to apply the law to the facts of the case; see also *charge*.

instrument. N. A formal written document; a writing that formally expresses some legal agreement, such as a contract, lease, will, deed, or bond. See also *negotiable instrument*.

insufficient. ADJ. Inadequate; not meeting needs. N. *insufficiency*.

insufficient evidence. N. The condition of not having enough evidence to support a claim at trial, determined by the court and resulting in a directed verdict for the defendant.

insufficient funds. N. The condition of having less money in a bank account than has been drawn on that account.

insular. ADJ. On an island; having to do with islands; isolated; provincial.

insurable. ADJ. Able to be insured.

insurable interest. N. A connection or relationship with a person or thing that is substantial enough to bring a real benefit or advantage to the person who wants to insure it, generally because the person or thing provides him or her with money or some other valuable thing, thus justifying the need or desire for insurance coverage.

insurance. N. A contract in which one party, the insurer, agrees to compensate the other party, the insured, for specified losses or damage to property or people in exchange for consideration, usually the payment of a premium.

insurance, automobile. N. Insurance that covers the owner or drivers of a vehicle from loss or damage to the vehicle and liability for personal injury caused by operation of the vehicle.

insurance, health. N. Insurance that covers illness, injury, and medical care for the insured.

insurance, life. N. A contract in which the insurer agrees to pay a specified sum to a named beneficiary when the insured dies.

insurance adjuster. N. A person who investigates and settles insurance claims.

insurance agent. N. A person who represents an insurance company, selling policies on its behalf.

insurance commissioner. N. A public official who supervises the insurance business within a state.

insurance defense. N. Legal work done by a law firm that specializes in defending claims brought against or covered by an insurance company, usually with a special fee arrangement giving the insurance company discounted rates for high volume work.

insurance policy. N. A contract of insurance.

insure. V. To promise to compensate someone for the loss of or damage to someone or something in exchange for payments of money; to assume the risk of loss or damage; to underwrite; see also *indemnify*.

insured. N. A person covered by an insurance policy.

insurer. N. A company or individual that insures people or things; an underwriter.

insurgent. N. A person who rises up against the government or authorities.

insurrection. N. A violent uprising against the government or authority; a rebellion by citizens against the government.

intangible. ADJ. Having no physical presence; difficult to define or grasp. See also *tangible*.

intangible asset. N. Property that has no physical substance but that nevertheless exists as a right, such as a patent, copyright, or goodwill; also called intangibles.

integrate. V. (1) To combine two or more things into one whole. (2) To desegregate.

integrated contract. N. A written contract that contains the entire and final agreement of the parties, and to which oral evidence cannot be admitted; also called an integration.

intent. N. Plan, resolve, or intention; desire to bring about a particular result; the state of mind of a person who wants to do a certain act and accomplish a particular result. V. *intend*. See also *motive*.

intent, general. N. In criminal cases, an intention to break a law but not necessarily to cause the specific result that occurred.

intent, legislative. N. A legislature's intended purpose in enacting a piece of legislation.

intent, specific. N. In criminal cases, an intention to commit a particular crime.

intention. N. A plan, desire, or aim; something that is intended.

intentional. ADJ. Deliberate; done consciously and purposely with an awareness of probable consequences; not accidental.

intentional infliction of emotional distress. N. A deliberate act done expressly to inflict emotional distress on its victim.

intentional tort. N. A tort committed deliberately with an express desire to harm.

inter alia. ADV. *(Latin)* Among other things; used to avoid listing all the details of a statute or other document while noting that they exist.

intercept. V. To catch or obstruct something on its way to a destination; to use electronic or other devices to obtain the contents of a communication done through some telecommunications device, such as a wiretap. N. *interception*.

interest. N. (1) A right, claim, or title to something. (2) A share or stake in some undertaking; a personal stake in a matter. (3) Money paid at a specified rate on a regular basis for the use of a loan or to delay the date of repayment of a loan.

interest, absolute. N. An interest in property that cannot be taken from its owner without his or her consent, no matter what happens.

interest, compound. N. Interest paid on top of interest already accrued, in addition to interest paid on principal.

interest, simple. N. Interest paid only on the principal of a loan.

interest, vested. N. A present interest in property that the owner is allowed to transfer in the present but might not be allowed to actually possess or enjoy until some time in the future.

interested party. N. A person with a legally recognized private interest in some matter.

interest rate. N. The percentage used to calculate interest due on a loan.

interim. N. In the meantime; during intervening time; temporary.

interim financing. N. A short-term loan held until long-term or permanent financing can be arranged for an enterprise; also called a bridge loan.

interim order. N. A temporary order issued to handle a matter until a specified event happens or until a final order is issued. See also *interlocutory*.

interlocking directors. N. People who serve on the boards of directors of two or more corporations simultaneously, resulting in a situation called an interlocking directorate, which can be used to restrict competition and is often illegal under antitrust law.

interlocutory. ADJ. Temporary; provisional; issued as a temporary stopgap measure while a lawsuit proceeds.

interlocutory order. N. An order issued by the court while a trial is still in process, determining an intermediate issue before coming to a final decision for the entire case.

internal network. N. A computer network restricted to a given workplace or facility, not accessible by the general public.

Internal Revenue Code. N. A federal statute in Title 26 of the U.S. Code setting forth laws on federal taxes, including income tax, estate tax, gift tax, excise tax, etc. ABBRV. *IRC*.

Internal Revenue Service. N. The federal agency that administers federal tax laws, assesses and collects taxes, audits taxpayers, and handles appeals by taxpayers who dispute their tax liability. ABBRV. *IRS*.

international agreement. N. An agreement between two or more nations that creates legal rights or obligations among them; a treaty, convention, or other such agreement between nations.

International Court of Justice. N. The United Nations' court, seated at The Hague, Netherlands, that provides advice on questions of law and the writing of treaties and settles legal disputes between nations; its decisions are enforceable by the U.N. Security Council.

international law. N. The body of law that governs relations between different countries, composed of custom and practice, rules and statutes, international treaties, and other sources.

international trade. N. Trade in goods or services across national borders.

Internet. N. A global network of computers, networks, and websites that allows the exchange of information through domain names, IP addresses, email, file sharing, and other mechanisms. See also *World Wide Web*.

Internet Corporation for Assigned Names and Numbers. N. A nonprofit corporation in California that manages the assignment of IP addresses and domain names for the U.S. Department of Commerce. ABBRV. *ICANN*.

Internet Protocol. N. (1) The set of rules governing communication among computers across a computer network or the Internet. (2) Intellectual property. ABBRV. *IP*.

Internet service provider. N. A company that sells consumers access to the Internet. ABBRV. *ISP*.

interpleader. N. An action in equity in which two or more parties who each claim property held by a third party submit the claim to a court to settle their rights, brought by the third party who fears that the claimants might pursue him or her to recover the property and does not want to be exposed to liability from several sources; often used by insurers in cases where several parties make conflicting claims on the same matter.

interpolate. V. To insert words into a document, thereby changing its meaning. N. *interpolation*.

interpret. V. To ascertain or explain the meaning of something, such as a statute, contract, or other document; to explain the meaning of the language of a law or other legal document without venturing into legal intentions and consequences. N. *interpretation*. See also *construe, construction*.

interrogate. V. To question; to ask questions of someone such as a suspected criminal, often in a close or formal way. N. *interrogation*.

interrogatories. N. During discovery before trial, written questions about the case presented by one party to the opposing party that must be answered under oath and returned to the questioning party.

interstate. ADJ. Existing in more than one state; carried on in or between two or more states.

interstate commerce. N. Trade, transportation of people or property, and all forms of commerce that involve the territory of more than one state in the United States.

Interstate Commerce Commission. N. A federal commission that regulates surface transportation between states, including trucks, trains, freight forwarders, oil pipelines, and other commercial carriers, in order to facilitate interstate commerce by ensuring that the public will have access to transportation that is reliable and reasonably priced. ABBRV. *ICC*.

interstate compact. N. An agreement between two or more states on a matter of interest to each of them.

intervene. V. To come between two things in such a way as to delay, obstruct, or change the course of events. N. *intervention*.

intervening cause. N. An independent event that occurs between a wrongful act and an injury and changes the expected course of events so that the result is not the one that would have been predicted, thus relieving the person who committed the original wrongful act of liability for the injury. See also *superseding cause*.

intervenor. N. A person who enters a lawsuit by intervention.

intervention. N. A procedure in which someone who is not originally a party to a lawsuit enters it to defend his or her own interest in the matter.

inter vivos. ADJ. *(Latin)* Between the living; describes gifts or transfers done from one living person to another. ADV. *inter vivos*.

intestacy. N. The condition of dying without a valid will.

intestate. ADJ. Without a valid will at the time of death. N. A person who dies without a valid will.

intestate succession. N. Disposition of the property of someone who dies intestate according to the rules of descent and distribution.

in the course of employment. ADJ. Occurring while an employee is at work or otherwise in his or her employer's service.

in toto. ADV. *(Latin)* Totally; completely; as a whole.

intoxicant. N. An intoxicating substance.

intoxicate. V. To make drunk; to cause someone to lose control of his or her physical and mental faculties.

intoxicated. ADJ. Drunk; under the influence of alcohol.

intoxication. N. Drunkenness; a state of losing control of one's physical or mental faculties due to the consumption of alcohol or another intoxicating substance, which renders one incapable of acting like a reasonable person of ordinary prudence would under the same circumstances.

intramural. ADJ. Within the walls; within the confines or boundaries of an organization or institution. See also *extramural*.

Intranet. N. An internal network; a computer network restricted to a secure area and specific users.

intrinsic. ADJ. Inherent; naturally part of something.

intrinsic evidence. N. Evidence produced by questioning a witness at trial.

intrinsic fraud. N. Fraud that occurs during trial through perjury, forged documents, or hiding or misrepresenting evidence, which affects the outcome of the trial.

intrinsic value. N. The inherent value of a thing, which remains constant regardless of place, time, or special features that affect its market value.

inure. V. (1) To take effect; to benefit someone; to vest. (2) To accustom someone to something.

invalid. ADJ. Not valid; not legally adequate; void.

invasion of privacy. N. The wrongful and unwarranted intrusion into or publicizing of someone's private affairs by another person or the government.

invent. V. To design or create some new thing that did not exist before; to create a story, often intending to deceive.

invention. N. The process of creating some new thing, especially a device or machine; something invented.

inventor. N. A person who invents something.

inventory. N. A detailed list of property, such as goods in stock or the complete contents of an estate. See also *first-in, first-out, last-in, first-out*.

invest. V. (1) To spend money on an enterprise in the hope that it will result in a profit; to give time or energy to a cause in the hope that it will generate good results. See also *investment*. (2) To bestow on someone an office or a right. (3) In feudal times, to bestow a grant of land on someone in a ceremony called investiture.

investee. N. A company whose shares are bought by an investor.

investigate. V. To examine the facts surrounding an incident as part of a formal inquiry into the matter. N. *investigation*. ADJ. *investigatory*.

investigatory powers. N. Powers given to governmental agencies to investigate violations of laws and the possible effects of proposed laws.

investment. N. The expenditure of money on an enterprise in the hope of making a profit; assets or securities bought in the hope of earning a profit.

investment banker. N. A financial institution or broker that buys newly issued securities and sells them to investors.

investment company. N. A company primarily in the business of trading securities, using its capital to invest in other companies.

investor. N. Someone who buys shares in a company or otherwise invests money.

invitee. N. A person who enters another's property after being invited.

invoice. N. A list of goods contained in a shipment along with the price due for them; a bill. V. To send an invoice to someone for goods or services provided.

involuntary. ADJ. Done unwillingly, without choice; accidental or unintentional.

involuntary confession. N. A confession made unwillingly and without free choice by someone whose rights against self-incrimination have been violated by threat of violence, coercion, improper promises, etc.

involuntary conversion. N. The unintentional loss of property through theft, destruction, seizure, or condemnation.

involuntary servitude. N. Slavery; forcing someone to work for someone else.

iota. N. The Greek letter "i," i.e., the smallest letter of the Greek alphabet; a miniscule amount, the smallest possible amount of something.

IP. ABBRV. Internet Protocol.

IP address. N. Internet Protocol address; a computer address; the unique set of digits that computers use to identify a specific computer or device in a network.

IPO. ABBRV. Initial public offering.

ipso facto. ADV. *(Latin)* By the very fact itself; through the effect of a fact or act.

IRA. ABBRV. Individual retirement account.

IRC. ABBRV. Internal Revenue Code.

irrelevant. ADJ. Not applicable to the matter at hand; immaterial. N. *irrelevance*, *irrelevancy*.

irreparable. ADJ. Impossible to repair.

irreparable injury. N. An injury for which no adequate legal remedy exists, usually addressed by an injunction.

irrevocable. ADJ. Unable to be withdrawn or revoked.

IRS. ABBRV. Internal Revenue Service.

ISP. ABBRV. Internet service provider.

issue. N. (1) A problem or question; a topic for debate. (2) The act of sending something out formally; promulgation. (3) Children; descendants. (4) The act of offering corporate securities for sale. V. To send out or distribute; to promulgate; to offer something up for sale.

issue of fact. N. A disagreement about facts in a legal controversy, i.e., when one party suggests one version of facts and the other disagrees.

issue of law. N. A question about the law applicable to a case when the facts of the matter are undisputed.

issue preclusion. N. The barring of an issue from further litigation because it has already been settled conclusively at trial.

IT. ABBRV. Information technology.

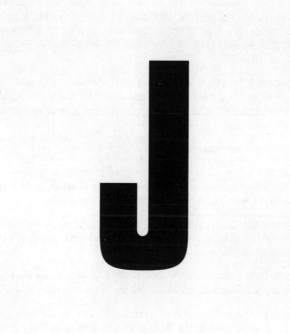

J. ABBRV. "Judge" or "justice"; used as a title for a person holding that office.

JAG. ABBRV. Judge Advocate General.

jail. N. A building used to confine people held in legal custody either awaiting trial for a criminal offense or serving a prison sentence after conviction; usually used for short-term confinement. V. To imprison; to put someone in jail. See also *prison, correctional institution.*

jailhouse lawyer. N. An inmate in a correctional institution who has no formal legal training but has studied the law independently, who helps fellow inmates prepare appeals and provides legal advice to them.

JD. ABBRV. Juris doctor.

Jencks Act. N. A law requiring the government to provide a criminal defendant in a federal case with copies of witness statements made against him or her in order to prepare a defense.

jeopardy. N. Risk or danger; the danger of being convicted that is a natural accompaniment to being a defendant in a criminal trial. See also *double jeopardy.*

Jim Crow laws. N. Laws used in the first half of the twentieth century to segregate the races. See also *segregate, desegregate.*

job. N. (1) A position of employment. (2) A task, usually paid. (3) A crime such as robbery. V. To buy and sell goods or stocks.

jobber. N. (1) A person who buys and sells stocks or goods; a wholesaler or middleman. (2) A person who works casually doing odd jobs for pay.

John/Jane Doe. N. A fictitious name given to a party to a lawsuit who wishes to remain anonymous or whose name is unknown; a fictitious name given to a hypothetical character for purposes of argument.

join. V. To combine or unite; to unite with another party in a lawsuit; to add a cause of action or issue to a lawsuit. See also *joinder*.

joinder. N. The act of uniting parties or causes of action to a lawsuit.

joinder, compulsory. N. The mandatory addition of a party to a lawsuit if his or her presence is necessary to provide complete relief to the current parties, or if his or her interests will be substantially affected by the lawsuit.

joinder, permissive. N. The voluntary joining of a lawsuit by a party who is not indispensable to the action but who does have a claim for relief arising out of it.

joinder of actions. N. Combining two or more causes of action into a single lawsuit.

joinder of parties. N. The addition of one or more parties to a lawsuit.

joint. ADJ. Shared; united. N. A marijuana cigarette.

joint and several. ADJ. Both shared and individual.

joint and several liability. N. Liability for an enterprise shared by two or more people that can be applied to the group as a whole or to individuals, so that each is individually responsible for performing the entire obligation and each can be sued independently for failure to fulfill it, while at the same time the group is also responsible for the obligation and can be sued as a whole.

joint bank account. N. A bank account shared by two or more people who each have equal right to it.

joint enterprise. N. An enterprise undertaken by two or more people who agree on a common purpose and share control of the project and a financial interest in it.

joint liability. N. Liability owed by two or more people together.

jointly. ADV. Done together.

joint venture. N. A commercial enterprise similar to a partnership, in which two or more parties join together for the purpose of carrying out a single commercial enterprise, for which they share assets, liability, and control.

journal. N. (1) A daily record of transactions, business, proceedings, appointments, events and occurrences, etc. (2) A periodical publication covering a particular profession or field.

journalists' privilege. N. A privilege that protects journalists and other media professionals from being forced to reveal confidential sources of information in some cases.

joyriding. N. Taking an automobile without the owner's permission in order to use it temporarily but not intending to keep it permanently.

J.P. ABBRV. Justice of the Peace.

judge. N. An officer who presides over and decides cases in a court. V. To decide a legal case; to form an opinion about a matter. ABBRV. *J.*

judge advocate. N. A military lawyer or legal officer; an officer in the Judge Advocate General's corps.

Judge Advocate General. N. A title used by military senior legal officers. ABBRV. *JAG*.

judge-made law. N. Case law created by judges who interpret statutes in what some consider to be an extreme or ideologically motivated way.

judgment. N. (1) The ability to form opinions and make decisions. (2) The court's final decision in a trial; the amount of money awarded to the prevailing party by the court.

judgment, final. N. A judgment that ends a legal controversy by conclusively stating whether or not the plaintiff is entitled to relief.

judgment, foreign. N. A judgment issued by a court in another state or country.

judgment, money. N. A judgment that awards a party a sum of money.

judgment notwithstanding the verdict. N. A judgment by the court for one party after receiving a verdict for the other, following a motion for a directed verdict; also called judgment n.o.v., non obstante veredicto.

judgment on the merits. N. A judgment rendered after the parties have presented their cases and the court has determined which party is in the right on the basis of facts and evidence presented.

judgment proof. ADJ. Describes a person not worth suing for monetary damages because he or she is insolvent, has no property within a jurisdiction, or is otherwise protected from a judgment for money recoveries.

judicial. ADJ. Related to the office of judge, judgments, the administration of justice, or courts; related to the interpretation and application of laws.

judicial activism. N. A form of legal action in which a judge writes opinions and renders decisions based on progressive ideas of social justice instead of basing his or her decisions strictly on judicial precedent and a restrained interpretation of legislation.

judicial authority. N. The power that comes as part of the office of judge; the power to hear cases and render decisions; also called judicial power.

judicial branch. N. The branch of government consisting of courts and other entities that exist to interpret and enforce laws.

judicial immunity. N. A judge's immunity from civil liability for anything done in his or her official capacity.

judicial notice. N. A practice in which the court will recognize certain facts without requiring one of the parties to produce evidence proving them, usually in the case of facts that are universally acknowledged to be true or facts that the judge or jury already know.

judicial review. N. (1) The power of the courts to review the acts of other branches of the government, usually in order to determine that the law is properly applied to a matter, especially in constitutional matters; review by the Supreme Court of acts by the legislature, as established in the case *Marbury v. Madison.* (2) Review of a trial court's decision by an appellate court.

judiciary. N. A collective term for judges; the bench; the judicial branch of the government.

jump bail. V. For a criminal defendant to leave the jurisdiction or fail to appear at trial after bail has been posted for him or her, causing whoever posted bail to forfeit it. See also *bail, bondsman.*

jural. ADJ. Relating to the law, justice, rights, or obligations.

juridical. ADJ. Having to do with legal proceedings, judges, or the administration of justice.

juris. ADJ. *(Latin)* Of law.

jurisdiction. N. The power to make judicial decisions; a court's or judge's power to investigate the facts of a matter, apply law to them, and declare a judgment. (2) The territory in which a particular court can exercise its authority; the system of courts within a particular area. ADJ. *jurisdictional*.

jurisdictional amount. N. The amount of money required to be involved in a controversy in order to give a court jurisdiction over it.

juris doctor. N. The degree received by someone who completes law school. ABBRV. *JD*.

jurisprudence. N. (1) The philosophy or science of law. (2) The body of law formed by cases and interpretations of them; a system of law.

jurist. N. A scholar of the law; a lawyer or judge.

juror. N. A member of a jury.

jury. N. A group of people selected and sworn to hear the evidence in a case and decide what the true facts are; usually composed of a cross section of the community. See also *grand jury*, *hung jury*, *petit jury*.

jury, blue ribbon. N. A jury composed of experts, professionals, or other people who are exceptionally qualified, rather than a cross section of all members of a community.

jury challenge. N. A party's rejection of a potential juror while selecting a jury for trial.

jury instructions. N. A statement made to the jurors by the judge at the conclusion of testimony but before the jurors begin deliberating, in which the judge describes the law that applies to the matters in controversy and explains how the jury should apply it.

jury panel. N. The group of people summoned to court on a particular day to serve as jurors if chosen.

jury selection. N. The process of choosing members of a jury from a panel of potential jurors, done by the parties to a lawsuit at the start of trial.

jury trial. N. A trial that takes place before a jury, in which the jury hears the testimony and sees evidence and then renders a decision about the facts in accordance with the judge's instructions. See also *bench trial.*

jus cogens. N. *(Latin)* Compelling law; a peremptory norm; in international law, a principle that is widely accepted to be true by a large number of states and individuals, such as the belief that genocide and slavery are wrong.

jus in bello. N. *(Latin)* Law in war; law governing actions during wartime.

just. ADJ. Fair; lawful; morally right.

just cause. N. A legitimate or fair reason for doing something; a reason that will legally justify an action.

just compensation. N. Compensation given to an owner whose property is taken through eminent domain that is fair both to the owner, who is losing property, and to the public, who is paying for it.

justice. N. (1) Fairness; fair and just administration of law; fair treatment or behavior. (2) A judge; a magistrate; a judge sitting on the Supreme Court of a state or country.

Justice Department. N. The federal department that enforces federal laws and represents the federal government in legal matters, under the direction of the attorney general.

justice of the peace. N. A magistrate with minor local authority, who hears minor criminal and civil cases, performs marriages, and handles other civil matters; most states have replaced justices of the peace with other courts and officers. ABBRV. *J.P.*

justiciable. ADJ. Able to be tried in court; presenting real interests instead of merely hypothetical or abstract ones.

justiciable controversy. N. A controversy involving a real issue that can be settled by a court, involving a present claim made by one party and another party disputing it.

justifiable. ADJ. Excusable; defensible; able to be proven to be reasonable or correct. See also *homicide, justifiable.*

juvenile. N. A child; a person below the age of legal majority. ADJ. Childish or youthful; relating to children or young people.

juvenile court. N. A court that hears cases involving children and teenagers, particularly over juvenile delinquents and neglected children.

juvenile delinquent. N. A minor who commits a crime or engages in regular criminal activity. See also *delinquent child.*

kangaroo court. N. A court that is completely biased against one party and therefore disregards that party's rights and delivers a judgment or verdict that is unfair to him or her; a trial in a kangaroo court is considered a sham without legal authority.

Keogh plan. N. A retirement plan for self-employed people with benefits similar to those enjoyed by employees with employer-sponsored retirement plans.

key number system. N. A system of organizing published cases by numbering each point of law with a key number, making it easy for legal researchers to locate relevant topics and cases.

kickback. N. A payment made by a seller to a buyer or agent in order to persuade him or her to enter into the transaction; illegal in most cases.

kidnap. V. To unlawfully and forcibly take and carry away a person. N. *kidnapping*.

kidnapping for ransom. N. The abduction and holding of a person in order to demand money in return for the victim's release. See also *abduct, false arrest, ransom*.

kite. V. To write fraudulent checks; to write checks on an account with insufficient funds in the hopes that funds sufficient to cover the check will be deposited before the check is presented to the bank for payment. N. *kiting*, *check kiting*. See also *float*.

know. V. To be aware of; to have information about something; to understand.

knowingly. ADJ. With awareness; consciously; with understanding of the circumstances and the implications of an act.

knowledge. N. Awareness of or familiarity with something; actual information; awareness of the positive and negative aspects of something.

Kyoto Protocol. N. An amendment to the United Nations Framework Convention on Climate Change that requires signatory nations to reduce their greenhouse gas emissions to an assigned level.

L

labor. N. (1) Work, especially manual work. (2) A collective term for workers. V. To work, especially at hard physical jobs.

labor dispute. N. A disagreement between employees and their employer about terms and conditions of employment, including pay, safety, hours, etc.

laborer. N. A person who engages in physical work for wages.

labor relations. N. The relationship between employers and employees, usually as personified by management and employees.

labor union. N. An organization of workers in a particular field that exists to handle disputes between the workers and their employers, working under the assumption that the workers have more power when they join forces and negotiate as a unit; also called a labor organization.

laches. N. An unreasonable delay in asserting or enforcing a claim.

laches, estoppel by. N. A doctrine that prevents a person from suing for some grievance that happened far in the past or otherwise seeking to enforce some right that he or she should have addressed long ago, on the assumption that the party with the claim has been negligent in not bringing it, that the defendant would have a hard time defending against it because it is so old, and that often the defendant has been put at a disadvantage because the would-be plaintiff has delayed so long.

laissez-faire. ADJ. *(French)* Allow to do; an economic doctrine stating that the free market should be allowed to operate free of governmental interference.

lame duck. N. A public official still in office after the election but before the inauguration of his or her successor.

land. N. (1) Soil or earth, including plants growing on it and rocks embedded in it. (2) Property, especially in the form of land; real property.

land, tenements, and hereditaments. N. A legal term encompassing all types of real property.

landed. ADJ. Consisting of land; owning land.

landlord. N. A person who owns real property and rents it to tenants. See also *lessor*.

landmark. N. (1) A feature of the landscape or an object placed on it that marks the boundary of a piece of property. (2) A building or natural object that is easy to spot, or that has some historical or cultural significance. (3) An important event that marks a turning point or a significant moment.

landmark decision. N. A decision by the Supreme Court that changes the established law in an area.

land mine. N. An explosive device laid on the surface of the earth or hidden just underneath it, intended to explode when a person or vehicle touches it.

land trust. N. A form of trust in which a trustee holds legal title to a piece of property but the beneficiary has the power to direct the trustee, manage the property, and receive income from it; also called an Illinois land trust.

lapse. N. The expiration of a right or privilege due to failure to exercise it or otherwise maintain it; the end of a legacy or right due to the death of the person who held it or to the expiration of a specified period of time; failure of a bequest or testamentary gift; the termination of an insurance policy if the policyholder does not pay the premium. V. *lapse*.

larceny. N. Taking the property of another person without the owner's consent and with the intention of making it the property of someone else.

larceny, grand. N. The taking of property with a high monetary value, set by statute.

larceny, petit. N. The taking of property with a low monetary value, set by statute. Also called petty larceny. See also *burglary, theft, robbery.*

lascivious. ADJ. Overtly sexual; lewd.

last clear chance. N. A doctrine that allows a plaintiff to recover from a defendant if the defendant had the last clear chance or opportunity to avoid the accident, regardless of the plaintiff's own negligence.

last-in, first-out. N. A method of inventory that assumes that the goods most recently bought are the first ones to be sold, and that goods still in inventory at the end of the year are the ones bought long ago. See also *first-in, first-out.* ABBRV. *LIFO.*

last will and testament. N. A will; the most recent will created by a deceased person; traditionally, the word "will" referred to the disposition of real property and the word "testament" to the disposition of personal property.

latent. ADJ. Hidden; existing but not yet obvious or apparent.

latent ambiguity. N. Language that appears to be clear and understandable but that in fact presents ambiguities or confusion when someone tries to apply it.

latent defect. N. A defect in an object that is not apparent on reasonable inspection or through the use of ordinary care.

launder. V. To move money through different businesses, accounts, and banks in order to conceal its origins; the federal crime of obscuring the source of money obtained through illegal means such as drug dealing, racketeering, and other crimes. N. *laundering*.

law. N. (1) A system of rules created by a society to regulate behavior and punish crimes. (2) A statute. (3) The professional field concerned with the rules that regulate society.

law, at. ADJ. Pertaining to law; related to the law or the legal profession.

law enforcement. N. Seeing that people follow laws and catching and punishing lawbreakers; the work done by police.

lawful. ADJ. Legal; permitted by law.

lawless. ADJ. Not conforming to law; not controlled by law.

law of the case. N. The doctrine that if a court decides an issue of law, the determination will stay the same throughout subsequent trials of the same facts unless a higher court reconsiders the issue and issues a new determination.

law of the land. N. The established law of a society, especially the principles of due process and other rights too fundamental to be abolished by government; in the United States, the Constitution and laws made by its authority.

Law of the Sea. N. United Nations Convention on the Law of the Sea; an international agreement that sets rules for the use of the world's oceans, establishing territorial boundaries and governing the management of marine resources.

law review. N. A professional journal published by a law school containing scholarly articles on legal topics by experts and students, usually compiled and edited by a staff of students chosen for their excellent academic record.

Law School Admission Test. N. A test that is required for admission to most law schools. ABBRV. *LSAT*.

laws of war. The laws that govern the actions nations may take when they are at war. See also *Geneva Conventions, jus in bello*.

lawsuit. N. An action at law or equity; a dispute brought before a court for determination.

lawyer. N. An attorney; a person who has studied law or who practices law.

lay. ADJ. Not professional or expert in a particular field; nonecclesiastical or nonclergy.

lay judge. N. A judge who has not studied law.

layman. N. A person who is not a professional or expert in a particular field, e.g., in legal situations, a nonlawyer.

layoff. N. The firing of one or many employees in response to business conditions, not for any wrongdoing of the employee; the temporary or permanent termination of one or more workers. See also *downsize*.

lay witness. N. A witness who is not an expert in the field on which he or she is called to testify; see also *expert*.

lead counsel. N. The head lawyer on one side of a lawsuit who is in charge of managing the case and all other attorneys and other people working on it.

leading case. N. A case that is recognized as determining the law on a particular topic and is often cited for that purpose.

leading question. N. A question in which the questioner hints or suggests to the witness the answer he or she would like to receive; not allowed during direct examination.

lease. N. A contract in which the owner of a piece of property allows someone else to possess it exclusively for a specified period of time in return for payment. V. To allow someone to use property for a period of time in exchange for payment; to rent. See also *let, lessor, lessee, sublease*.

lease, month-to-month. N. A tenancy without an actual lease, in which the lessor pays rent monthly and either party can terminate the arrangement with one month's notice.

lease, proprietary. N. A lease held by a resident in a cooperative apartment.

leasehold. N. An estate in real property held by lease, usually of a fixed duration; see also *freehold*.

leave. N. Permission.

leave of absence. N. A period of time in which a person has permission to be absent from work or duties, after which he or she intends to return.

leave of court. N. The court's permission to do a particular act.

legacy. N. A bequest; money or property left to someone by a will.

legacy, absolute. N. A bequest that comes into effect immediately without any conditions or restrictions.

legacy, alternate. N. A bequest in which the testator leaves a recipient one of several things without specifying which.

legacy, contingent. N. A bequest that will take effect when and if a specified event occurs.

legacy, demonstrative. N. A bequest of money that is to be paid out of a specific fund.

legacy, general. N. A bequest of money or goods to be paid out of the general assets of the estate.

legacy, residuary. N. A bequest of all personal property not otherwise disposed of by will, i.e., the residue.

legacy, specific. N. A bequest of a specific item designated by the testator.

legal. ADJ. (1) Having to do with law; related to principles of law as opposed to equity. (2) In accordance with law; lawful. ADV. *legally*.

legal age. N. The age at which a person can enter into contracts and conduct business on his or her own behalf, or the age at which a person can marry; majority.

legal aid. N. A nonprofit system that provides legal assistance to people who cannot afford to pay for lawyers themselves.

legal capacity to sue. N. The right to bring a lawsuit; the condition of being of sound mind, being of legal age, and suffering from no legal restraints or other impediments to bringing a lawsuit.

legal cause. N. The conduct or event that directly causes an injury; proximate cause.

legal detriment. N. Injury or disadvantage caused to someone who acted in such a way as to change his or her legal position or assume a liability or duty based on a promise that another person made but did not keep.

legal duty. N. An obligation required by law, such as the duty of parents to care for their children or the duty arising from a contract; also called a legal obligation.

legalese. N. The formal language used in legal documents; especially refers derogatorily to unnecessarily complex and opaque language that is extremely difficult to understand.

legal fiction. N. An assumption that certain facts are true that is made by the court in order to render a legal decision without delay.

legal name. N. A person's official name registered with the government, usually consisting of one or more given names recorded on the person's birth certificate, the parents' or father's family name, and possibly a new family name acquired upon marriage.

legal secretary. N. A secretary with special expertise in legal matters.

Legal Services Corporation. N. A corporation established by Congress in 1974 that provides funding for legal assistance in noncriminal proceedings for people who cannot afford to pay for legal counsel. See also *legal aid*.

legal tender. N. Money that can be used to pay for things; all coins and currencies of the United States, regardless of when they were issued.

legatee. N. A person who receives a legacy.

legislate. V. To create or pass a law or resolution.

legislation. N. The act of making laws; laws created by a legislature.

legislative. ADJ. Holding the power to create laws; pertaining to the creation of laws. N. *legislative act*, *legislative branch*, *legislative history*, *legislative immunity*, *legislative power*.

legislator. N. A member of a body that creates laws.

legislature. N. The group of people who make laws for a state or country.

Legum Magister. N. (*Latin*) Master of laws; a post-graduate degree offered by law schools to students who have done advanced study in a legal specialty or to foreign lawyers who have taken a certain number of classes at an American law school. ABBRV. *LL.M.*

lemon. N. A defective or unsatisfactory automobile.

lemon laws. N. Laws passed by many states that provide relief to people who purchase new automobiles that turn out to be defective.

lend. V. (1) To let someone use something temporarily, on the understanding that it will be returned; to allow someone to borrow something. (2) To provide someone with money that he or she must eventually pay back, usually with interest.

lender. N. A person or organization that lends something, particularly money.

lending. N. The act or business of lending something, especially money. See also *loan*.

lessee. N. A person who holds property through a lease; a person who rents property; a tenant. See also *lease, lessor*.

lesser included offense. N. A crime that is inherently part of a more serious crime; e.g., assault is an inherent part of the more serious crime of assault and battery, or attempt is an inherent part of any crime that is actually completed.

lessor. N. A person who rents or leases property to someone else; a landlord.

let. V. (1) To rent; to allow someone to use property in exchange for payment; to grant a license to use property. (2) To award a contract for a project to one of several applicants who have submitted bids.

letter of credit. N. A promise made by a bank or other financial institution to another bank or financial institution that it will honor demands for payment on behalf of a specified customer under specified conditions.

letter of intent. N. A document that records the intention of the parties to it to enter into a contract or take some other action but that is not itself a formal contract.

letter of the law. N. A strict, literal, word-for-word interpretation of laws and statutes. See also *spirit of the law.*

leverage. N. (1) The use of borrowed money to try to earn much more through investment, in the hopes that the profits will outweigh the interest owed on the debt. (2) The ratio of a business's debt to equity.

leveraged buyout. N. A method by which outside investors or a corporation's own management buy the outstanding stock of a corporation using money borrowed from outside sources, and using the purchased company's assets as security for the loan.

levy. V. (1) To impose a tax, fee, or fine on someone; to raise or collect. (2) To seize money or property. (3) To begin to wage war. N. (1) A tax or other sum collected from people. (2) Raising money through seizing property and selling it. (3) The enlisting of troops; a group of enlisted soldiers.

lewd. ADJ. Sexually indecent; provoking lust. See also *lascivious, indecent.*

lewdness. N. Sexual indecency, especially performed in public or in the presence of people who might be offended by it.

lewd and lascivious cohabitation. N. The crime of a man and woman living together without being married.

LexisNexis. N. A privately owned online legal research system that provides access to reported decisions, federal and state statutes, law review articles, and many other materials; also called Lexis. See also *Westlaw*.

liability. N. The condition of being responsible for something; something for which someone is responsible; an obligation or duty to do something or pay a sum of money; a possible claim against a person or business.

liability insurance. N. Insurance that covers an individual against claims against him or her made by third parties.

liable. ADJ. Responsible; legally answerable for something; obligated or accountable.

libel. N. A written, printed, or published false and malicious statement that injures someone's reputation; the written form of defamation. ADJ. *libelous*. See also *defamation, slander*.

liberal. ADJ. Open to new opinions and interpretations; not strict, conservative, or narrow-minded; in favor of individual liberty; generous. See also *construction*.

liberalize. V. To remove restrictions.

liberties. N. Specific instances of freedom from restrictions; rights or privileges. See also *civil liberties*.

liberty. N. Freedom; freedom from restrictions except for those imposed by law to prevent people from interfering with the liberty of others.

license. N. (1) A permit that allows someone to do some act; permission to do something that would be illegal without that permission. (2) Permission to use property owned by someone else, which does not give the licensee an exclusive right of possession; see also *lease*.

license fee. N. A fee imposed by the government for granting a license or a privilege to do something; also called a license tax.

licensee. N. A person who receives a license; a person who has the right to use property or do some action through a license.

licensor. N. A person who grants a license.

lie. V. (1) To intentionally make a false statement; to tell an untruth. (2) For an action or claim to be sustainable or admissible. N. A falsehood or untruth told intentionally to mislead someone.

lien. N. A claim placed on property to act as security for a debt owed by the owner, held until the owner pays the debt and kept if the owner never pays.

lien, artisan's. N. A lien that allows an artisan or craftsman to hold an item he or she has made until receiving payment for it.

lien, equitable. N. A lien enforceable in equity, not at law.

lien, floating. N. A lien that affects not only inventory and assets owned by the debtor at the time the agreement is made, but also property acquired afterward.

lien, judgment. N. A lien that a judgment creditor is entitled to file against a judgment debtor's property, often in order to sell the property at a sheriff's sale.

lien, materialman's. N. See *lien, mechanic's.*

lien, mechanic's. N. A lien that allows builders, tradesmen, suppliers, and others who provide materials or labor for construction or maintenance of buildings to attach the land or buildings in question to secure payment for their work and materials.

lien, tax. N. A lien that the state may place on a taxpayer's property if he or she fails to pay taxes.

life estate. N. An estate in property that lasts until the person holding it dies, or until some other specified person dies.

life expectancy. N. The number of years a person is expected to live, based on age and sex and calculated by actuarial tables and statistics.

life insurance. See *insurance.*

life interest. N. A claim to or interest in property that ends at the death of the person holding the interest or of some other person; see also *life estate, life tenant.*

life tenant. N. A person who holds a tenancy on land that ends at his or her death or at the death of another person; such a tenancy is called a life tenancy. See also *life estate.*

LIFO. ABBRV. Last-in, first-out.

like-kind exchange. N. An exchange of an item of property for another item of property of a similar type and value, usually nontaxable.

limit. V. To restrict; to set boundaries. N. A boundary or restriction.

limitation. N. A restriction; a restriction of the time in which a lawsuit can be filed; a restriction of who can receive an estate in property or the uses to which an estate may be restricted. See also *statute of limitations*.

limited. ADJ. Restricted in size, time, or extent.

limited jurisdiction. N. Jurisdiction over only specific kinds of cases or otherwise restricted by statute; see also *special jurisdiction*.

limited liability. N. Liability for corporate losses that is restricted in some way, usually to the amount that an investor or shareholder has placed in the corporation and not reaching personal assets.

limited liability company. N. A business organization, often managed by its members, with limited liability and limited ability to transfer ownership. ABBRV. *L.L.C.*

limited partnership. N. A form of partnership in which one or more general partners manage the business and are personally responsible for its debts, and one or more limited partners contribute money and earn profits but do not run the business and are not liable for its debts.

lineage. N. Family descent or ancestry.

lineal. ADJ. In a direct line from a particular relative, such as grandparent to parent to child; see also *collateral*.

lineal descendant. N. A person who is directly descended in a straight line from an ancestor.

lineal heir. N. A person who inherits directly from a lineal ancestor or ascendant; see also *descent*.

line of credit. N. An amount of credit available for a specified time to a consumer that the consumer may access as he or she chooses; a standing loan available for a preset time period.

lineup. N. A procedure used by police to identify criminal suspects, in which a suspect and several similar people are lined up in front of a wall and a witness is asked to identify the one who committed the crime.

link. V. To connect one website or computer with another. N. A place on a website that, if clicked, will connect the user to another website.

liquid. ADJ. In cash or readily converted into cash; holding a large amount of cash and working capital.

liquid assets. N. Cash or items that can be quickly converted into cash.

liquidate. V. (1) To convert assets into cash; to sell assets. (2) To settle; to pay debts; to settle the affairs of a business by determining debts and apportioning assets. N. *liquidation*.

liquidated damages. N. The amount of damages that a party to a contract agrees to pay if he or she breaches it.

liquidity. N. The amount of cash available to a person or business; the ease with which a person or business can obtain cash.

lis pendens. N. *(Latin)* A pending lawsuit; a doctrine that requires purchasers of property or other people with an interest in property subject to a lawsuit to be bound by the outcome of the litigation.

lis pendens, notice of. N. A public notice informing the community that a particular property is subject to litigation and that prospective purchasers of the property will be bound by any judgment affecting it.

list. N. A document containing several items of the same type, such as a court calendar or schedule, or a registry of voters. V. To compile a list; to register; to put a property up for sale with a real estate agent.

listed stock. N. Stock in a company that meets the Securities and Exchange Commission's requirements and is traded on an organized stock exchange; also called a listed security.

listing. N. (1) Putting real estate up for sale; entering an agency agreement with a real estate agent to sell a piece of property. (2) Entering into a contract to place a company's stock on a stock exchange.

list price. N. The publicly advertised price of an item.

litigant. N. A party to a lawsuit; a plaintiff or defendant.

litigate. V. To bring a dispute to a court of law; to bring or defend a lawsuit in court.

litigation. N. A lawsuit or legal action; the act of bringing or defending a lawsuit. ADJ. *litigious*.

litigator. N. A lawyer who represents parties in lawsuits in courts of law; a specialist in litigation.

living wage. N. A wage sufficient to meet ordinary living expenses. See also *minimum wage*.

living will. N. A document created by a person while still in relatively good mental condition stating in advance his or her wishes for medical treatment if and when he or she is no longer able to communicate and provide informed consent; see also *advance directive, durable power of attorney*.

L.L.C. ABBRV. Limited liability company.

LL.M. ABBRV. *(Latin)* Legum Magister.

Lloyd's of London. N. A group of private insurance underwriters based in London, England, that originally specialized in marine insurance but now will agree to underwrite a wide variety of risks.

loan. N. Something that is borrowed, especially money; the act of lending something to someone, with the intention of having it returned at some future time. V. To lend; to borrow.

loan, personal. N. A secured or unsecured loan to be used for personal purposes as opposed to commercial ones.

loan, secured. N. A loan that is secured with property or securities; also called a collateral loan.

loan commitment. N. A promise made by a bank or other lending institution to a prospective purchaser of real estate that it will lend him or her a specified sum at a specified interest rate to purchase a particular property if it is done within a specified period of time.

loaned servant. N. An employee hired out to another employer for a particular job, who comes under the control of the temporary employer and for whom the temporary employer becomes liable.

loan shark. N. A person who lends money at extortionate interest rates, usually illegally.

loansharking. N. The act of lending money at excessively high interest. See also *extort, usury*.

lobby. V. To attempt to influence a politician on a particular issue. N. A group of people who work to influence politicians on an issue; an attempt to influence politicians on an issue.

lobbyist. N. A person who works to influence politicians on particular issues and to persuade them to support or argue against particular items of proposed legislation.

local government. N. The government of a geographical region smaller than a state, such as a city or county, with control over local matters.

lockdown. N. Confining prisoners to their cells temporarily in order to restore security after a riot or other emergency.

lockout. N. An employer's refusal to allow employees to work during periods of negotiation; the employer's version of a strike.

locus. N. *(Latin)* A site; a place.

locus contractus. N. The place where a contract was made.

locus delicti. N. The place where an offense occurred.

locus in quo. N. The place in which, i.e., the place where something occurred.

logrolling. N. A method used by legislators to pass legislation without actually persuading fellow lawmakers of the validity of the proposed law, done by combining several unrelated matters into one bill in an effort to attract the votes of people who support individual parts of it, or by exchanging favors such as agreeing to vote for one another's bills.

loiter. V. To stand around idly; to move slowly and purposelessly. N. *loitering*.

long arm statute. N. A state statute that gives the state personal jurisdiction over nonresident defendants in matters that affect local residents and property.

long-term. ADJ. Occurring over a long period of time.

long-term capital gain or loss. N. A gain or loss that occurs from the sale of capital assets that have been held for the required length of time, usually at least one year.

long-term debt. N. Debt with a maturity date at least one year in the future.

long-term financing. N. A loan or mortgage that has a term of one year or more.

lookout. N. (1) A person who stands near the place where a crime is being committed to watch for police or other witnesses; a person stationed to watch for potential danger. (2) The watchfulness and diligence that a driver of an automobile must use while driving.

loophole. N. An ambiguity in a law; an inadequacy in a law that allows a person to legally avoid complying with it, especially in tax laws.

loss. N. The fact or act of losing something; something that is lost; the detriment or damage resulting from the destruction or ruin of something; injury; expense.

loss, casualty. N. The destruction of property by an unexpected cause such as fire or flood.

loss of earning capacity. N. Damage to a person's ability to earn money in the future.

lost property. N. Property that is no longer in its owner's possession due to the owner's negligence or carelessness and that cannot be found or recovered.

lot. N. (1) An item or collection of items delivered or sold as one unit. (2) A plot of land. (3) A set of shares of stock to be traded; see also *odd lot*.

lottery. N. A game of chance in which people pay money for a chance to win a prize that is awarded at random.

love and affection. N. The emotional support and kind feelings shared by close relatives such as parents and children or husbands and wives; love and affection can serve as adequate consideration for a gift between relatives.

loyalty oath. N. An oath of allegiance to a government or other institution, required of some public officials.

LSAT. ABBRV. Law School Admission Test.

lump sum. N. A single payment of an entire amount due. See also *installment*.

lying in wait. N. The act of hiding in order to ambush someone or attack suddenly.

lynch. N. For a mob to kill someone for a suspected but unproven offense, usually by hanging, without the approval or authority of the law.

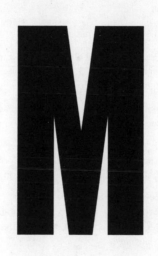

Maastricht Treaty. N. The treaty signed in Maastricht, the Netherlands, in 1992 that created the European Union.

machination. N. Scheming or plotting, usually to carry out some evil purpose.

mafia. N. A body of organized criminals who use extortion, threats, and violence to influence business or government; see also *organized crime, mob.*

mafioso. N. A member of the mafia.

magistrate. N. A public official with judicial, executive, or legislative power granted by the government, often functioning as a judge over minor matters or a justice of the peace.

magistrate's court. N. A court over which a magistrate presides, handling small claims and minor matters.

Magna Carta. N. *(Latin)* Great Charter; an agreement signed by King John in England in 1215, guaranteeing political rights and liberty to his nobles and forming the foundation of English rights and privileges.

Magnuson-Moss Warranty Act. N. A federal statute that requires warranties for consumer products to be written in clear, easily understandable language.

mail. N. Letters or packages transported from sender to recipient through a postal system. V. To address a package or letter, place the proper postage on it, and deliver it into the keeping of a postal system.

mailbox rule. N. A doctrine in contract law stating that an offer is accepted at the time a written acceptance is deposited in the mail.

mail fraud. N. Using letters sent through the mail to defraud people out of money.

maim. V. To injure so as to cause permanent damage to some part of the body; to cripple someone.

maintain. V. To support; to continue; to keep something in a condition to continue and to prevent decline or decay; to continue to prosecute a lawsuit once beginning it.

maintenance. N. (1) The upkeep of property. (2) Providing financial support for another person.

majority. N. (1) A number greater than half of a total; the larger group or number. (2) The age at which a person becomes an adult.

majority rule. N. A form of government in which the desire of the largest group within the whole determines how the entire state, nation, or organization will act.

majority vote. N. A vote in which the person who receives the greatest number of votes is declared the winner.

maker. N. A person who makes or creates something; a person who creates a law; a person who signs a check or promissory note.

malfeasance. Bad conduct; wrongdoing; a wrongful or unlawful act, particularly by a public official.

malice. N. Evil intention; an intention to do a wrongful act or commit a crime without any justification or excuse.

malice aforethought. N. A state of mind in which a person deliberately plans to commit a crime before actually performing it, characterized by cruelty and a disregard for the consequences to human life and social duties.

malicious. ADJ. Intending to do harm; done out of ill will and without justification.

malicious abuse of legal process. N. Intentionally using the legal process for an improper purpose.

malicious arrest. N. Arresting on criminal charges a person who is known not to have committed a crime or arresting a person without probable cause.

malicious prosecution. N. Criminal or civil litigation brought without probable cause and out of malice; if the defendant prevails in such a case, he or she may bring an action for the tort of malicious prosecution.

malinger. V. To pretend to be sick or disabled to get out of work or to keep receiving disability compensation.

malingerer. N. A person who malingers.

malpractice. N. Incompetence or improper conduct by a professional performing professional duties.

malpractice, legal. N. Failure by an attorney to use the degree of skill or care that should ordinarily be exercised in a situation.

malpractice, medical. N. Failure by a physician to use the degree of skill or care that should ordinarily be exercised in a situation.

malum in se. ADJ. *(Latin)* Bad in itself; describes an act that is inherently wrong in itself without regard to what the law says.

malum prohibitum. ADJ. *(Latin)* Bad because it is prohibited; describes an act that is wrong because it is prohibited by law.

mandamus. N. *(Latin)* We command; a writ issued by a superior court to a lower court, corporation, or officer, ordering it to do some act that is a duty required of it by law.

mandate. N. (1) A judicial order or command directing that some action be taken, especially from a higher court to a lower one. (2) Authority granted to a person to do some act, usually granted to an elected official by the electorate. V. (1) To require that something be done. (2) To give someone authority to do something.

mandatory. ADJ. Required; compulsory.

manifest. ADJ. Evident; obvious. N. A document listing the cargo and passengers on a ship or aircraft.

manifesto. N. A public declaration of political principles issued by a sovereign or politician; a formal document issued by an executive officer of a state declaring its reasons for taking some international action.

manipulate. V. To influence someone unfairly; to control someone's actions; to buy or sell a security in order to give a false impression about its value and thus influence the purchasing or selling decisions of others. N. *manipulation*. ADJ. *manipulative*.

Mann Act. N. A federal statute that makes it a crime to transport a woman or girl across state lines for immoral purposes such as prostitution; also called the White Slave Traffic Act.

manslaughter. N. The unlawful and unjustifiable killing of another person without premeditation or malice aforethought.

manslaughter, involuntary. N. Accidental or unintentional killing of a person through negligence or recklessness.

manslaughter, voluntary. N. The intentional but not premeditated killing of a person in the heat of passion.

Marbury v. Madison. n. An 1803 U.S. Supreme Court case that formalized the concept of the judicial review of statutes, enshrining the principle that the courts could invalidate laws passed by legislatures if they found them unconstitutional.

margin. N. (1) An edge or border; the place where water meets land. (2) The difference between two prices, such as the selling price of an item and its cost of production. (3) The amount paid to a securities broker by a customer when using the broker's credit to buy securities. ADJ. ***marginal***.

margin transaction. N. The purchasing of securities using a combination of cash and a loan extended by the broker making the purchase.

marijuana. N. Cannabis; a plant whose leaves can be smoked as an illegal drug; also spelled marihuana; also called pot, grass, weed, Mary Jane.

marital. N. Related to marriage.

marital agreement. N. An agreement or contract between a married couple or a couple about to get married, usually stating which partner owns what marital property.

marital communications privilege. N. The doctrine that a person does not have to disclose confidential communications made by his or her spouse during a legal marriage, and that such communications are inadmissible at trial; see also *husband-wife privilege*.

marital property. N. Property acquired by either spouse during a marriage, which is subject to equitable division if the parties divorce unless they made a marital agreement that allocated it; also called marital estate.

marital rights. N. The rights that constitute the basis of marriage and that a husband and wife are entitled to expect from one another.

marital status. N. The condition of being single, married, divorced, separated, or widowed.

maritime. ADJ. Related to the sea and seafaring; connected with all bodies of navigable water and commerce upon them.

maritime law. N. The body of laws governing travel and commerce on navigable waters.

market. N. (1) A place where goods and services are bought and sold. (2) The demand for a particular good or service; the state of commerce in general. (3) The actions of supply and demand on commerce; the free market.

marketable. ADJ. Able to be sold. N. *marketability*.

marketable title. N. Title to property that is free from encumbrances such that a reasonable person would accept it, and that can be sold or transferred without impediment.

marketplace. N. The world of commerce and trade.

market price. N. The price for an item that a buyer will pay and a seller will accept on the open market; the current price for an item; also called market value.

marriage. N. A legally recognized union between a man and a woman as husband and wife. V. *marry*.

marriage, common law. N. A union between a man and a woman who have not been married by ceremony but who have agreed to live together as husband and wife and have assumed marital duties.

A majority of states in the United States do not now recognize common law marriages. See also *domestic partner*.

marriage, same-sex. N. A union between two men or two women who live together as spouses; not legally recognized by most states. See also *domestic partner; marriage, common law.*

marriage certificate. N. A document certifying that a couple is legally married.

marriage license. N. A document issued by the state authorizing two people to marry within a stated period of time.

marshal. N. A public officer who enforces laws; the head of a police or fire department; a sheriff. V. To arrange; to put in order. See also *United States Marshal.*

marshalling assets. N. Arranging assets into the order in which they will be used to pay debts.

martial law. N. Government by the military instead of civilians during times of war or extreme civil unrest.

master. N. (1) A person with authority over another; an employer. (2) The presiding officer in a court of equity, also called a master in chancery or master in equity. (3) An officer appointed to represent a court in some matter, also called a special master.

master and servant. N. The relationship between an employer and an employee in which the employee performs services for the employer in return for pay, and the employer directs the employee and has the right to fire him or her.

master plan. N. The long-term plan for some governmental project, such as the plan for the urban development of a city.

master-servant rule. N. A rule stating that an employer is responsible for conduct by an employee while the employee is working for him or her.

material. ADJ. Essential; important; relevant to establishing a cause of action or arriving at a judgment; see also *immaterial*. N. *materiality*.

material alteration. N. A change to a document that alters its original meaning or its legal effect.

material evidence. N. Evidence that influences the judge's or jury's perception of the facts in a case; evidence with a real bearing on the issues.

material fact. N. A fact that is relevant and important to the matter at hand and that would influence the actions of other parties if made known to them; a fact that would cause someone to decide to enter or not enter a contract.

material witness. N. A witness who is the only person, or one of very few people, who can testify about a particular fact.

maternal. ADJ. Having to do with mothers and motherhood.

maternal line. N. A line of descent traced through mothers.

maternity. N. The condition of motherhood. See also *paternity*.

maternity leave. N. Leave granted a worker during pregnancy, or after the birth or adoption of a new child.

matricide. N. The killing of a mother by her child; a person who kills his or her own mother.

matrimonial action. N. A lawsuit related to the marital status of the parties, such as an action for divorce, separation, or annulment.

matrimony. N. The state of marriage; the ceremony in which two people are married. ADJ. *matrimonial*.

matter. N. A situation or state of affairs; the facts that comprise a cause of action or defense.

matter in controversy. N. The situation that is the basis of a lawsuit.

matter of fact. N. The factual issues to be ascertained at trial; also called a question of fact.

matter of law. N. A question of the proper law to apply to the facts of a case, to be determined by the judge; also called a question of law.

matter of record. N. An issue that can be proven by the official record on which it has been entered.

mature. ADJ. Fully developed; due for payment. N. *maturity*.

maturity date. N. The date on which a note or other commercial obligation comes due.

maturity value. N. The amount due for a mature note or other obligation.

maxim. N. A short statement of a principle or rule of law, often used in deciding equity cases.

mayhem. N. (1) Violent disorder or chaos. (2) The crime of maliciously injuring, maiming, or dismembering someone so as to render the victim permanently unable to fight.

McCain-Feingold Act. N. The Bipartisan Campaign Reform Act of 2002, a federal law that sets rules for campaign finance, limiting the amounts of money that contributors can donate and regulating the types of advertising that campaigns may use to raise money.

means. N. (1) Resources, especially financial. (2) The action or method that allows something to happen.

mediate. V. To intervene in a dispute in order to help the parties resolve it.

mediation. N. A form of alternate dispute resolution in which a neutral third party, the mediator, hears the testimony of both parties to a dispute and tries to help them agree on a solution, but cannot impose a decision on them.

Medicaid. N. A health insurance program run by the U.S. Department of Health and Human Services that pays for health care for low-income individuals, the disabled, and several other categories that people may fall under.

Medicare. N. A health insurance program run by the U.S. Department of Health and Human Services that pays for health care for people who are at least 65 years old and certain other individuals.

meeting of minds. N. The state of agreement about the terms and conditions of a contract that the parties to it must reach for it to be validly created.

member. N. A person or business that belongs to a larger group or organization.

member bank. N. A bank that is affiliated with the Federal Reserve System.

member firm. N. A securities brokerage firm that belongs to a particular stock exchange.

memorandum. N. (1) An informal document that records the details of a transaction, event, or agreement, or discusses some matter. (2) A document that examines the facts of a case and applies the law to it to see whether it has merit or not, usually written by a law clerk or low-level attorney at the request of a higher-level attorney, and considered attorney work product; also called a memorandum of law or a memo.

memorandum of understanding. N. A legal document that expresses an agreement between two parties but that is not as formal or binding as a contract. ABBRV. *MOU*.

menace. V. To threaten, especially with the prospect of injury. N. A threatening person or thing; a danger. ADJ. *menacing*. See also *assault*.

mens rea. N. The mental state that occurs when committing a crime, i.e., guilt, criminal intent, or knowledge that a crime is being committed; one of the four mental states in which a crime may be committed, i.e., intentionally, knowingly, recklessly, or negligently.

mens rea, general. N. A general intention to commit a crime.

mens rea, specific. N. The specific mental state that is necessary to convict someone of particular crimes.

mental anguish. N. Extreme distress, anxiety, and any other mental pain that is extreme enough to merit damages for the victim.

mental capacity. N. A person's ability to understand what he or she is doing or the effects that other people's actions will have on him or her; see also *capacity*.

mental cruelty. N. In marriage, behavior by one spouse that endangers the mental health of the other or is so humiliating and unpleasant that it makes the other's life miserable.

mercantile. ADJ. Related to merchants, trade, and commerce; commercial.

mercantile law. N. Commercial law; the law that governs merchants, trade, and commerce.

merchant. N. A person who buys and sells goods, usually buying wholesale and selling at retail; a trader; a person who imports and exports goods for sale.

merchantable. ADJ. Salable; able to be sold; of the type described and fit for the purpose for which it is sold. N. *merchantability*.

Mercosur. N. A free trade agreement between Argentina, Brazil, Paraguay, Uruguay, and several other South American nations that are associate members.

mercy killing. N. Euthanasia; killing a person or animal because continued life would be intolerable due to a painful, incurable illness or severe injury.

merge. V. To combine two or more things together into one whole.

merger. N. (1) The combination of two or more entities, rights, or other things into a single whole, especially the absorption of the minor entities, rights, or things into the largest of them. (2) The combining of two or more corporations into one, with one of them absorbing the others into itself. (3) The absorption of one estate into another when one person comes into possession of both of them. (4) Sentencing a person convicted of two or more crimes for only one of them. (5) After a plaintiff receives judgment in his or her favor, the combination of that judgment with other possible issues arising out of the original claim, thereby making it impossible to sue again on the same cause of action. (6) In a divorce action, substituting the final judgment for other property settlement agreements.

merits. N. The legal substance of a claim or defense.

mesne. ADJ. Intermediate; in the middle.

mesne profits. N. (1) Profits occurring between two points in time. (2) Profits earned from land by a person who has no right to it, recoverable by the landowner.

message board. N. A type of Internet forum in which users can post and respond to messages on various topics.

meta tags. N. Codes written in a computer language such as HTML or XML that identify particular types of text or images on a web page or document.

metes and bounds. N. Boundaries of property; a method of measuring and describing land boundaries using distances and angles from surrounding properties and landmarks.

MFN. ABBRV. Most favored nation.

military. ADJ. Related to war, the armed forces, and soldiers.

military jurisdiction. N. As listed in the Constitution, the three kinds of military authority over civil matters: military law, which governs the military during peacetime and war; military government, in which a military commander appointed by the president supersedes civilian laws during times of civil and foreign war; and, martial law, ordered by the president during times of dire emergencies.

military law. N. The branch of law that regulates the military and applies only to members of the armed services.

militia. N. An organization of citizens, civilians or military that defends a locality, state, or nation, but that is not part of a standing army; an organization of so-called citizen soldiers, such as the National Guard.

mineral. N. A solid inorganic substance naturally occurring in the earth, often obtained by mining, drilling, or quarrying, such as coal, oil, gas, iron, gold, uranium, etc.

mineral rights. N. The right to take minerals out of a particular piece of land.

minimum contacts. N. The minimum level of contact with a forum state that a nonresident defendant must have to be subjected to personal jurisdiction in the courts of that state without offending due process of law; usually intentional business activity in the forum state is enough.

minimum wage. N. The federally established lowest hourly wage that employers engaged in interstate commerce must pay their employees, or the equivalent established by an individual state, set at a level to allow workers to maintain their health and well-being.

mine. N. An opening made in the earth to allow the extraction of minerals.

mining. N. The process or business of extracting minerals from the earth.

mining lease. N. A lease that allows the lessee to enter land to search for minerals on it and to extract them if found.

minister. N. (1) A member of the clergy, particularly of Protestant Christian denominations. (2) The head of a governmental department. (3) A diplomatic official who represents one state or nation to another. (4) *(Archaic)* An agent; someone who acts for someone else. V. To care for; to meet someone's needs.

ministerial act. N. An act done by an agent or subordinate who is acting on orders from a superior.

minor. N. A person below the age of majority; a child or juvenile. ADJ. Small; of less importance.

minority. N. (1) The smaller group or number of a whole; a number less than half of a total; the opposite of majority. (2) The condition of being a minor; childhood. (3) A disadvantaged group of people; a group of people that comprises a relatively small part of the whole population and that suffers due to its race, religion, sex, etc.

minority stockholder. N. A stockholder who holds very few shares in a corporation and thus is unable to vote effectively for corporate directors.

minutes. N. A transcript of a meeting or event; a record of court proceedings.

Miranda Rule. N. A rule requiring that before a person is interrogated about a crime he or she be informed of legal protections against self-incrimination and the right to counsel, a procedure called the Miranda warning or reading someone his or her rights; evidence obtained from questioning done without first reading the Miranda warning is inadmissible in court (except for impeachment purposes).

Miranda v. Arizona. n. A 1966 U.S. Supreme Court case that held that the police must inform criminal suspects of their right to remain silent during police questioning and their right to an attorney, which developed into the Miranda warning.

misadventure. N. An accident; an unfortunate mishap.

misappropriate. V. To dishonestly take something that belongs to someone else and use it for oneself; to use someone else's property for a purpose for which it was not intended; also called misapply. N. *misappropriation*.

miscarriage. N. (1) An unsuccessful outcome, especially due to mismanagement. (2) The premature termination of a pregnancy before the fetus is able to survive outside the womb. V. *miscarry*.

miscarriage of justice. N. Errors made by a court that damage the rights of a party sufficiently to warrant reversal of the decision.

miscegenation. N. The genetic mingling of races; interracial marriage.

mischief. N. Harm; trouble; the act of damaging property or injuring a person intentionally or recklessly.

misconduct. N. Improper behavior; neglect of duties; mismanagement.

misconduct in office. N. Unlawful or corrupt behavior by a public official in the conduct of official duties.

miscreant. N. A person who breaks a law or a rule; a person who behaves badly. ADJ. *miscreant*.

misdelivery. N. Delivery of goods to the wrong recipient or the wrong destination; delivery of goods damaged by the carrier entrusted with their transport; failure to deliver goods at all.

misdemeanor. N. A minor crime, less serious than a felony and usually punished by less severe penalties.

misfeasance. N. Doing a legally required duty in the wrong way.

misjoinder. N. An improper joinder.

mislead. V. To give someone the wrong idea or impression about something; to deceive. ADJ. *misleading*.

misnomer. N. An inaccurate name; a mistake made in recording someone's name.

misrepresent. V. To make a false or inaccurate statement; to give the impression by words or behavior that a situation is different from what is in fact the case. N. *misrepresentation*.

mistake. N. An incorrect or wrong action or belief; an act or omission caused by ignorance or misconception about the true situation.

mistake, mutual. N. A mistake made by both parties to an agreement.

mistake, unilateral. N. A mistake made by only one party to an agreement.

mistake of fact. N. An error caused by ignorance or misconception of a fact.

mistake of law. N. An error occurring when a party understands the facts but is ignorant or confused as to how the law applies to them.

mistrial. N. An invalid trial; a trial terminated before a judgment is reached due to circumstances such as a hung jury, lack of jurisdiction, or another fundamental problem.

misuse. V. To use something in an improper or incorrect way; to use a product in a way not intended or reasonably foreseen by its manufacturer. N. *misuse*.

mitigate. V. To make something less severe or serious. N. *mitigation*.

mitigating circumstances. N. Circumstances that make a crime or offense less serious without excusing the act.

mitigation of damages. N. A doctrine requiring the victim of a tort or breach to use reasonable diligence and ordinary care to minimize injury or damage.

mob. N. (1) A large and unruly group of people, especially a group engaged in illegal and destructive behavior; see also *riot*. (2) The mafia; organized crime in general. V. For a large group of people to swarm over and overwhelm an area.

Model Rules of Professional Conduct. N. A set of rules created by the American Bar Association and adopted by many states that govern the conduct of attorneys.

modus operandi. N. *(Latin)* A way of operating; a way of doing things; especially used to refer to a criminal's habitual methods; also called m.o.

molest. V. To engage in sexual touching, up to and including sexual intercourse, with an unwilling partner.

monetary. ADJ. Having to do with money.

money. N. Coins, paper currency or banknotes, and other mediums of exchange authorized by a government; wealth.

money demand. N. A claim made by a plaintiff for recovery of a specified sum of money.

money judgment. N. A final judgment by a court ordering the defendant to pay a sum of money to the plaintiff.

money order. N. A negotiable instrument purchased by the person who wants to pay a sum of money from a bank, post office, or other third party that makes its credit available, and made payable to a named recipient.

money supply. N. All money in the economy at a given time.

monopoly. N. Exclusive possession or control of a supply of some commodity or an industry by one or a few people or businesses; a market condition in which a single person or company controls the entire trade in something. V. *monopolize*.

Montreal Convention. N. An international treaty created in 1999 that establishes rules for the compensation of victims of air disasters.

moot. ADJ. Uncertain or unsettled; subject to debate. V. To raise an issue for debate; to discuss.

moot case. N. A case that seeks a decision on some issue that has no actual controversy or no practical application because the issue has already been resolved.

moot court. N. A mock court set up by a law school to try hypothetical cases as an exercise in oral advocacy for law students.

moral. ADJ. Concerned with character, the distinction between right and wrong, proper social interactions, and ethics.

moral certainty. N. Certainty about something that is beyond a reasonable doubt but not quite absolute; enough certainty about an issue that a reasonable man or woman of sound mind would feel justified in acting on the assumption that it is, in fact, the case.

moral turpitude. N. Depravity, dishonesty, or vileness; conduct that grossly violates acceptable standards of morality and behavior.

moratorium. N. A temporary stop to or prohibition of a particular activity; a temporary period in which debtors may postpone payment of debts.

mortal. ADJ. Deadly or fatal; related to death.

mortality. N. Death; the number of deaths from a particular cause or at a particular time or place; the condition of being subject to death.

mortality tables. N. Actuarial tables that insurance companies use to determine how long a person is likely to live.

mortgage. N. An interest in real property held by a creditor who lends money to a debtor to purchase the property and takes title to or a lien on the property as security for the loan. V. To give a creditor an interest in property as security for a loan.

mortgage, adjustable rate. N. A mortgage in which the interest rate is tied to an index and periodically moves up or down as the index does. ABBRV. *ARM*.

mortgage, balloon payment. N. A mortgage in which the borrower pays regular interest payments for a period and then must pay the entire principal at once.

mortgage, fixed-rate. N. A mortgage with an interest rate that remains the same throughout the life of the mortgage.

mortgage broker. N. A firm or person who arranges mortgages between borrowers and lenders.

mortgagee. N. A person who lends money to another through a mortgage.

mortgagor. N. A person who borrows money to acquire title to property and pledges that property as security for the debt.

mortmain. N. *(French)* Dead hand; the state of property owned by an ecclesiastical or other organization.

most favored nation. N. A nation that is accorded the most favorable rights and privileges, especially trade rights, that can be granted by another nation. ABBRV. *MFN*.

motion. N. A formal application to the court asking for a rule or order in favor of the applicant, such as a grant of summary judgment, of judgment notwithstanding the verdict, to dismiss a complaint, or a new trial. See also *move.*

motion in limine. N. A motion made before trial asking the court to prevent the other party from introducing evidence that would be too prejudicial to the party making the motion.

Motion Picture Association of America. N. A nonprofit trade association that lobbies on behalf of film studios, particularly in the realm of copyright, digital rights management, and free speech. See also *Digital Millennium Copyright Act.* ABBRV. *MPAA.*

motion to suppress. N. In a criminal case, a request to exclude evidence that has been obtained illegally.

motive. N. The reason for doing some act; the idea or circumstances that cause someone to do something.

MOU. ABBRV. Memorandum of understanding.

movant. N. A party making a motion.

move. v. To make a motion.

MPAA. ABBRV. Motion Picture Association of America.

multifarious. ADJ. Of various types; having multiple parts.

multifarious suit. N. A lawsuit in which dissimilar causes of action or parties are joined incorrectly.

multilateral. ADJ. Involving the participation of at least three parties, especially governments or nations.

multiplicity. N. A large number or great variety of something.

multiplicity of actions. N. Several lawsuits on the same matter brought by different plaintiffs against the same defendant; also called multiplicity of suits.

municipal. ADJ. Related to a city or town or its government, or another local government; occasionally used in reference to state or national government.

municipal bonds. N. Securities sold by a city, county, state, or other local government body to raise money for municipal expenses and projects, payable at a specified future date with interest that is exempt from federal and some state income tax.

municipal court. N. A city court with jurisdiction over local matters, including small civil matters and crimes occurring within the city.

municipality. N. The population of a specific area that has been incorporated and governs itself; a city, village, or town; also called a municipal corporation.

municipal ordinance. N. A law enacted by a municipality to regulate local affairs.

murder. N. The unlawful killing of a person by another person with malice aforethought. ADJ. *murderous*.

murder, first-degree. N. An unlawful killing that is willful, deliberate, and premeditated.

murder, second-degree. N. An unlawful killing without deliberation or premeditation but with malice aforethought.

murder, serial. N. The murder by one killer of several victims over a period of time.

mutilate. V. To injure badly; to deprive someone of the use of a limb; to inflict serious, disfiguring damage on someone or something; to damage or alter a document so that it becomes imperfect. N. *mutilation*.

mutiny. N. A rebellion by soldiers or sailors against their commanding officers. V. *mutiny*. ADJ. *mutinous*.

mutual. ADJ. Held in common by both parties; reciprocal.

mutual company. N. A company owned by members who also do business with the company, and who receive profits in proportion to their business with the company.

mutual fund. N. A fund run by an investment company that pools the contributions of various investors who purchase shares in the fund, and invests them in a selection of publicly traded securities.

mutual insurance company. N. An insurance company owned by the people it insures, who share in the company's profits.

mutuality. N. A mutual or reciprocal action, quality, or condition.

mutuality of obligation. N. The principle that both parties to a contract are either bound to it or not, but one party cannot be bound if the other is not.

mutuality of remedy. N. The principle that one party cannot receive an equitable remedy that the other party could not also receive.

n/a. ABBRV. (1) Not available; not applicable. (2) *(Latin)* Non allocatur; not allowed.

NAFTA. ABBRV. North American Free Trade Association.

name. N. The word or words used to identify a person, animal, business, or other entity. V. To give a name to someone or something.

named insured. N. The person designated on an insurance policy as having a contract for insurance.

narcotic. N. A pain-relieving drug that also causes drowsiness or stupor and is often addictive, many of which are used medically but also abused illegally. ADJ. *narcotic*.

NASDAQ. ABBRV. National Association of Securities Dealers Automated Quotations.

National Association of Securities Dealers Automated Quotations. N. A computerized information system used in trading securities. ABBRV. *NASDAQ*.

National Guard. N. A militia trained and equipped by the U.S. Army and Air Force that serves as reserve forces and can be mobilized by the president to help the armed forces with military operations or during states of emergency.

National Labor Relations Board. N. An independent agency established by Congress through the National Labor Relations Act that works to prevent unfair labor practices by either employers or labor unions, oversees union elections, and adjudicates claims. ABBRV. *NLRB*.

national origin. N. The country in which a person was born or from which his or her immediate ancestors emigrated.

National Rifle Association. N. A national advocacy organization that supports gun rights. ABBRV. *NRA*.

native. N. A person who was born in a particular place; a person who is a citizen of a place because he or she was born there, or because his or her parents are citizens. ADJ. *native*.

natural. ADJ. Caused by nature or existing in nature; not artificial.

natural affection. N. The emotional state that is supposed to exist naturally between parents and children, spouses, and siblings, and that can function as valuable consideration for a contract.

natural child. N. A child that is related to his or her parents by blood, not adoption.

natural death. N. Death from natural causes, such as illness or old age, and not caused by violence or accident.

naturalization. N. The process of becoming a citizen of a country if one was not born there.

naturalize. V. To become a citizen of a country other than one's place of birth.

naturalized citizen. N. A person who has earned citizenship by fulfilling residence and other requirements, as opposed to merely being born in a nation or to citizen parents.

natural law. N. Moral rules and principles believed to govern human behavior naturally, as an inherent part of human nature, regardless of laws enacted by people; see also *positivism*.

natural life. N. A person's actual physical life that ends with physical death.

natural person. N. A human being; an actual person instead of an artificial entity such as a corporation.

navigable. ADJ. Able to be traveled; describes waters accessible to boats, or roads accessible to vehicular traffic.

navigable waters. N. Waterways that can be traveled down for commerce.

n.b. ABBRV. *(Latin)* Nota bene, meaning note well, observe; used to draw a reader's attention to an important point.

necessary. ADJ. Required; needed; essential.

necessary and proper clause. N. Language in Article I of the U.S. Constitution authorizing Congress to pass laws that are necessary and proper to carrying out the powers granted to the government by the Constitution.

necessary parties. N. Parties who must be included in a lawsuit because complete relief would be impossible without them.

necessity. N. Something that is required or must be done; the state of being required.

negative. ADJ. (1) Characterized by absence rather than presence. (2) Expressing refusal, denial, or disagreement.

negative condition. N. A requirement in an agreement that something must not happen.

negative covenant. N. A covenant that prevents someone from doing something, such as selling goods in the same region as someone else.

negative easement. N. An easement that prevents a landowner from doing certain things to the property.

negative evidence. N. Evidence showing that something is not the case.

neglect. V. To fail to do something; to fail to care for someone or something; to disregard or ignore. N. The state of being uncared for or ignored; failure to do something.

neglected child. N. A child whose caregivers fail to provide the required level of care for his or her physical, mental, and emotional needs.

negligence. N. Failure to use the proper care in doing something, i.e., the amount of care that an ordinarily prudent person would use under the same circumstances. ADJ. ***negligent***.

negligence, contributory. N. A plaintiff's negligence that is at least a partial proximate cause of the injury.

negligence, criminal. N. Negligence that can constitute a crime; such carelessness or disregard for the safety of others that it makes the actor criminally liable.

negligence, gross. N. Failure to use even the slightest care.

negligence, ordinary. N. Failure to use ordinary care.

negligence, willful, wanton, or reckless. N. Negligence done with complete disregard to the risks and with conscious indifference to the consequences. See also *comparative negligence*.

negligence per se. N. Conduct that is treated as negligence because it violates a statute.

negotiable. ADJ. Able to be transferred to another person; modifiable.

negotiable instrument. N. A legal document signed by its maker that promises unconditionally to pay a specified sum at a specified time to the person who presents it or to order, i.e., "pay to the order of Mr. X"; a check, money order, draft, note, certificate of deposit, or other similar document, as long as it can be transferred to another person. Also called negotiable paper. See also *commercial paper*.

negotiate. v. To discuss a matter in an effort to reach agreement, often suggesting different possibilities for consideration and acceptance or refusal; to bargain. (2) To transfer the legal ownership of a negotiable instrument. N. *negotiation*.

nepotism. N. The practice by a public official or other person with power and influence of giving choice jobs to close relatives; preferential hiring of relatives.

net. N. The total amount remaining after all expenses and deductions.

net asset value. N. The value of a share of stock in a mutual fund or corporation, calculated by subtracting total liabilities from total assets and dividing by the number of outstanding shares; book value.

net cost. N. The total cost of an item minus any financial gain from it.

net estate. N. A gross estate minus funeral expenses, claims against the estate, mortgages and other debts, and any other proper deductions that must come from the estate during settlement.

net loss. N. The situation arising when expenses are greater than income; negative income.

net operating loss. N. The loss resulting when the expenses involved in operating a business are greater than the revenues it generates.

network. N. A group of computers that are linked to one another through electronic communications technology. V. To set out to meet people with the intention of using their acquaintance to further one's business or career ambitions.

net worth. N. The total assets of a person, business, etc., minus total liabilities; also called net assets.

neutral. N. Unbiased, disinterested; not taking either side of a dispute; neither positive nor negative. N. *neutrality*.

neutrality laws. N. Laws that govern warfare as it concerns neutral nations; laws passed by Congress that govern the United States when it functions as a neutral party while other nations are at war.

new. ADJ. Novel; fresh; appearing more recently than another similar item or person.

newly discovered evidence. N. Evidence discovered after a trial is concluded and judgment rendered that could not have been discovered before trial and that can be grounds for a new trial if it probably would result differently.

new matter. N. In pleading, a new issue with new facts that has not been already alleged by a party and added by an amended or supplemental pleading.

next friend. N. A person who acts on behalf of an infant, incompetent, or other person who is not sui juris and is therefore unable to represent himself or herself adequately in the action; the next friend is not a party to the suit and acts as an officer of the court; see also *ad litem*, *guardian*.

next of kin. N. The living person or people most closely related by blood to someone; the person or people who will take a decedent's estate under the rule of descent and distribution.

nil. N. *(Latin)* Nothing; shortened form of Latin word "nihil," meaning "nothing"; used in writs and judgments to convey various negative meanings.

nisi. ADJ. *(Latin)* Unless; used to describe an order, judgment, etc., that will take effect unless some specific thing happens.

NLRB. ABBRV. National Labor Relations Board.

no fault. ADJ. Used to describe a situation in which the fault of the parties is irrelevant to the outcome, such as an insurance policy in which the insurer will pay for damage regardless of whether the insured was at fault in causing it; see also *divorce*.

nolo contendere. N. *(Latin)* "I do not want to contend," or "I am unwilling to contest it"; a plea used by a defendant in a criminal case that neither admits nor denies charges but has most of the effects of a guilty plea.

nominal. ADJ. Existing in name only, having no real presence; merely stated, not actually existing; so small as to be strictly symbolic.

nominal damages. N. A very small sum awarded as damages to a plaintiff who has suffered no real compensable injury.

nominal party. N. A plaintiff or defendant joined to an action for jurisdictional or procedural reasons, not because of any injury or liability.

nominee. N. A person who has been nominated for a position.

non. PREFIX. *(Latin)* Not; used to negate a word.

nonacceptance. N. Refusal to accept something.

nonaccess. N. Lack of opportunity for sexual intercourse, used as a defense in paternity suits.

non compos mentis. ADJ. *(Latin)* Not of sound mind; insane. See also *compos mentis*.

nonconforming use. N. A use of property that began lawfully before the creation of a zoning restriction that makes it unlawful; see also *variance*.

nonconformity. N. An aspect of some object that does not conform to the prevailing standard for objects of that kind.

noncontestability clause. N. A clause in an insurance contract that prevents the insurer from contesting a policy due to mistake or fraud after a specified period of time.

nondelivery. N. Failure by a carrier to deliver goods to the proper recipient.

nondisclosure. N. Failure to disclose information or reveal facts.

nonexempt. ADJ. Not exempt; eligible for overtime pay under the National Labor Relations Act.

nonfeasance. N. Failure to perform a duty; failure by an agent to perform some obligation he or she has agreed to do for a principal; failure of a public official to do some duty required by law. See also *malfeasance, misfeasance*.

nonperformance. N. Failure to perform some duty or obligation; failure to perform according to the terms of a contract.

nonprofit. ADJ. Conducted for purposes other than making a profit, such as charity or scientific research.

nonprofit corporation. N. A corporation that does not distribute its income to shareholders or officers as profit and that engages in a purpose such as religion, charity, education, public safety, etc.

nonrecourse. ADJ. Not personally liable; without liability.

nonrecourse debt. N. A debt for which the borrower is not personally liable and that is instead secured by the purchased property, which the creditor can repossess if the debtor defaults.

non sequitur. N. *(Latin)* It does not follow; a statement that does not logically follow the statement or argument preceding it; ABBRV. non seq.

nonstock corporation. N. A corporation that does not issue shares of stock but instead grants members ownership through a membership charter or agreement, common among mutual companies and charities.

nonsuit. N. A judgment rendered against a plaintiff who fails to proceed to trial or prove his or her case by not producing enough evidence to support it; nonsuit is not judgment on the merits and does not preclude the plaintiff's bringing the same lawsuit again.

nonsupport. N. Failure to provide financial support to someone to whom a duty of support is owed, such as the failure of a parent to support a child.

no par stock. See *par*.

normal. ADJ. Regular; typical; conforming to an established standard.

North American Free Trade Agreement. N. A free trade aggreement between the United States, Canada, and Mexico. ABBRV. *NAFTA*.

no strike clause. N. A clause in an agreement between labor and management prohibiting employees from striking and instead requiring that disputes be solved in some other way, such as binding arbitration.

NOTAM. ABBRV. Notice to airmen.

notary public. N. A person with the authority to perform a limited range of legal functions such as administering oaths, witnessing signatures, drawing up contracts or deeds, taking depositions, etc.

note. N. (1) A written document in which a borrower promises to pay back a debt to a specified recipient at a specified time. (2) A short treatise on some legal subject written by a law student for a law review.

note, demand. N. A note payable on demand.

note, installment. N. A note that is paid in several installments over a period of time.

note, mortgage. N. A note promising payment for a property that serves as security for the debt.

not guilty. N. (1) A plea given by a criminal defendant who denies committing the crime in question. (2) A verdict given by the jury in a criminal trial if it finds that the state has not proved its case against the defendant beyond a reasonable doubt.

notice. N. Notification; warning or knowledge that a fact exists or that something will occur.

notice, actual. N. Information expressly given to a person so that there is no question whether or not it has been received, or information that he or she should have had because there was sufficient evidence available.

notice, constructive. N. Information that a person is assumed to have because he or she should have discovered it through normal diligence.

notice, legal. N. Notice that the law requires to be given, such as by advertising in a newspaper; also, notice implied by law such as actual notice or constructive notice.

notice act. N. A recording act that gives priority to a bona fide purchaser who is the first to record the claim and who has no knowledge of other claims.

notice of dishonor. N. Notice that a check or other negotiable instrument has been dishonored.

notice to airmen. N. A notice filed at an airport to notify pilots of hazards in the area. ABBRV. *NOTAM*.

notice to appear. N. Notice summoning a defendant to appear in court.

notice to quit. N. Notice given by a tenant informing the landlord that the tenant intends to move out; also, notice given by a landlord informing the tenant that he or she must move out.

notify. V. To inform someone of something; to give notice. N. *notification*.

notorious. ADJ. (1) Famous; well-known, especially for some bad behavior or evil deed. (2) Open; easy to observe and not concealed.

notorious possession. N. Open and unconcealed possession of real property; see also *adverse possession*.

nov. *(Latin)* Non obstante verdicto, notwithstanding the verdict; see also *judgment*.

novation. N. The replacement of an old contract with a new one, usually substituting a new party for one of the original ones.

N.O.W. ABBRV. Negotiable order of withdrawal.

N.O.W. account. N. A kind of interest-bearing checking account.

NPT. ABBRV. Nuclear Nonproliferation Treaty.

NRA. ABBRV. National Rifle Association.

NRC. ABBRV. Nuclear Regulatory Commission.

NSF. ABBRV. Nonsufficient funds.

NSF check. N. A check written for an amount greater than the sum in the account on which it is written.

Nuclear Nonproliferation Treaty. N. An international treaty created in 1968 that requires its members not to make new nuclear weapons, not to assist other nations in making nuclear weapons, and to get rid of their own nuclear weapons, while still being allowed to develop and use nuclear fuel for power generation. ABBRV. *NPT.*

nuclear proliferation. N. The spread of nuclear weapons and related materials to nations that have not previously had nuclear weapons.

Nuclear Regulatory Commission. N. A federal agency that regulates the civilian use of nuclear materials. ABBRV. *NRC.*

nugatory. ADJ. Ineffectual or invalid; useless; of no importance.

nuisance. N. A person, thing, or activity that causes inconvenience or annoyance; anything that prevents a person from freely enjoying the use of his or her own property, endangers his or her health, or offends. See also *abate.*

nuisance per se. N. Something that is a nuisance all the time under any circumstances.

null. ADJ. Invalid; void; with no legal force; also called null and void.

nullify. V. To invalidate; to make null and void. N. *nullification*.

nullity. N. Something that is legally invalid; the state of being legally invalid.

nuptial. ADJ. Related to marriage.

nurture. V. To care for; to raise a child.

oath. N. The act of swearing that something is true; a promise to tell the truth in court or perform some act, often sworn before a witness or invoking a supreme power.

oath, under. ADJ. Describes the state of a person after swearing an oath.

oath of allegiance. N. An oath binding the swearer to some nation or leader.

oath of office. N. An oath sworn upon taking some office, promising to perform the duties of the office properly.

obiter dictum. N. *(Latin)* Something said in passing; incidental remarks or opinions made by a judge that are not essential to judgment in a case.

object. N. Purpose; goal; aim. V. To protest; to express disapproval; in court, to protest that the opposing party's action or statement is improper or illegal.

objection. N. The act of protesting an action or statement of the opposing party in order to draw the court's attention to illegality and impropriety and to preserve the issue for appeal.

objective. N. Purpose or goal. ADJ. Unbiased, not influenced by outside sources.

obligation. N. A duty; something that a person is required to do; a binding agreement that requires a person to do something; a document containing a binding agreement. V. *obligate*. ADJ. *obligatory*.

oblige. V. To make someone legally bound to do something or pay a sum of money.

obligee. N. The person who is owed the performance of some duty or the payment of money; a promisee.

obligor. N. The person bound to perform some duty or pay money; a promisor.

obloquy. N. Blame; public criticism or disgrace; reproach; public verbal abuse reproaching someone for some act.

obscene. ADJ. Morally offensive; against accepted standards of decency, especially in a sexual way; appealing to sexual interests and without serious political, literary, scientific, or artistic value. N. *obscenity*.

obscure. ADJ. Hidden; not easily discovered; hard to understand. V. To conceal; to make difficult to understand.

obsolescent. ADJ. Becoming obsolete. N. *obsolescence*.

obsolete. ADJ. No longer used; out of date; still in existence but no longer observed due to irrelevance to changed circumstances.

obstruct. V. To hinder; to get in the way of something; to block or impede. N. *obstruction*.

obstruction of justice. N. Hindering the process of justice in court or of judicial acts, such as by influencing jurors or preventing an officer of the court from performing his or her duty.

obvious. ADJ. Clear; easily seen or understood; apparent.

obvious risk. N. A risk that is easily discovered by a person of ordinary intelligence.

occupancy. N. Occupying or taking possession of a property with title to it.

occupant. N. A person who occupies a property; a person who possesses and uses property; a person who holds a particular public office.

occupation. N. (1) A job or profession. (2) The act of taking possession of a property or land; the condition of being possessed.

occupational. ADJ. Related to a particular job or profession; related to work.

occupational disease. N. A disease caused by a particular job or resulting from long-term exposure to conditions at a particular job.

occupational hazard. N. A risk that is an accepted aspect of a particular job, as a natural consequence of working conditions and actions.

Occupational Safety and Health Act. N. A federal law intended to reduce workplace injuries, illnesses, and deaths, administered by the Occupational Safety and Health Administration. ABBRV. *OSHA.*

occupy. V. (1) To reside in; to hold; to fill. (2) To conquer and inhabit a land or nation with an army.

occur. V. To happen; to exist.

occurrence. N. Something that happens; an event or incident.

odd lot. N. A unit of stock containing fewer shares than the usual one hundred or ten shares that make up units for sale.

of counsel. ADJ. Describes an attorney who assists in the preparation of a case but is not the lead attorney on it, or an attorney who is semi-retired from a firm or works at it part-time.

of course. ADV. Used to describe an action that is a person's right, which does not need justification or permission, usually in the phrase "as a matter of course."

offend. V. To commit an illegal act; to break a rule.

offender. N. One who commits an illegal act.

offense. N. An illegal act; an act that violates criminal laws; a felony or misdemeanor.

offense, criminal. N. A violation of a criminal law; a crime.

offer. V. To present something to someone to be accepted or rejected. N. An expression of willingness to do something or pay a sum of money; a promise to enter into an agreement if the promise is accepted.

offer and acceptance. N. The two necessary components of a contract; a proposal by one party that is accepted by the other.

offering. N. A quantity of stock issued for sale at a fixed price.

offer of proof. N. A presentation of evidence at trial for acceptance by the court; often done in situations where an objection to a party's line of questioning has been sustained but the court gives the party the opportunity to show privately, away from the jury, evidence showing the relevance of the question.

office. N. (1) An official position of authority, often with a government or corporation. (2) A room or building in which business is transacted or in which a professional works or maintains headquarters.

office, home. N. A room or area in a dwelling set aside as a professional workplace.

office, public. N. An official governmental position that gives a person holding it some degree of governmental powers to be used to benefit the public.

officer. N. (1) A person who holds an office. (2) A member of the armed services with authority to command. (3) A member of the police force. (4) A person entrusted with the management of a corporation.

official. N. A person who holds an office. ADJ. With the authority of a public body; done by an officer.

offshoring. N. The practice of a business having some or all of its operations performed in a foreign country by local workers, usually for cost reasons.

of record. ADJ. Officially recorded; entered onto official records.

oligarchy. N. Rule of a nation, institution, etc., by a few, i.e., by a small group of people.

oligopoly. N. A market condition in which only a few sellers control the entire trade in some product; see also *monopoly*.

ombudsman. N. An official in a government or company whose job is to hear, investigate, and remedy complaints.

omission. N. The failure to do some duty or required action; the exclusion or leaving out of something or someone; overlooking something or someone. V. *omit*.

omnibus. ADJ. Containing several components or items.

omnibus bill. N. A piece of proposed legislation that addresses several different matters, often combined in order to force the executive to accept laws that he or she does not want in order to avoid defeating the whole package.

omnibus clause. N. A clause in an automobile insurance policy extending liability coverage to people other than the named insured; also, a clause in a will that passes on property not known or mentioned at the time the will was drafted.

on demand. ADJ. When requested or on presentation, usually used to describe a negotiable instrument that is payable when presented instead of on a specified date.

one person, one vote. N. A form of allocating legislators by district so that every citizen gets equal representation, in that seats in the legislature are apportioned by population.

on its face. ADJ. Upon immediate inspection; used to describe a law that is void or unconstitutional by its very wording, usually because it does not address the issue it is intended to address.

online. ADJ. On a computer network; on the Internet.

on or about. ADV. Approximately; in the vicinity of; used to describe an act that happened around a particular time without having to specify a date or time, or something that is near a person without necessarily being physically on him or her.

on the merits. ADV. Based on the facts of a case and the rights of the parties involved.

on the person. ADV. In physical contact with the body or in the clothing being worn.

onus. N. *(Latin)* Burden; a duty or responsibility.

open. V. (1) To allow access to something. (2) To create or establish, e.g. a business, bank account, or legal case. (3) To begin a trial. ADJ. (1) Visible; frank; not hidden or secretive. (2) Allowing access; not closed.

open account. N. (1) An unsettled account; an account intended to be used for future transactions. (2) An account on which a buyer can make repeated transactions on credit.

open and notorious. ADJ. Conspicuous, public, with no attempt at concealment; see also *adverse possession*.

open court. N. A court open to the public, to which anyone conducting themselves properly may be admitted.

opening statement. N. A speech made by an attorney at the start of a trial describing the facts and issues of the case and arguments that the attorney will make.

open shop. N. A workplace that employs people without regard to whether they belong to a union; see also *closed shop*.

open source. ADJ. With regard to software, freely distributed, with source code that is freely available and modifiable, without any restrictive licenses.

operate. V. To function; to run something. N. *operation*.

operating expenses. N. The money required to run something, such as a business.

operating system. N. The software that performs the essential tasks a computer must do in order to function, such as allocating memory, controlling devices, supporting software applications, and providing access to files. ABBRV. *OS*.

operation of law. N. The automatic effects of law; used in situations when the rights or liabilities of parties are determined by application of law, and not through their own private agreements.

operative. ADJ. Most relevant, meaningful, or significant; describes the word or words that carry the most important meaning in a sentence, or that cause a contract or document to take effect.

opiate. N. A drug derived from opium; a narcotic; a substance or drug with addictive properties and other effects similar to morphine.

opinion. N. (1) A statement written by a judge explaining his or her decision in a case. (2) A statement written by an attorney for a client explaining his or her evaluation of the facts and law in a case. (3) Personal beliefs, views, or judgments on a matter.

opinion, concurring. N. An opinion written by a judge who is part of a panel of judges, agreeing with the conclusion of the majority opinion but not necessarily with the reasoning.

opinion, dissenting. N. An opinion written by one of a panel of judges disagreeing with the majority opinion.

opinion, expert. N. A statement made by an expert explaining his or her evaluation of facts from a qualified perspective.

opinion, majority. N. An opinion shared by a majority of the judges on a panel.

opinion, plurality. N. An opinion shared by less than the majority of the judges on a panel as to reasoning but that agrees with the conclusion of the majority.

oppress. V. To force someone to stay in a position of hardship; to dominate; to use one's authority to inflict harm or cruelty on someone. N. *oppression*.

option. N. The right to choose something; something that can be chosen.

option contract. N. A contract in which one party promises to keep an offer open (such as an offer to sell property) for a specified period of time, usually in return for consideration. See also *stock option*.

oral. ADJ. Verbal; stated in speech, not in writing.

oral argument. N. A verbal statement made by counsel before a court arguing in support of a position.

oral confession. N. A verbal statement confessing to having committed a crime.

oral contract. N. A contract that is made verbally, or partly verbally and partly in writing.

oral evidence. N. Evidence provided through the speech of a witness.

order. (1) A command or direction; a direction issued by a court to direct an action or determine a point of law. (2) A request or instruction to buy something or have something made. (3) The arrangement of several items or people in a sequence. V. *order*.

order instrument. N. A negotiable instrument made payable to a particular person, through language such as "pay to the order of"; also called order paper.

ordinance. N. A law, statute, or rule, usually enacted by a municipal or other local government.

ordinary. ADJ. Common; usual; normal.

ordinary and necessary expenses. N. Expenses that are normal, expected, and appropriate to the conduct of a business.

ordinary care. N. The degree of care that a person of normal prudence would exercise in a given situation.

ordinary course of business. N. The usual activities and events that occur during the usual conduct of a particular business or of commercial activity in general.

ordinary income. N. Earnings from work or business as opposed to income from investments.

organic law. N. The fundamental law of a state or country that serves as a basis for all other laws and social organization; it may be written, such as a constitution, or unwritten.

organized crime. N. Systematic, large-scale crime organized and executed by professional criminals; see also *mafia, mob, racketeering.*

original. ADJ. First; present at the beginning; created directly by a particular person, not copied.

original document rule. N. A rule that a party must produce the original of a document offered as evidence unless it is not available.

original jurisdiction. N. Jurisdiction to try and judge a case at its beginning, as opposed to on appeal.

OS. ABBRV. Operating system.

OSHA. ABBRV. Occupational Safety and Health Act.

ouster. N. Wrongfully forcing someone off his or her own property. V. *oust*.

outcome. N. A result.

outcome test. N. The principle that a diversity case should have the same outcome whether brought in federal or state court.

outline. N. A summary of the key points of a document, argument, or topic, arranged as a list; a summary of the key points of a law school class done by a law student or a commercial publisher, created as a study aid. V. *outline*.

outline group. N. A group of law students who collaborate on an outline for a class, such as by each contributing an outline of one week of class so as to compile a complete set of notes for the semester.

out-of-court. ADJ. Arranged privately, outside of court or trial, by parties to a lawsuit.

out-of-court settlement. N. An agreement reached privately by the parties to a lawsuit, settling their grievances and ending the lawsuit without intervention by the court.

out-of-pocket. ADJ. Having to do with the expenditure of cash, especially of a financial loss paid personally.

out-of-pocket expense. N. A necessary expense paid directly by a person who intends to recover the cost from someone else at a later time (such as when a tenant pays for repairs to rental property and expects reimbursement from the landlord).

out-of-pocket loss. N. In a warranty or breach of contract case, the difference between the purchase price and the actual value of an object.

outrage. N. The tort of intentional infliction of severe emotional distress; an extreme insult or violent injury.

outsourcing. N. The practice of a business hiring another company or outside individuals to perform some of its work; subcontracting. See also *independent contractor*.

outstanding. ADJ. Undone; remaining to be done or paid.

outstanding balance. N. The money still to be paid on a debt.

outstanding check. N. A check that has been written and given to its recipient but has not yet been deducted from a bank account.

overbroad. ADJ. Used to describe a statute that covers too many situations, i.e., that, while legitimately forbidding certain conduct, inadvertently also prohibits constitutionally protected activities. N. *overbreadth*. See also *void, vague.*

overdraft. N. The condition of drawing more money out of an account than it has in it, such as by writing a check for too great an amount.

overdue. ADJ. Not having been done or paid by the appointed date; delayed.

overhead. N. Operating expenses of a business aside from cost of materials or labor.

overreaching. N. Using fraud or a superior bargaining position to take advantage of someone else in a commercial transaction.

overrule. V. To reverse or annul; to overturn or void the decision of another court.

overt. ADJ. Open; visible; not concealed.

overt act. N. In criminal law, an open act done as part of a crime.

over-the-counter market. N. A securities market of dealers who buy and sell securities that are not listed in a securities exchange, done primarily over the telephone or online.

overtime. N. Time worked in addition to normal working hours.

overtime pay. N. Wages paid for overtime worked, usually at a higher rate than ordinary hourly pay.

own. V. To possess; to hold title to property.

owner. N. A person or business that has legal title to property.

ownership. N. The state of owning property, with a right to possess, use, and dispose of it.

oye. N. A word meaning "hear ye," cried by a bailiff to mark the beginning of a court session; pronounced "oh yes."

ozone layer. N. A portion of the atmosphere surrounding the Earth that contains a high concentration of ozone, a molecule that plays an important role in absorbing excess ultraviolet radiation from the sun.

P

p.a. ABBRV. (1) Professional association. (2) Per annum, meaning yearly.

pacifist. N. A person who thinks war and violence are always unjustifiable, and who refuses to participate in war or military activities. See also *conscientious objector*.

pact. N. An agreement between two or more parties.

pain and suffering. N. Physical and mental distress or injury, for which damages may be recovered in a tort action.

palimony. N. Financial support similar to alimony given to a partner in a terminated nonmarital relationship; see also *domestic partner*.

pander. V. To cater to someone's immoral lusts and desires, such as by providing pornography; to procure a prostitute for someone. N. A pimp.

panderer. N. A pimp.

panel. N. A group of people joined together for some united purpose, such as a group of judges who sit together to hear the same case, or the group of jurors summoned to court for jury duty.

paper. N. A document, including letters, contracts, account books, promissory notes, and anything else that can be written or printed on paper; a written or printed instrument.

paper money. N. Banknotes; documents printed by a government, backed by its credit, and used as currency.

paper profit or loss. N. Profit or loss that exists on the books but has not been converted into cash.

par. N. (1) A standard or norm used as a benchmark for comparison, such as the value of one nation's currency compared to another's (also called par of exchange), or the normal number of strokes used to complete a golf course. (2) The face value of a stock, bond, or negotiable instrument, as opposed to market value; also called par value.

par, above. ADJ. Selling for more than face value.

par, at. ADJ. Selling at face value, when face value and market value are equal.

par, below. ADJ. Selling for less than face value.

paralegal. N. A person with some legal training who assists an attorney in preparing cases, documents, and other legal tasks.

paramount. ADJ. Most important; of highest rank; supreme.

paramount title. N. The superior of two titles to the same property, i.e., the one that will prevail over the other.

paramour. N. A lover, usually of a married person committing adultery.

paraphernalia. N. (1) Equipment used for a particular activity. (2) *(Archaic)* A married woman's own personal property, apart from a dowry, that she could keep after the death of her husband.

parcel. N. (1) A package. (2) A quantity of something, such as a piece of land or an estate. V. To divide something into portions and distribute them to various recipients.

pardon. V. To forgive; to release a convicted criminal from liability for his or her crime; to absolve. N. An act by a governor, president, or other government official releasing a convicted criminal from punishment for a crime and reinstating his or her former level of civil liberties.

pardon, conditional. N. A pardon that becomes or remains valid as long as the pardoned person does or does not observe some specified condition.

pardon, full. N. A pardon removing all legal consequences from a conviction.

pardon, general. N. A pardon issued to a group of people who have all committed the same offense, usually political; see also *amnesty*.

parens patriae. N. *(Latin)* Parent of the country; the doctrine that it is the role of the government to look out for those who cannot take care of themselves.

parent. N. (1) A father or mother, natural or adoptive. (2) A company or organization that controls several subsidiaries, often called a parent company. ADJ. *parental*.

parental liability. N. Parents' liability for the actions of their minor children.

parental rights. N. A parent's rights in regard to his or her children, including the right to custody, discipline, control over a child's earnings and property, and to be supported by a grown child.

parish. N. (1) An administrative district of a Christian church. (2) In Louisiana, a territorial division equivalent to a county.

parity. N. (1) Equality, particularly of pay or status; equivalence of goods. (2) A method of regulating prices for farm goods by making them equivalent to prices set on a particular date. (3) One country's value in terms of another's at a particular rate of exchange. See also *par*.

parliament. N. A legislature, such as the highest legislature of the United Kingdom. ADJ. *parliamentary*.

parliamentary law. N. Rules governing procedure in a legislature; also called parliamentary procedure.

parody. N. A work such as a film, literary work, or song that imitates another work in a humorous, ironic, or satirical way.

parole. N. The release of a convict from prison before the end of his or her sentence on the condition that the former prisoner follow certain rules and commit no more crimes.

parolee. N. A person released from prison on parole.

parole officer. N. An official who supervises parolees.

parol evidence. N. Verbal or spoken evidence; spoken testimony by a witness.

parol evidence rule. N. A rule that prevents the parties to a written agreement from altering it with spoken provisions or oral agreements.

partial. ADJ. Not complete or entire; affecting only part of something.

partial loss. N. Loss of only part of something, as opposed to total loss.

participate. V. To take part in something; to do something with other people; to share. N. *participation*.

partisan. ADJ. Associated with and espousing the views of a particular political party.

partition. V. To divide into sections. N. The division of property between co-owners so that each gets an individual interest in a part of it.

partner. N. (1) A person who shares the profits and risks of some business or other enterprise with one or several other people. (2) A spouse or domestic partner. V. To join with someone else as partners.

partner, general. N. A partner who participates in all management, profits, and losses, and is personally liable for all partnership debts; also called a full partner.

partner, limited. N. A partner whose liability for partnership debts is limited to his or her share of contributed capital, and who has only a limited share of profits or losses.

partner, silent. N. A partner who shares profits and losses but does not participate in the management of the enterprise; also called a dormant partner.

partnership. N. An association between two or more people who call themselves partners and share the profits and risks of a business or some other undertaking.

partnership, general. N. A partnership in which partners share profits, losses, and management equally, regardless of the contributions to capital made by each of them.

partnership, limited. N. A partnership with at least one general partner and at least one limited partner.

party. N. (1) A person or entity involved in some transaction or matter; a person or entity on one side of a lawsuit or other dispute. (2) An organized political group that tries to make its own views the law of the land by participating in elections and working for common goals in government; also called a political party. See also *third party*.

party wall. N. A wall built on the border between two pieces of property that is shared equally by both owners.

passport. N. A document issued by a national government that identifies its bearer as a citizen of that country with permission to travel abroad and return home under the home nation's protection.

passport control. N. A security checkpoint at an entrance point into a country where officials inspect and approve the passports of those wishing to enter.

patent. N. (1) An exclusive right granted by the government to manufacture and sell an invention for a specified period of time. (2) A document granting land from a government to a person. V. To obtain a patent for an invention. ADJ. Obvious; readily apparent.

patent pending. N. A notice placed on an object informing others that its inventor has applied for a patent on it and is awaiting the government's decision.

Patent and Trademark Office. N. The federal agency that issues patents and trademarks as part of the Department of Commerce.

patent troll. N. An individual or business that acquires patents without planning to manufacture the patented items but intending to sue anyone who infringes on the patents.

paternal. ADJ. Having to do with fatherhood and fathers; showing the care expected of a father.

paternity. N. Fatherhood; the state of being a father. See also *maternity*.

paternity suit. N. A lawsuit brought to identify the father of a child and demand child support payments from him.

patient-physician privilege. N. A privilege exempting confidential communications between patients and their doctors from discovery.

patient's bill of rights. N. A statement of patients' rights adopted by many hospitals and health care providers, and made law by the federal government and several states, that covers topics such as confidentiality, consent to treatment, and dignity.

Patient Self-Determination Act. N. A federal law requiring health care facilities to inform patients of their rights under state law to create advance directives to dictate how they should be cared for if they become incapacitated; see also *living will, durable power of attorney.*

patricide. N. The killing of one's own father; a person who kills his or her father.

patrimony. N. Property inherited from one's father; property inherited from either parent or other ancestors; heritage.

patron. N. (1) A person who supports or protects someone or something, usually with financial contributions. (2) A regular customer of a business. V. *patronize.*

patronage. N. (1) The support given by a patron. (2) Regular business given by customers to a store, theater, etc.

patronage, political. N. The (generally improper) use of a political office to provide friends and relatives with government jobs or protection.

pauper. N. A destitute person; a person so poverty-stricken that he or she must be supported by the public. See also *indigent.*

pawn. V. To give an object of personal property to another person, called a pawnbroker, as security for a loan.

pay. V. To give money in exchange for goods or services, or to discharge a debt. N. Compensation; wages; payment.

payable. ADJ. Due to be paid; required to be paid.

payment. N. The amount paid for something; the act of paying for something; satisfaction of a debt or obligation.

payment in due course. N. Payment to the holder of a negotiable instrument on or after its maturity date in good faith and with no known defects in title.

payment into court. N. A party's depositing with the court money or other property while a lawsuit is in progress, after which the court will pay out the money and property according to the judgment or other settlement.

payout. N. A taxable payment, such as a dividend, drawn from a company's earnings and made by that company to its shareholders.

payroll. N. A list of all the employees in a company and the amounts they are paid; the total amount a company pays its employees.

payroll tax. N. Taxes paid on wages, salary, or income, including income tax, Social Security tax, and unemployment tax.

peaceable. ADJ. Peaceful; free from arguments, conflict, or violence.

peaceable possession. N. Continuous possession of property without any adverse claims on it.

peculate. V. For a public officer to steal public funds entrusted to him or her; to embezzle. N. *peculation*.

pecuniary. ADJ. Related to money; financial.

pecuniary bequest. N. A bequest of money.

pecuniary loss. N. A loss of money or any anticipated economic benefit, such as a child's support by a parent.

penal. ADJ. Related to punishment or penalties.

penal code. N. The codification of criminal law; criminal statutes.

penal institution. A correctional institution, such as a prison, jail, or penitentiary.

penalize. V. To impose a punishment on someone.

penalty. N. A punishment.

penalty clause. N. A clause in a contract or agreement that describes a penalty for a breach, default, or other infraction, usually not enforceable by a court.

pendente lite. ADJ. *(Latin)* Pending the lawsuit; describes matters that must be put on hold to await the outcome of a lawsuit that will determine how they are settled.

pendent jurisdiction. N. Discretionary jurisdiction by a federal court over a state law claim that arises out of the same matter that simultaneously creates a federal claim.

pending. ADJ. About to happen; begun but not yet completed; awaiting settlement.

penitentiary. N. A prison, usually for the incarceration of people convicted of felonies or serious crimes.

pen register. N. A device that records the numbers dialed on a telephone; see also *eavesdrop, wiretapping*.

pension. N. A regular payment made to a person after retirement by his or her former employer or by the government, usually from a fund to which the person contributed while working.

pension plan. N. A plan established by an employer to provide retirement benefits to employees.

per annum. ADV. *(Latin)* Yearly. ABBRV. *p.a.*

per capita. ADJ. *(Latin)* By heads; according to the number of people; counting individuals and dividing something among them equally. ADV. *per capita*.

per curiam. ADV. *(Latin)* By the court; by a court's or judge's decision.

per diem. ADJ. *(Latin)* By the day. ADV. Daily. N. A daily allowance of money.

peremptory. ADJ. Absolute; final; indisputable.

peremptory norm. N. A principle of international law that is so important and so widely accepted that no state is permitted to deviate from it, such as the prohibitions on genocide, slavery, or piracy.

perfect. ADJ. Complete; without flaw or defect; having fulfilled the requirements to make something enforceable at law. V. To make perfect; to finish; to fulfill all requirements necessary for some transaction.

perfidy. N. Treachery.

perform. N. To do some act in fulfillment of a promise; to take the required steps to meet an obligation; to accomplish something. N. *performance*.

performance bond. N. A bond given as surety by a building contractor to a customer to ensure that the contractor will complete the project, and that the customer may use to pay for completion if the contractor defaults.

peril. N. Danger; risk; the risk that is covered by an insurance policy.

periodic. ADJ. Occurring regularly at intervals.

periodic alimony. N. Alimony paid in a specific amount at intervals, such as monthly; also called permanent alimony if it lasts for the recipient spouse's lifetime.

periodic tenancy. N. A tenancy that lasts for a specified period, such as a year, and that cannot be terminated except at the end of the rental period.

perjury. N. The crime of intentionally lying under oath during a judicial proceeding, such as at trial.

permanent. ADJ. Fixed; continuing or lasting without interruption; intended to stay in the same place or the same condition indefinitely.

permanent abode. N. A fixed residence; a long-term home that the resident intends to stay in indefinitely.

permanent disability. N. A disability that impairs a person's earning capacity for the rest of his or her life.

permanent employment. N. Employment that will continue until terminated by either employee or employer.

permission. N. Being allowed to do something; authorization.

permissive. ADJ. Allowed but optional.

permissive counterclaim. N. A counterclaim that a defendant is allowed to bring regarding a matter that is completely different from the one brought by the plaintiff in the original complaint. See also *joinder, use, waste*.

permit. V. To authorize or consent to something; to allow. N. An official document authorizing someone to do something.

perpetrate. V. To commit a crime or other wrongful act. N. *perpetration*.

perpetrator. N. A person who commits a crime.

perpetual. ADJ. Never ending; continuing without interruption or end.

perpetuity. N. (1) Something that lasts forever; the condition of lasting forever. (2) A restriction on property that makes it impossible to transfer forever, or for a period beyond that allowed by law; an estate with such a restriction on it. See also *rule against perpetuities*.

perquisites. N. The fringe benefits and special rights and privileges that go with a position; also called perks.

per se. ADV. *(Latin)* In itself; intrinsically; by its very nature.

person. N. A human being; an individual, corporation, partnership, trustee, labor organization, government, or other entity with defined legal responsibilities and rights.

personal. ADJ. Related to or belonging to an individual.

personal effects. N. Movable property and chattels owned by an individual, particularly all goods owned by a person at the time of death; also called personal property or personalty.

personal holding company. N. A company with few shareholders and a large percentage of income through passive sources such as rents or royalties.

personal injury. N. Physical injury to a person's body; also refers to a branch of law specializing in torts arising out of physical injuries.

personal injury lawyer. N. A lawyer who specializes in bringing lawsuits on behalf of plaintiffs who have suffered physical injuries.

personal liability. N. Liability for a matter extending to an individual's personal funds and property.

personal representative. N. A person who handles the affairs of someone who cannot do so him- or herself, such as a child, an incapacitated person, or a deceased person; see also *executor*.

persona non grata. N. *(Latin)* A person who is not pleasing; an unwelcome, undesirable, or unwanted person.

per stirpes. ADJ. *(Latin)* By roots or by shoots, as of a tree; a form of distribution of an estate in which each recipient takes a share according to the proportion that would have fallen to his or her deceased ancestor; the opposite of per capita. E.g., Grandmother has three daughters, A, B, and C. A is still alive but B and C are dead. A has one child, B has one child, and C has four children. If Grandmother dies and leaves $300,000, under a per stirpes arrangement, A will inherit $100,000 and her child will inherit nothing; B's child will take his dead mother's share of $100,000; and C's four children will divide their mother's share of $100,000, each receiving $25,000.

persuade. V. To use arguments and reasoning to induce someone to adopt a particular opinion on a matter. N. *persuasion*.

petit. ADJ. *(French)* Small; see also *petty*.

petition. N. (1) A formal written request presented to some authority asking that something be done, often signed by a large number of people who express their support for the proposed action; a formal written request to a court asking it to take some judicial action. (2) In a court of equity, an application to the court asking for relief on some matter that functions as a complaint does in a court of law; in most jurisdictions today, the term "complaint" is used instead of petition. V. To bring a petition.

petitioner. N. (1) A person who presents a petition to some authority. (2) A person who brings a legal action by means of a petition either in a court of equity or a court of appeals.

petit jury. N. A trial jury that has the job of hearing testimony, seeing evidence, and using the information to determine issues of fact and reach a conclusion about them, such as a verdict in a criminal case. See also *grand jury*.

petty. ADJ. Small; unimportant; trivial; an English corruption of the French word "petit."

phishing. N. Using email and misleading websites to entice users to provide their credit card numbers, bank account numbers, passwords, usernames, and other confidential information in order to use that information for criminal purposes such as theft.

picket. N. A group of people carrying signs and standing or marching outside a place of business in a peaceful protest against working conditions, labor practices, union grievances, or other sources of disagreement. V. To participate in a picket.

picketing. N. The act of participating in a picket.

pierce the corporate veil. V. To impose personal liability for corporate activities on individuals associated with the corporation, doing away with the protection against personal liability that ordinarily accompanies corporate status, usually in cases in which directors or managers were using the corporation to commit fraud or other crimes for their own personal gain.

pimp. N. A person who finds clients for prostitutes in exchange for a share of their earnings. V. To work as a pimp. See also *pander*.

piracy. N. (1) The practice of attacking and robbing ships at sea; see also *hijack*. (2) The unlawful copying and distribution of copyrighted works such as software or recordings of music.

pirate. N. A person who commits acts of piracy.

place of business. N. A place where a business is run or where someone works; see also *domicile*.

place of business, principal. N. The main or most important location of a business's operations; the management headquarters or center of operations.

plagiarize. V. To copy someone else's words or ideas and pass them off as one's own. N. ***plagiarism***. See also *copyright*.

plain error. N. An obvious error made by a trial court that substantially affects a defendant's rights and warrants a reversal of the judgment and a new trial.

plain meaning. N. An interpretation of a statute arrived at by reading its words and interpreting them according to their general, common meaning, usually without considering legislative history or other evidence to determine the intent of the people who drafted it.

plaintiff. N. A person who files a complaint to start a lawsuit.

plaintiff in error. N. An appellant; one who brings an appeal; "appellant" is the term more commonly used today.

plaintiff's attorney. N. An attorney who specializes in representing plaintiffs.

plaintiff's firm. N. A law firm that specializes in bringing lawsuits on behalf of plaintiffs, usually for a contingency fee. See also *defense firm.*

plain view. N. Those things that can be immediately seen without special effort because they are sitting out in the open and are unconcealed; incriminating evidence in plain view can be taken by police without a search warrant.

plan. N. A benefits plan or health plan; a package of employee benefits.

plan year. N. The one-year period in which a given benefits package remains in place, after which members and plan components may be modified.

plat. N. A map showing the property lines, roads, and other land-marks of an area; also called a plot.

plea. N. (1) In criminal law, a defendant's response to the charges brought against him or her. (2) Formerly, at common law or equity, one of several kinds of pleading that have now been made obsolete under the Rules of Civil Procedure.

plea bargain. N. An agreement made between a criminal defendant and the prosecutor in which the defendant agrees to plead guilty to a lesser offense in exchange for a lighter punishment after conviction.

plead. V. (1) In criminal law, to answer charges brought by the pros-ecution. (2) To make or file a pleading in a lawsuit; to file a pleading in response to a plaintiff's complaint.

pleading. N. A document containing a party's side of a lawsuit, such as a plaintiff's complaint or a defendant's answer, in which the party lists the facts that support his or her side of the case and presents them to the court at the beginning of a lawsuit.

pleading, affirmative. N. An answer filed by a defendant that states the existence of facts that contradict the plaintiff's allegations, rather than simply denying those allegations.

pleading, amended. N. A pleading that either corrects or expands an earlier pleading.

pleading, code. N. Pleading done according to the requirements of a procedural code. See also *Federal Rules of Civil Procedure*.

pledge. N. (1) A promise. (2) An object given as security for a promise, contract, debt, or other obligation.

pledgee. N. A person who receives a pledge as security.

pledgor. N. A person who gives a pledge to someone else.

plenary. ADJ. Absolute; complete; full.

plenary action. N. A full trial on the merits; see also *summary*.

plenary session. N. A meeting of a legislature or other group attended by all members.

Plessy v. Ferguson. n. The 1896 U.S. Supreme Court case that held that separate but equal facilities for different races were constitutional.

plurality. N. (1) In voting for more than two candidates, the number of votes for the candidate who wins more than any other but does not receive a majority. (2) On an appellate court with a panel of judges, an opinion joined by the greatest number of judges without being a majority; i.e., on a panel of nine judges, if four judges agree on an opinion, two judges agree with the result but not the reasoning, and three dissent, the opinion with four judges is a plurality.

plutocracy. N. Government by the wealthy; a group of wealthy people who control the government.

plutocrat. N. A wealthy person who uses his or her wealth to gain political power.

pocket veto. N. A president's or governor's method of rejecting a bill submitted by the legislature toward the end of a legislative session by simply refusing to accept or reject it and letting it die through inaction, rather than rejecting it outright with a veto.

point. N. (1) An argument; a distinct proposition or issue of law; the relevance or reason of some argument. (2) In real estate, a fee of 1% of a loan amount paid to the lender when the loan is created. (3) In securities, a measure of value, often worth one dollar.

point reserved. N. A difficult legal issue set aside at trial for later consideration so that the court can proceed with other issues.

police. N. An organization maintained by a government to preserve public order, prevent crimes, and apprehend criminals. V. To maintain order; to enforce laws.

police court. N. A local or municipal court with jurisdiction over minor criminal matters.

police power. N. A government's power to preserve the peace and public order through the use of a police force and criminal laws that restrain personal freedom and property rights.

policy. N. (1) The principles that guide the actions of a government, business, or other entity or individual. (2) A contract of insurance. (3) A lottery.

policyholder. N. A person who owns an insurance policy.

political. ADJ. Related to government and public affairs.

political question. N. A question that a court will not decide because it should be decided by another branch of government, such as the legislature.

political subdivision. N. Any geographical area that is governed by a particular governmental entity, such as a county or school district.

politician. N. A person engaged in politics, particularly one elected or running for public office.

politics. N. The activities of a government and those associated with it.

poll. V. (1) To record votes or opinions from people. (2) To ask the members of a jury individually what their own decision is before the jury's verdict is recorded. N. A record of votes cast in an election; a place where votes are cast (also called polls); a list of voters.

poll tax. N. A tax paid by a person in exchange for the right to vote in elections; a tax on individuals of a particular class, such as all males over 21 years of age.

polygamy. N. Simultaneous marriage to more than one person.

polygraph. N. A lie detector; a device that monitors heart rate, breathing, and other physical aspects of a person being questioned to predict the likelihood that he or she is telling the truth, but with debatable reliability.

ponzi scheme. N. A kind of pyramid scheme in which a perpetrator promises high returns on an investment and uses money submitted by later investors to pay off earlier investors, but eventually runs out of money or disappears and the scheme collapses. See also *Securities and Exchange Commission*.

pool. N. (1) A group of people or organizations, especially those involved in the same business, who combine resources to benefit one another and to reduce competition. (2) A common fund contributed to and shared by a number of people, either in legitimate business or in gambling. V. To combine resources or funds.

pop-under ad. N. An advertisement that opens a new window under the active window when the user visits a particular website. See also *banner ad*.

pop-up ad. N. An advertisement that opens in a new window on top of the active window when a user visits a particular website.

pornography. N. Literature, photography, or other printed or visual material that depicts sex organs or sexual activity, intended to cause erotic stimulation rather than education. ADJ. *pornographic*. See also *obscene, prurient interest*.

port. N. A harbor; a place where ships can load and unload, and where customs and duties are collected; a city or town with such a harbor.

portfolio. N. The collective investments held by a person or institution.

port of departure. N. The port or airport from which a ship or aircraft begins its journey.

port of entry. N. A place where a ship, aircraft, or other vessel, and its passengers or cargo, enter a country, where customs and duties are paid and immigration procedures observed.

positive law. N. Law created by a government and human institution to run society; see also *natural law*.

positivism. N. The belief that laws exist to run society and are valid because they are enacted by humans, and ideals or worries about justice should not limit their application.

possess. V. To own; to hold without owning; to control something; to occupy physically.

possession. (1) The act of holding or controlling something; having visible control over something; physically occupying a property. (2) A belonging; something that is held or owned.

possessory action. N. A lawsuit in which the plaintiff's objective is to recover possession of real property, as opposed to recovering title to it.

possessory interest. N. The right to possess property, i.e., to occupy it or control it and to exclude others from it.

possibility. N. Something that could happen but will not necessarily happen; a contingent interest in property.

possibility of a reverter. N. A chance that an estate will return to the person who granted it if certain conditions occur.

post. N. (1) Mail; letters and packages and the system that delivers them. (2) A job; an assigned duty or position, such as that held by a soldier. (3) A military base. V. (1) To mail a letter or package. (2) To hang a sign or notice in some public place, such as a sign warning away trespassers from property. (3) To enter an amount in a bookkeeping ledger; to accept a negotiable instrument, pay it, and record the payment. (4) To furnish bail. ADV. *(Latin)* After.

post-conviction. ADJ. After conviction of a criminal offense.

post-conviction relief procedures. N. Court actions that allow a criminal defendant to challenge a conviction on constitutional grounds; ABBRV. PCR actions.

post-date. V. To enter a date on an instrument that is later than the date on which it is written.

post hoc ergo propter hoc. ADV. *(Latin)* After this, therefore because of this; the mistaken reasoning that if something happens after an event, it was necessarily caused by that event.

posthumous. ADJ. After death.

posthumous child. N. A child born after the death of his or her father.

post-mortem. ADJ. After death. N. An examination of a dead body to determine cause of death.

post-nuptial. ADJ. After marriage.

post-nuptial agreement. N. An agreement made between spouses settling their property rights if they should divorce or if one should die. See also *prenuptial agreement.*

pound. N. (1) A place for the detention of illegally parked automobiles or stray animals. (2) A unit of weight used in the United States and the United Kingdom. (3) The basic unit of currency in the United Kingdom and several other nations.

pourover. N. A provision in a will directing that estate property be placed in a previously established trust, or that property be moved from a trust to a will.

power. N. Authority; the ability or liberty to do something.

power, constitutional. N. The authority to act in particular matters granted to branches of the government by the Constitution; see also *implied powers, enumerated powers, Commerce Clause, necessary and proper clause.*

power, corporate. N. A corporation's power to act in particular matters that are necessary to its operation.

power of acceptance. N. The power held by a person who receives an offer to create a contract by accepting it.

power of appointment. N. Authority given by a donor or testator allowing a donee to choose the beneficiaries of a fund, trust, or estate; title to the transferred property passes directly from the donor or testator to the beneficiaries chosen by the donee.

power of appointment, special. N. A power of appointment that limits the possible beneficiaries to members of a specified group.

power of attorney. N. The authority to act for someone else in legal matters; a document conferring that authority to someone.

practicable. ADJ. Possible under given circumstances; feasible in actual practice.

practice. N. (1) Customary action or procedure; the established procedures of law and court proceedings. (2) The exercise of a profession or religion. V. To carry out the daily activities of a profession such as law or medicine, or of a religion; to work as a professional in a particular field.

prayer. N. A formal request in a complaint or petition in equity asking for relief for the plaintiff's grievance; also called a prayer for relief or demand for relief. V. ***pray***.

preamble. N. An introductory statement; an introductory section of a statute, constitution, etc., that explains the reason for its creation and the objects it is meant to achieve.

precarious. ADJ. Uncertain; likely to break, fall, or fail; not securely held.

precarious loan. N. A loan that must be repaid whenever the lender demands it; a loan that is likely not to be repaid.

precatory. ADJ. Expressing a request, wish, or recommendation, as when a testator expresses a wish in his or her will.

precedent. N. A previously decided case that serves as a guide for deciding subsequent cases that have similar facts or legal questions. See also *condition precedent*.

precept. N. (1) A moral rule. (2) A written order, warrant, or writ.

preempt. V. (1) To act before someone else in order to prevent him or her from doing something; to forestall someone else's action. (2) In property, to settle or cultivate land before anyone else in order to acquire a right to purchase it and exclude other settlers; to purchase something before someone else has the chance to purchase it.

preemption. N. (1) Acting before someone else; forestalling. (2) Purchasing something before someone else has the opportunity to do so. (3) A doctrine holding that federal laws take precedence over state laws in certain situations, and that states may not pass laws that are inconsistent with federal ones.

preemptive rights. N. The right of someone who already holds shares of stock in a company to purchase additional shares of a new issue before they are made available to others.

prefer. V. (1) To place before others; to treat one person better than another; to like one thing better than another. (2) To prosecute; to submit a charge, such as a criminal charge; to bring an indictment.

preference. N. (1) Favor shown to one person above others. (2) Placing one creditor in front of others; paying one creditor to the exclusion of or harm to other creditors.

preferential. ADJ. Favoring one person or group over another.

preferential debt. N. A debt that will be paid before others.

preferential shop. N. A workplace in which union members receive better treatment than nonunion employees.

preferment. N. Promotion to a position.

preferred. ADJ. Favored; receiving better treatment than other similar people or objects.

preferred creditor. N. A creditor who receives payment ahead of other creditors of the same debtor.

preferred stock. N. Stock that received dividends or distributions ahead of common stock.

prejudice. N. Bias; prejudgment not based on actual experience or evidence; injury to a party that results from preconceived notions about the facts. V. To cause prejudice; to harm. ADJ. *prejudicial*.

preliminary. ADJ. Initial; introductory; preparatory to something more important.

preliminary hearing. N. An initial hearing on a criminal charge to give the judge a chance to determine whether the prosecution has enough evidence to bring the charge to trial.

premeditate. V. To consider an act before doing it; to think out and plan a crime before committing it. N. *premeditation*.

premise. N. A logical proposition or assertion forming the basis of a subsequent assertion; in a legal document such as a contract, the introductory language that explains why the document has been created. V. To base an argument on a proposition.

premises. N. Land and the buildings on it.

premium. N. (1) A reward given for services rendered; a bonus; a sum added to wages or interest. (2) The fee paid for an insurance policy. ADJ. Superior; of better quality and usually of a higher price than ordinary goods.

prenatal. ADJ. Before birth; related to or during pregnancy.

prenuptial. ADJ. Before marriage.

prenuptial agreement. N. An agreement signed by a couple before they marry arranging for ownership of assets owned individually by each of them before marriage. See also *post-nuptial agreement*.

preponderance of the evidence. N. The usual standard of proof in civil cases, in which the evidence of one side is more likely to be true than the evidence of the opposing side; evidence that is more probable than not.

prerogative. N. A right or privilege that is exclusive to a person, office, or class.

prerogative writ. N. A writ issued by a court through its discretionary powers, not in common use under the Federal Rules of Civil Procedure.

prescribe. V. (1) To direct, guide, or recommend; to order that some action be taken. (2) To claim the right to use something based on a history of having used it for a long time; to claim an easement to land on the basis of having used the land for a period of time already.

prescription. N. (1) A recommendation or order given by some authority, such as a doctor's prescription. (2) The acquisition of an easement through continuous use of some property; such an easement is called a prescriptive easement.

pre-sentence report. N. A report on a convicted criminal including employment history, education, prior arrest and conviction history, family background, and sentencing recommendations intended to help the trial court set a suitable sentence.

presentment. N. (1) A written accusation of a crime created and signed by the members of a grand jury and presented to the court. (2) The act of presenting a negotiable instrument to the person responsible for paying it in order to receive payment.

preside. V. To hold the position of authority in a gathering or meeting; to be in charge of something; to sit in authority over a court.

president. N. (1) A person with authority over others; one who presides. (2) An elected head of a republic.

presume. V. To suppose that something is true based on available evidence; to assume or infer that something is the case.

presumption. N. The act of presuming; the use of existing facts to infer other facts that are assumed to be true until they are rebutted; an assumption that must be made by a court if certain facts are shown and that will stand until other facts are presented to rebut it.

presumption, conclusive. N. A presumption that is so strong it cannot be rebutted by contradictory evidence, which makes it effectively not a presumption, but a rule of law.

presumption, rebuttable. N. A presumption that can be overturned by contrary evidence, but that becomes conclusive if contrary evidence is not presented.

presumption of innocence. N. In criminal law, the assumption that a person is innocent until proven guilty.

presumption of legitimacy. N. The assumption that a child born to a married woman is the offspring of her legal husband.

presumptive. ADJ. Presumed, inferred, or supposed; giving reason to assume the existence of a fact.

presumptive evidence. N. Evidence that is accepted as true until rebutted by contradictory evidence.

pretermit. V. To omit, especially to omit a child or heir from a will, usually in cases where the child or heir was not born when the will was created. N. *pretermission*.

pretrial. ADJ. Before trial begins.

pretrial conference. N. A conference held by the court between the beginning of a lawsuit or criminal prosecution and the commencement of trial in which the attorneys for both sides define issues, discuss discovery, take other steps to make the trial run smoothly, and possibly settle the dispute.

pretrial intervention. N. A program under which minor criminal defendants are not convicted, but instead sent straight to probation where they are given an opportunity to correct their behavior.

prevail. V. (1) To win. (2) To be common or widespread.

prevailing party. N. The party to a lawsuit who receives judgment in his or her favor.

prevaricate. V. To speak evasively; to act in a deceitful manner. N. *prevarication*.

preventive detention. N. Confinement of a criminal defendant before trial without the option of bail in cases where the defendant would pose an immediate risk to the public if released pending trial.

price. N. The amount of money asked or paid for something; the cost of some object or service. V. To set a price.

price discrimination. N. Asking different prices from different buyers for the same item.

price fixing. N. Conspiring with other individuals or companies in the same business to set prices instead of letting them be set by market forces, usually to restrict competition.

price fixing, horizontal. N. Price fixing done by businesses selling the same items, i.e., competitors.

price fixing, vertical. N. Price fixing done between levels of production, such as between retailer and manufacturer, manufacturer and supplier, etc.

priest-penitent privilege. N. A privilege exempting confidential communications made between a priest and a confessor in the confessional from discovery.

prima facie. ADJ. *(Latin)* First face; at first sight; based on first impressions; the initial view of something, accepted as true until disproven.

prima facie case. N. An initial case; a case with sufficient proof to stand trial and withstand a motion to dismiss or for a directed verdict, which will be accepted as true until the defendant proves otherwise.

prima facie evidence. N. Evidence sufficient to establish a claim or defense until rebutted by contrary evidence.

primary. ADJ. First; principal; most important. N. A preliminary election to choose candidates for a subsequent major election.

primary evidence. N. The best and most important evidence in a case.

primary jurisdiction. N. The principle that where an administrative agency has jurisdiction over a dispute, the courts will not hear the case until the agency has heard it first.

prime. ADJ. First; most important.

prime contractor. N. A general contractor; the contractor who is ultimately responsible for an entire project and the work of subcontractors.

prime cost. N. The true price paid for something; the true cost of an item, including the material and labor used to produce it.

prime interest rate. N. The lowest interest rate for short-term unsecured loans charged by a lender to its customers with the best credit.

primogeniture. N. (1) The condition of being a firstborn child. (2) The right of succession that belongs to a firstborn child; in feudal times, the eldest son's right to inherit the entire estate of his father, leaving nothing for younger sons.

principal. ADJ. Most important; main. N. (1) The person with the highest authority in some organization; the chief, such as the principal of a school. (2) A person who directs an agent to act on his or her behalf. (3) A person who commits a crime; the person directly responsible for a crime. (4) A sum of money invested or borrowed, on which interest is paid or charged.

principle. N. A fundamental truth, especially a moral truth, that serves as a basis for action; a rule of action or procedure.

prior. ADJ. Existing or occurring before something else; preceding.

prior inconsistent statement. N. A statement made earlier outside of court by a witness that contradicts his or her statement made on the witness stand.

priority. N. Precedence; something that is ranked higher than something else; the condition of being more important than someone or something else.

prior restraint. N. A restriction placed on a kind of free expression before it has actually been used, e.g., a prohibition placed on a certain kind of publication before anyone has created such a publication.

prison. N. A jail or penitentiary; a building used to house convicted criminals.

prisoner. N. A person confined to a prison; a person confined against his or her will.

prisoner at the bar. N. A person who is being tried for a crime.

privacy. N. The state of being left alone, free from observation of and interference with personal relations.

privacy, right of. N. The right to be left alone, without unwarranted scrutiny or interference by the public or government in personal matters, without unwanted publicity, and with the right to make choices about one's own personal and family life; the right of privacy is not specifically guaranteed by the Constitution but the Supreme Court has found that various Constitutional guarantees include many aspects of privacy.

private. ADJ. The opposite of public; run by an individual or group for commercial purposes, as opposed to being run by the government; holding no public office; belonging to one particular person or group of people.

private foundation. N. A charitable or educational organization run by a private group, not by the government.

private offering. N. Offering securities for sale to private individuals but not to the public.

private practice. N. The work done by a professional such as a doctor or lawyer who works for his or her own profit and not for the benefit of the government or the public.

private sector. N. The part of the economy not controlled by the government, in which private citizens work for their own profit.

privilege. N. (1) A right, immunity, or advantage held by only one or a few people, or only by a particular group or class. (2) An exemption from duties or requirements imposed on most people; a release from an obligation or liability.

privileged communication. N. A communication that does not have to be revealed during discovery because it occurred in a special situation, such as information revealed to a doctor by a patient or from one spouse to another. See also *attorney-client privilege, patient-physician privilege, marital communications privilege, priest-penitent privilege*.

privileges and immunities. N. A phrase used in the Constitution to refer to rights and protections held by all U.S. citizens by virtue of their citizenship, such as the right to travel from state to state and to be accorded the same rights granted to citizens of those states, the right to vote in federal elections, and the right to do business in various states.

privity. N. A relationship between parties that occurs when they share an interest in or right to some property or matter, such as two people who enter a contract, or a deceased person and his or her heir, or two people who own the same piece of property one after the other.

privy. N. A person who shares privity with another; a person with an interest in an action or property. ADJ. Sharing in private information.

probable. ADJ. More likely than not. N. *probability*.

probable cause. N. Reason to believe that a particular fact is more likely true than not; when considering doing search and seizure, reasonable grounds supported by evidence to assume that the search or arrest is justified, i.e., that a crime has been committed or that the property to be seized is associated with a crime.

probate. N. A formal court procedure in which a will is proven to be valid or invalid; the entire process of settling the estate of a deceased person. V. To establish that a will is valid.

probate court. N. A court that handles wills, estates, and the appointment of guardians for orphaned children.

probation. N. A sentencing procedure in which, instead of imprisoning a person convicted of a crime, the court releases him or her to the supervision of a probation officer, with the understanding that a violation of the terms of probation will result in a prison sentence.

probationary period. N. A specified time during which an employer may assess the skills and suitability of a new hire and may choose to terminate the employee if he or she is deemed not suitable.

probative. ADJ. Proving something.

probative evidence. N. Evidence that proves what it is intended to prove.

probative value. N. The quality or level of proof offered by a particular piece of evidence.

pro bono. ADJ. *(Latin)* For the sake of good; describes work done without compensation for the public good. ADV. ***pro bono***.

procedure. N. A method of doing something; the formal steps and methods used in conducting a lawsuit. See also *civil procedure, criminal procedure, Federal Rules of Civil Procedure, Federal Rules of Criminal Procedure*.

proceeding. N. A lawsuit or legal action; a step or event that is part of a lawsuit; a hearing, inquest, investigation, or other action that takes place before a judicial officer.

proceeds. N. Money earned from some enterprise or activity.

process. N. (1) A series of actions taken to achieve some result; a normal method or procedure. (2) A summons, writ, warrant, or other document ordering someone to appear in court; a court's exercise of jurisdiction over someone.

process server. N. A person who is legally authorized to deliver process documents to a defendant, such as a sheriff. See also *service of process*.

proclaim. V. To announce or publish; to make an official or public declaration.

proclamation. N. The act of announcing something officially or publicly; an official or public announcement, especially of some governmental action or policy; a bailiff's announcement that the court is about to do something.

proctor. N. An agent or proxy; a person who manages another person's affairs.

procuration. N. Appointing an attorney or agent to act on one's behalf; acting as a proxy or agent for someone.

procurator. N. A person who acts on someone else's behalf.

procure. V. (1) To obtain something; to obtain a prostitute for someone. (2) To persuade someone to do something. N. *procurement*.

procurer. N. A person who procures; a pimp.

produce. V. (1) To make, manufacture, or create. N. *product*. (2) To present for viewing or examination; to present a witness or exhibit to the court.

products liability. N. A doctrine of tort law that holds manufacturers and sellers liable for injuries caused by defective products they introduce into the marketplace.

profession. N. (1) An occupation or job that requires extensive formal training and usually certification by some body of professionals within the field, such as with law or medicine. (2) A declaration of belief; a public declaration or announcement. V. **_profess_**.

professional. ADJ. Relating to a profession. N. A practitioner of a profession.

professional association. N. (1) A group of people in the same profession who work together in an organization similar to a corporation, also called a professional corporation. (2) A group of professionals who organize themselves to advance education, lobbying, or other interests held by all of them. ABBRV. *p.a.*

proffer. V. To offer; to offer or hold out something as proof or evidence.

profit. N. Financial gain; income greater than the costs and expenses involved in earning it. V. To earn a profit; to benefit.

pro forma. ADJ. *(Latin)* For the sake of form; as a matter of form, rather than based on facts; for politeness. (1) Describes judgments rendered to facilitate further proceedings rather than on the basis of facts. (2) Describes accounting statements showing anticipated income before it actually occurs. ADV. **_pro forma_**.

prohibit. V. To prevent; to forbid by law or rule. N. **_prohibition_**.

promise. N. A binding declaration that a person will do a certain act, which gives the person receiving the promise the right to expect performance. V. To declare or assure someone that one will definitely do some act.

promisee. N. A person who receives a promise.

promisor. N. A person who promises something.

promissory. ADJ. Implying or containing a promise.

promissory estoppel. N. A condition that arises when someone promises something to another person who relies on that promise and takes action that would hurt him or her if the promise is not kept; a court will find that such a promise is binding if there is no other way to avoid injustice to the injured party.

promissory note. N. A document in which the maker promises to pay a certain sum of money on a specified date.

promote. V. (1) To encourage or support. (2) To raise someone to a higher position or rank. (3) To form a corporation and raise capital for it. N. *promotion*.

promoter. N. A person who founds a corporation.

promulgate. V. (1) To make widely known; to publish. (2) To put a statute into effect; to announce a statute or rule officially. N. *promulgation*.

proof. N. The use of evidence or argument to establish a fact; evidence offered at trial to show the truth of some proposition.

proper. ADJ. Correct; appropriate; suitable.

proper care. N. The degree of care an ordinary person of ordinary prudence would use in a given situation.

proper lookout. N. The degree of attention, care, and prudence an ordinary person of ordinary prudence driving a car would use while driving under similar conditions.

proper party. N. A party with an interest in a lawsuit who could be joined and whose presence would help the just settlement of the matter, but without whom the lawsuit could still continue.

property. N. That which is or can be owned, possessed, used, and disposed of; those things owned by someone; possessions, land, buildings, and all rights and interests that can be owned.

property, common. N. Property shared by two or more owners, such as tenants in common or husband and wife; property owned by all citizens and held in trust by the government.

property, intangible. N. Property with no physical existence, such as a copyright.

property, movable. N. Objects that can be moved; chattels.

property, personal. N. All property other than real property that is owned by a person.

property, private. N. Property held by a private citizen or entity, not available for public or governmental use.

property, public. N. Property owned by the community or citizenry or by a government.

property, real. N. Land, buildings, and other immovable objects fixed to the ground.

property settlement. N. The disposition of marital property between spouses after a divorce.

property tax. N. A tax levied by the government on the value of property owned by taxpayers.

proportional representation. N. System of election that distributes seats in proportion to the number of votes cast for particular candidates or parties.

propose. V. To suggest or offer an idea for consideration. N. *proposal*.

proprietary. ADJ. Related to ownership; acting like an owner; owned by a particular person or company; sold under a trade name. N. An owner or proprietor.

proprietary function. N. A function or duty that a municipal government performs on behalf of its citizens.

proprietary information. N. Trade secret information in which a person has an ownership interest.

proprietary name. N. A trade name or trademark; a registered name of a product that may not be used without the owner's permission.

proprietary rights. N. Rights over property that an owner has by virtue of ownership.

proprietor. N. A person who owns a business; a person with legal rights or title to a business.

proprietorship. N. A business owned by one person, usually not incorporated; synonymous with *sole proprietorship*.

pro rata. ADJ. *(Latin)* According to the rate; proportional or proportionately. ADV. *pro rata*.

prorate. V. To distribute proportionately.

prorogue. V. To discontinue or suspend a session, as of a legislature, without dissolving it; to end a legislative session; to postpone.

proscribe. V. To forbid an action; to denounce, outlaw, or condemn a person. N. *proscription*.

pro se. ADV. *(Latin)* For oneself; appearing on one's own behalf; describes a person who represents himself or herself in a lawsuit.

prosecute. V. (1) To begin legal proceedings against someone, especially by the state against an accused criminal. (2) To continue to carry out some action, intending to complete it.

prosecution. N. The act of prosecuting; the party prosecuting a case; a criminal action.

prosecutor. N. An attorney who prosecutes criminal cases on behalf of the state.

prospective. ADJ. Future; expected to happen in the future.

prospective law. N. A law scheduled to be enacted at some future date and that will apply only to cases arising after it is enacted.

prospectus. N. A document issued by a corporation disclosing its financial information to current and prospective investors.

prostitute. N. A person who engages in sex acts for money.

prostitution. N. The practice of selling sex for money. See also *pander, pimp*.

protect. V. To keep someone or something safe; to keep intact; to preserve something that exists. N. *protection*. ADJ. *protective*.

protectionism. N. The policy of limiting trade with foreign nations in an attempt to protect domestic producers.

protective custody. N. The confinement of a person to protect him or her from harm, either self-inflicted or inflicted by others.

protective order. N. An order issued by a court to protect a party from the abusive discovery, service of process, or other aspect of the legal process.

protective tariff. N. A duty or tariff on imported goods intended to discourage imports and protect domestically manufactured goods.

pro tem. ABBRV. Pro tempore.

pro tempore. ADJ. *(Latin)* For the time being; temporary or provisional; used to describe someone holding an office temporarily. ADV. *pro tempore*. ABBRV. *pro tem*.

protest. N. (1) A formal statement objecting to something; a statement of disapproval or dissent, often made to avoid implying consent by silence. (2) A written declaration witnessed by a notary that a bill or note has been presented for payment and refused. V. *protest*.

protocol. N. (1) Proper procedure, behavior, and etiquette at a diplomatic occasion or government function; the procedural rules for an organization, government, or situation. (2) A draft of a treaty or other diplomatic document; the minutes to a diplomatic meeting, signed by participants. (3) An addition to a treaty or international convention.

prove. V. To establish the truth of something by using evidence and arguments. See also *proof*.

provide. V. To stipulate a condition in a legal document.

provision. N. A requirement or condition stated in a legal document.

provisional. ADJ. Temporary; arranged as a temporary measure to keep affairs in order until a permanent solution can be arranged.

provisional government. N. A temporary government created to keep order until a permanent government can be installed.

provisional remedy. N. A temporary remedy given to a plaintiff to meet a present need while a lawsuit is in progress.

proviso. N. A condition or stipulation added to an agreement or contract.

provoke. V. To cause someone to act, usually by deliberately annoying or irritating him or her. N. *provocation*.

proximate. ADJ. Closest in relationship, time, physical distance, or causal connection; immediate; direct. See also *cause*.

proxy. N. A substitute, deputy, or agent; a person authorized to act on behalf of someone else, especially someone allowed to vote for stockholders in a corporate election.

prudent. ADJ. Cautious; careful; showing concern about the future. N. *prudence*.

prudent man rule. N. A rule guiding investment by trustees in some states, limiting a trustee's investments to securities that a prudent person of reasonable intelligence and discretion would choose to provide a decent income and preserve capital.

prurient. ADJ. Showing excessive fascination with nudity, sexual matters, or excrement.

prurient interest. N. An excessive interest in sex, nudity, wanton behavior, lasciviousness, etc.

psychoactive. ADJ. Altering brain chemistry to affect mood, perception, and behavior. Synonymous with *psychotropic*.

psychotropic. ADJ. See *psychoactive*.

public. ADJ. (1) Concerning all people or an entire community. (2) Shared; common to or belonging to all the members of a community. (3) Done or provided by the government; involved in the government. (4) Open; unconcealed. N. The citizenry; the community; all people.

publication. N. Making something public; preparing and issuing a book, article, or other document for sale to the public. V. *publish*.

public defender. N. An attorney employed by the government to represent criminal defendants who cannot afford to pay for a lawyer.

public domain. N. The body of knowledge and creative works, including works of film, music, literature, and inventions, whose copyrights are not owned by anyone and are thus considered available for free use by anyone.

public figure. N. A person who is famous or well-known in a community or in society in general, such as a famous athlete, actor, or politician.

public good. N. The well-being of the entire community.

public interest. N. An interest or concern important to an entire community or all of society.

public office. N. A position that exists to do some job necessary to and on behalf of the government, held by a public official who is elected by the people and exercises some sovereign powers of the government.

public policy. N. The principles that guide a government in its administration, in an effort to maintain the well-being and order of the state and its citizens; also, the principle that a contract or transaction that harms the public good is illegal.

public property. N. Property owned by the citizenry or the government as opposed to a private individual.

public purpose. N. The intention or objective of benefiting or serving the public; used to describe government actions done to benefit the community directly; also called governmental purpose.

public record. N. Documents filed in government offices that are open to the public for examination, such as records of real estate transactions.

public sector. N. The part of the economy controlled by the government, not by private individuals working for profit. See also *private sector*.

public service. N. Work done by a corporation that serves the needs of the public, such as transportation or utilities.

public service corporation. N. A privately owned corporation that provides a public service, usually with a franchise from the state.

public use. N. Benefit to the entire community brought about through the use of property condemned by the government through eminent domain.

public utility. N. A company that supplies a service, such as electricity, water, or gas, that is so essential to the public that the government will allow it to use public property and to function as a monopoly in exchange for government regulation of price and the requirement that it serve all customers without discrimination.

publish. V. (1) To prepare a book or document and issue it for sale to the public. (2) To make information widely known, such as by advertising in a newspaper. (3) To inform witnesses that one is signing a document as one's will. N. *publication*.

puff. V. To exaggerate the quality of goods in advertising or in describing them to prospective buyers, intending to make them look good and improve the chances of someone purchasing them but not actually misleading the customer because the puffing is done as an expression of opinion, not a statement of fact.

punish. V. To inflict a penalty on someone as retribution for a crime or misdeed. N. *punishment*.

punitive. ADJ. Intended as punishment; related to punishment.

purchase. V. To buy; to acquire something by exchanging money or other valuable consideration for it. N. *purchase*.

purchaser. N. A person who buys something.

purchaser for value. N. A person who gives valuable consideration in exchange for the item purchased.

purloin. V. To steal.

purposely. ADV. Intentionally; done with conscious intent and awareness of likely consequences.

pursue. V. To chase; to try to accomplish something; to engage in some activity. N. *pursuit*.

pursuit of happiness. N. An inalienable right listed in the Declaration of Independence; includes freedom to pursue an occupation of one's choice, the right to have a family, freedom from discrimination or oppression, freedom of contract, and other personal freedoms necessary to create a life of one's own choosing and to one's own satisfaction.

purview. N. Within the scope of something, such as a statute; the enacting portion of a statute.

putative. ADJ. Reputed; generally assumed to be; supposed.

putative father. N. A man who is assumed to be the father of a child born out of wedlock.

putative spouse. N. A person who believes he or she is legally married to someone although the marriage is actually invalid.

pyramiding. N. The use of paper profits from existing investments to buy more investments.

pyramid scheme. N. A sales scheme, often illegal, in which a buyer of goods is promised a commission for every additional buyer he or she finds and recruits to be a seller, and in which the people at the top of the pyramid collect payments from all the bottom tiers but the people at the bottom usually lose money. See also *Securities and Exchange Commission*.

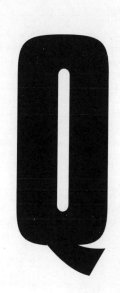

qualified expenses. N. Expenses that meet certain criteria, such as specific medical expenses.

qualify. V. (1) To be eligible for or entitled to something by meeting a required condition. (2) To meet the criteria for becoming a member of a profession or to hold an office. (3) To restrict the meaning of something; to add reservations to a statement. N. *qualification*. ADJ. *qualified*.

quality. N. (1) The standard of excellence of an item as compared to other similar items; the comparative rank of a person or thing; excellence. (2) A characteristic; a unique attribute that can be used to distinguish one thing or person from another.

quantum meruit. N. *(Latin)* As much as one deserves; used to describe a reasonable sum to pay to a person for some service if the price is not specified in a contract; used to prevent the unjust enrichment of someone who has received services under circumstances that should have notified him or her that the plaintiff providing the service expected to be paid.

quarantine. N. A period of time, condition, or place of isolation for someone who has been exposed to an infectious disease, intended to prevent the disease from spreading into the community. V. *quarantine*.

quarterly. ADJ. Four times a year. ADV. *quarterly*.

quash. V. To reject, suppress, or end; to make legally invalid.

quasi. ADJ. *(Latin)* Almost, as if; apparently but not actually; seemingly.

quasi contract. N. An obligation similar to a contract imposed by the law when two parties have made no promises to one another but when one party has benefited from services provided by another in such a way that the benefited party would be unjustly enriched if the court did not find the existence of an obligation.

quasi in rem jurisdiction. N. Jurisdiction based on a defendant's interest in property within the court's jurisdiction, even when the defendant does not actually live there.

quasi judicial. N. Describes the actions and powers of administrative officers and agencies that can perform some judicial tasks, although they are not in fact judges or courts.

query. N. A question. V. To ask a question.

question. N. (1) A sentence worded in such a way as to search for and discover information; an interrogatory statement to a witness asking him or her for information. (2) A point that is not settled and is open to debate; a doubt about some matter. V. To ask someone for information; to interrogate. See also *hypothetical; matter of fact, matter of law.*

quick. ADJ. Alive.

quickening. N. The point at which a pregnant woman feels the fetus move inside her womb.

quid pro quo. N. *(Latin)* Something for something; giving one valuable thing in exchange for something else.

quiet enjoyment. N. Undisturbed use of land or buildings that one is leasing.

quiet title. V. To determine title to land in court by bringing all interested parties into court and allowing them to attempt to establish their claims; this court proceeding is called an action to quiet title.

quit. V. (1) To leave a place; to give up possession of property. (2) To stop some activity; to resign from a job. ADJ. Rid of or free from something.

qui tam. ABBRV. *(Latin)* Who also. Qui tam pro domino rege quam pro si ipso in hac parte sequitur; someone who sues in this case on behalf of the ruling king as much as if on his own behalf; used to name a legal action brought by an individual plaintiff on behalf of the state or government as well as on the plaintiff's own behalf, such as a case brought by a whistleblower.

quitclaim. N. The act of giving up a claim on someone else or relinquishing a title to something. V. *quitclaim*.

quitclaim deed. N. A deed in which a person transfers whatever title he or she has to property, without guaranteeing that he or she has any title at all.

quorum. N. The minimum number of members or delegates that must be present at a meeting of a body to validate any decisions made or business transacted at that meeting.

quota. N. A goal; a fixed number of objects or people that are allowed or desired someplace; a proportional share of something.

quote. V. (1) To copy or read words verbatim from a source, such as a statute or document. (2) To state a price for something or the cost of doing a job; to state an official price for the sale of securities. N. *quotation*.

q.v. ABBRV. *(Latin)* Quod vide; which see; used to direct a reader to another part of a document for more information about a topic.

race. N. (1) An ethnic group. (2) An election.

race act. N. A recording act that allows the first person to record a deed to take precedence over others who record deeds to the same property subsequently, even if the first person to record knows of other claims to the land.

race notice act. N. A recording act that allows the first person to record a deed to take precedence over those who record deeds to the same property subsequently, unless the first person to record knows of other unrecorded claims to the land.

racial. ADJ. Related to ethnicity or race; because of race.

racial profiling. N. The use by law enforcement officers of racial quotas instead of actual grounds for suspicion in their selection of people to stop for questioning.

racism. N. Prejudice against members of a particular ethnic group or race.

Racketeer Influenced and Corrupt Organizations Act. N. A federal law designed to fight organized crime. ABBRV. *RICO*.

racketeering. N. Engaging in a conspiracy to commit business fraud, extortion, or coercion; using threats to extort money, goods, or services from business owners. See also *mafia, organized crime, Racketeer Influenced and Corrupt Organizations Act*.

radar. N. A device that uses electromagnetic waves to track the position, speed, and direction of motion of a vehicle, commonly used by police officers to detect people driving automobiles faster than the legal speed limit.

radical. ADJ. Politically extreme, most often extremely liberal; supporting extreme change or complete reform of a system of government. N. *radical*. See also *revolution*.

raise. V. (1) To increase; to make higher; to increase the face amount on a check, usually by forgery. (2) To suggest; to bring up a topic for consideration; to introduce an issue to the court, as through pleadings. (3) To collect money, as by asking for donations; to gather taxes. (4) To care for a child until adulthood. N. An increase in salary or compensation.

ransom. N. A sum of money or other valuable item demanded for the release of a prisoner, especially a kidnapped person. V. *ransom*.

rape. N. The crime of having sexual intercourse with someone without his or her consent and against his or her will; synonymous with *sexual assault*. V. *rape*.

rape, statutory. N. The crime of having sexual intercourse with a person below a statutorily prescribed age of consent, regardless of whether the victim consented and how old the victim claimed to be.

ratable. ADJ. Able to be estimated; proportional; able to be measured according to some system of proportions.

ratable estate. N. An estate with a value that can be appraised, usually for taxes.

rate. N. (1) A measure or value relative to some other measure or value; a proportion. (2) A price; a fee; a charge per unit of service or goods. V. To measure or assess according to a standard.

rate, exchange. N. The price of one nation's currency relative to another's.

rate, interest. N. The percentage of interest that a lender charges as a fee for lending money.

rate, tax. N. Amount of tax to be paid determined by a percentage of income or price.

rate of return. N. The percentage of profit made on an investment.

ratify. V. To approve, affirm, or confirm something, such as a law or contract; to make something valid. N. *ratification*.

rational basis test. N. A test applied by a court to determine whether a law challenged on constitutional grounds has a rational basis for existence, i.e., that it is intended to and does accomplish some legitimate governmental objective, that it is reasonable and not arbitrary, and that it treats all similar people the same way.

ravish. V. To rape; to have sexual intercourse by force and against the victim's will. N. *ravishment*.

reactionary. ADJ. Extremely conservative; opposed to social and political reform; not liberal. N. *reactionary*.

real estate. N. Land and the buildings attached to it; see also *property, real*.

real estate investment trust. N. An investment company that invests in real estate, distributes income to shareholders, and is given special income tax treatment. ABBRV. *REIT*.

real evidence. N. Evidence consisting of actual things that can be seen and inspected by the jury at trial; see also *demonstrative evidence*.

realize. V. To make money from something; to receive profits from investments. N. *realization*.

realized gain or loss. N. Actual and identifiable gain or loss received by selling property or an investment. See also *recognize*.

real party in interest. N. A person with the legal right to enforce a claim and to benefit from a lawsuit if successful.

real property. See *property, real*.

realty. N. Real estate; real property.

reapportion. V. To change the way something is distributed; to change the boundaries of legislative districts or to change the number of representatives per district in order to keep representation proportional to population. N. *reapportionment*. See also *gerrymander*.

reargument. N. Presentation to the court of more oral arguments on an issue it has already heard, in cases where it seems that an important point has been overlooked or where there might be some confusion about facts.

reason. N. (1) A cause, motive, or explanation for something. (2) Common sense; mental ability to think, distinguish between right and wrong, and to discern and interpret facts. V. To think about facts and form a judgment based on them; to attempt to persuade someone to think a certain way through the use of evidence and logic.

reasonable. ADJ. Appropriate; based on common sense and good judgment; fair and just.

reasonable belief. N. A belief based on facts, circumstances, and information trustworthy enough to make a person of ordinary intelligence and caution believe something is the case, commonly used when deciding to arrest someone or conduct a search and seizure without a warrant; see also *probable cause*.

reasonable care. N. The care that a person of ordinary prudence and competence would use in a similar situation. See also *care, ordinary*.

reasonable doubt. N. Enough uncertainty that a person has committed a crime, based on evidence or lack thereof, that a person of ordinary prudence and logical ability would hesitate to find him or her guilty.

reasonable person. N. A hypothetical person with ordinary intelligence, prudence, caution, and good judgment who is interested in protecting his or her own interests and the safety and well-being of others, used as a benchmark for measuring the behavior of a defendant in a negligence case; also called a reasonable man or reasonable woman in cases where gender is a factor.

reasonable time. N. A fair and appropriate amount of time to do something under given circumstances.

rebut. V. To respond to an argument or claim with contrary arguments and evidence; to refute.

rebuttable presumption. N. A presumption that can be refuted with evidence; an assumption that is held to be true until refuted by evidence.

rebuttal. N. The opportunity given to a defending party to respond to and refute the arguments presented by the party presenting a case in chief, or to the party who initiates a closing argument after the other party has responded to that argument; an oral argument responding to and refuting an initial case.

rebuttal evidence. N. Evidence offered to refute or combat claims made and evidence presented by an opposing party.

recall. V. (1) To revoke; to reverse or cancel a judgment. (2) To remove an elected official from office before the end of his or her term. (3) To order an official, particularly a diplomatic official, to come back home and often to relinquish his or her office. (4) To notify consumers of a manufacturing defect in a product and allow them to return the product for repair or replacement. N. *recall*.

recapitalize. V. To reorganize the capital structure of a corporation; to rearrange the stocks, bonds, and other securities of a corporation, especially to acquire more capital and reduce debt. N. *recapitalization*.

recapture. V. (1) To collect tax that was previously claimed by a taxpayer as a deduction or credit. (2) To take back something that has been captured by an enemy. N. *recapture*.

receivable. ADJ. Due; ready to be collected. N. An amount that is owed to a business; an account that records amounts due.

receiver. N. A person or business appointed by a court to manage property owned by an insolvent person or business that is the subject of a lawsuit, to hold the property and preserve it for the benefit of those who will ultimately receive it.

receivership. N. The state of an insolvent business or person whose property has been put under the care of a receiver for management, preservation, and distribution at the end of a lawsuit; the equitable proceeding in which a receiver is appointed.

receiving stolen property. N. The crime of receiving and accepting property or goods known to be stolen; see also *fence*.

recess. N. A break in a court or legislative session in which official proceedings are suspended for a short time.

recidivism. N. The practice of committing crimes regularly.

recidivist. N. A repeat offender; a person who habitually and regularly commits crimes. ADJ. *recidivist*.

reciprocal. ADJ. Mutual; affecting both parties equally; done in return for something.

reciprocal contract. N. A bilateral contract; a contract in which each party does something for the other.

reciprocal law. N. A law that extends rights and privileges to citizens of another state in exchange for the other state extending its rights and privileges to the first state.

reciprocity. N. An agreement or relationship between states, countries, or people, in which the rights and privileges of one are observed in the other; e.g., an attorney who is a member of a bar in one state is allowed to practice law in states that have reciprocity with the first state.

reck. V. *(Archaic)* To pay attention to something.

reckless. ADJ. Without regard to the consequence of one's actions; careless; indifferent. N. *recklessness*.

reckless disregard. N. Wanton or careless inattention to the safety of others or to consequences while conscious of risks, but without intent to cause harm.

reckless driving. N. Driving a vehicle without attention to risks, consequences, or the safety of others.

recognizance. N. A promise or obligation to do an act required by law, such as to appear in court on a particular date to answer criminal charges.

recognize. V. (1) To include money earned in taxable income. (2) To acknowledge; to confirm. N. *recognition*. See also *realize*.

recollect. V. To remember; to recall to mind. N. *recollection*.

reconcile. V. To settle a disagreement; to restore friendly relations between people, states, or nations; to correct discrepancies in a document or account. N. *reconciliation*.

record. N. An official written report about some event or transaction; written documents, audio and video tapes, and other documentary information. V. To write an account of some event or transaction to serve as an official version of what happened.

record date. N. A date by which a shareholder must be registered with a corporation in order to receive dividends and vote in elections.

recording act. N. A state statute that regulates the recording of real estate documents such as deeds, mortgages, and leases, with particular attention to those cases in which more than one person claims the same property.

Recording Industry Association of America. N. A trade organization that lobbies on behalf of recorded music producers, particularly in the area of copyright and file sharing. ABBRV. *RIAA*.

record notice. N. The public acknowledgement of a person's claim to property that occurs when the owner publicly records an instrument of conveyance, such as a deed.

record on appeal. N. The documents that constitute the history of a lawsuit, including pleadings, evidence, motions, briefs, and other papers filed with the court.

record owner. N. The person who is registered as the official owner of company stock. See also *public record*.

recoup. V. To recover; to reclaim something that had been lost; for a defendant to have a plaintiff's award for damages reduced through some claim the defendant has on the plaintiff. N. *recoupment*.

recourse. N. Assistance in difficulty; a source of help; a right to demand compensation.

recourse loan. N. A loan guaranteed by a guarantor or other endorser who agrees to pay the lender if the borrower defaults.

recover. V. (1) To return to a normal condition, as of a person's health or the economy. (2) To regain control or possession of something. (3) To receive compensation as a result of a lawsuit.

recovery. N. (1) A return to normal condition. (2) The act of recovering something; the restoration of a right or possession. (3) An amount awarded to the prevailing party in a lawsuit.

recrimination. N. An accusation made by an accused person against his or her accuser, especially in a divorce case.

rectify. V. To correct; to make something right. N. *rectification*.

recuse. V. For a judge to withdraw from hearing a lawsuit because of self-interest, bias, or other inability to render a fair and impartial decision; to object to a judge or jury on the grounds that he or she will not be impartial. N. *recusal*.

Red Cross. N. A group of humanitarian organizations in several countries that work to help people in need, such as disaster victims.

redeem. V. To buy something back; to exchange a coupon or negotiable instrument for money; to clear a debt, such as a mortgage; for a corporation to buy back its own stock. N. *redemption.*

redemption. N. The act of redeeming; regaining possession of something by buying it back. V. *redeem.*

red herring. N. (1) A misleading clue; a point in a case that might seem important but that is in fact irrelevant to the main issue. (2) In securities, a preliminary prospectus about a future stock issue not yet approved by the Securities and Exchange Commission, so-called because it is bordered in red to alert investors that it is not yet approved.

redline. V. To refuse to give someone a mortgage loan based on the neighborhood in which the prospective borrower lives; to refuse to insure a dwelling based on its neighborhood. N. *redlining.*

redress. N. Remedy; compensation for an injury. V. *redress.*

red tape. N. Excessive bureaucracy; the excessive requirements, paperwork, and technicalities that are part of doing business with a bureaucracy.

reductio ad absurdum. N. *(Latin)* Reduction to the point of absurdity; a method of arguing against a proposition by showing that its ultimate conclusion is absurd.

redundancy. N. The inclusion of words or arguments that could be omitted without harming the ultimate meaning; the inclusion of unnecessary material in a document or pleading.

redundant. ADJ. Unnecessary; superfluous.

re-entry. N. The act of resuming possession of property that one possessed formerly.

refer. V. (1) To direct attention or allude to something. (2) To send a matter to some other body; to send a case to a referee for investigation; to submit a contract to arbitration. N. *reference.*

referee. N. An officer appointed by a court to hear testimony from the parties to a case and report his or her findings to the court.

reference. N. (1) A citation; a mention of the source of information; a book or other document used as a source of information. (2) A person who provides information about another person, usually to a prospective employer; a letter from a person providing information about another person. (3) The act of referring a matter to another body. V. *refer.*

referendum. N. A state or local election in which the voters vote on an item of legislation or an amendment.

refinance. V. To replace an existing loan with a new one, usually at a lower interest rate; in securities, to issue new bonds to raise money for the payment of bonds about to mature.

reform. V. To correct; to change something to make it better; to change oneself or another person for the better; to correct a written instrument under court order.

reformation. N. A court-ordered rewriting of a contract or other instrument in cases where the instrument does not say what the parties intended it to say.

reformatory. N. An institution where juvenile criminals are sent instead of prison, with an emphasis on education and improved behavior; also called a reform school.

refugee. N. An individual who has been forced to flee his or her home due to war, fear of persecution, or natural disaster. See also *asylum*.

refund. N. A return of money paid to some person or institution, such as to a dissatisfied customer or to a taxpayer who has paid too much in taxes. V. (1) To return money already paid, such as to a customer or taxpayer. (2) To refinance; to fund a debt again; to sell new bonds to pay off a loan.

refuse. N. Rejected things; things that have been thrown away, such as garbage and trash. V. To decline to do something. N. *refusal*.

register. V. To enroll; to enter something in an official list or record. N. *registration*. N. (1) An official list; a compilation of public records. (2) An officer who keeps public records.

registered. ADJ. Recorded in some official list.

registered bond. N. A bond recorded in its purchaser's name on the books of its issuer, redeemable only by the purchaser.

registered mail. N. Insured first-class mail that is recorded when first mailed and at stops along the way to its destination as a safeguard against loss or damage.

registered representative. N. A person who has met certain qualifications and is allowed by the Securities and Exchange Commission to sell securities to the general public.

registered voter. N. A person whose name is listed on the rolls of voters for a particular state or county.

register of deeds. N. An officer responsible for recording property transactions in the public records.

register of wills. N. An officer who records wills and does other functions for the probate court.

registrar. N. A person who is responsible for a list of records, such as the officer who enrolls students at a university; a bank or trust company that keeps records of a corporation's securities transactions.

registration. N. (1) Enrollment; entry on an official list. (2) A company's submission of its financial status to the Securities and Exchange Commission in order to be allowed to sell securities. V. *register.*

registration statement. N. A document that companies selling securities must submit to the Securities and Exchange Commission, including information on the company's finances, the nature of the business, the purpose of the securities offering, and the identities of the managers and major stockholders.

registry. N. A book or record in which information is recorded.

regular. ADJ. Ordinary, usual, or common; conforming to laws or requirements.

regular course of business. N. The habitual and ordinary acts that a person does in the course of work, or that a company does as an inherent and regular part of the business in which it is engaged; see also *ordinary course of business.*

regulate. V. To control by rules.

regulation. N. A rule created and enforced by an authority; a rule created by a government agency to carry out the requirements of a law; the act of regulating. ADJ. *regulatory.*

rehabilitate. V. To restore a person or business to a normal level of health, freedom, reputation, dignity, finances, or other capacity; to improve the reliability of a witness whose credibility has been impeached by opposing counsel; to help a criminal improve his or her situation so as to abandon crime in the future. N. *rehabilitation*.

rehabilitative alimony. N. Alimony intended to help a divorced spouse acquire the skills needed to support himself or herself.

rehearing. N. A second hearing of a matter that the court has already considered; a retrial or reconsideration by the court in which a matter was originally heard.

reinstate. V. To restore to former status or position; to restore insurance benefits under a policy that had lapsed or been canceled; to put a lawsuit that has been dismissed back into the court process.

reinsure. V. For an insurer to enter into a contract with another insurer to share a risk already assumed by the first insurer. N. *reinsurance*.

REIT. ABBRV. Real estate investment trust.

rejoinder. N. A reply or response; an answer made by a defendant to a plaintiff's rebuttal.

relate. V. (1) To be connected, as by blood, marriage, or causation. (2) To recount; to narrate.

related. ADJ. To be connected to someone or something; belonging to the same type or family.

relation. N. (1) A person related to another by blood or marriage; a relative. (2) A connection or interaction between two people. (3) A narration of facts or events.

relation back. N. A principle in which some action is held to have occurred earlier than it did in fact occur; e.g., an amended complaint is still held to have been filed at the time of the original complaint for purposes of the statute of limitations.

relative. N. A kinsman or kinswoman; a person related to another by blood or marriage. ADJ. In relation or comparison to someone or something else.

release. V. To set free; to remove restrictions from someone or something. N. (1) The act of setting someone or something free. (2) Giving up a claim, right, debt, or interest; a document that gives up a claim, right, debt, or interest.

release on own recognizance. V. To release a defendant in a criminal case without bail, with only a promise from the defendant to return to stand trial.

relevant. ADJ. Closely connected or logically related to the matter at hand. N. *relevance*, *relevancy*.

relevant evidence. N. Evidence that is logically connected to the fact it is intended to establish.

reliance. N. Trust or confidence that someone will do something or that something will happen; a belief that something will happen that causes the believer to do something he or she would not have done otherwise. V. *rely*.

relief. N. (1) Assistance, especially money or food given to those in need; an act or benefit that alleviates some hardship or distress. (2) A replacement for someone who has been on duty. V. *relieve*.

remainder. N. Something that is left over; a part of an estate in land left over after the rest of the estate has been settled; a future interest in an estate.

remainderman. N. A person entitled to a future interest in an estate in land; a person who will take the remainder of an estate after all testamentary bequests are settled.

remand. V. (1) For an appellate court to send a case back to a lower court for reconsideration. (2) To place someone in custody, such as a defendant, while a trial is adjourned. N. *remand*.

remedial. ADJ. Intended to cure or to act as a remedy.

remedy. N. A means of compensating someone for an injury or enforcing a right.

remit. V. (1) To refer a matter to some authority for decision; to send a case back to a lower court. (2) To send money. (3) To cancel a debt; to refrain from punishing someone for a misdeed; to forgive. N. *remission*.

remitter. N. The process of restoring good title to property to a person who formerly had good title but currently does not.

remittitur. N. The reduction of a jury's excessive verdict or award of damages.

remote cause. N. An action or event that would not necessarily cause a particular result; see also *proximate*.

remove. V. (1) To take off; to take away; to eliminate. (2) To transfer a lawsuit from one court to another, especially from a state court to a federal one. N. *removal*.

render. V. (1) To provide something, such as help or payment. (2) To pronounce a judgment on a case or matter; to provide a verdict.

renounce. V. To formally abandon a claim or right; to reject or refuse to support; to give something up; for a wife to waive her rights under her husband's will and instead choose to receive a share of his estate according to statutory rules. N. *renunciation*.

rent. N. Money or another consideration paid to the owner of property or equipment for the right to use it. V. To pay for the use of something; to charge money in return for allowing someone to use one's property.

renunciation. N. The act of abandoning a claim or right; a document expressing abandonment of a claim or right; in criminal law, the affirmative defense of having abandoned criminal intent before committing a crime. V. *renounce*.

reorganize. V. To organize something differently; to change the structure of a corporation or other enterprise, such as when two corporations merge or a corporation changes its capitalization. N. *reorganization*.

repeal. V. To revoke or annul a law. N. *repeal*.

replevin. N. An action in which the owner of wrongfully taken goods recovers possession of them.

replevy. V. To deliver goods back to their rightful owner.

replication. N. In common law pleading, a plaintiff's reply to a defendant's answer.

reply. N. An answer or response; in pleading, a plaintiff's response to a counterclaim raised in the defendant's answer. V. To answer or respond.

report. N. An account of something that has happened; a formal written or oral statement made by an official who has investigated some matter. V. To provide an account of an event, either oral or written, based on investigation or observation.

reporter. N. A published volume of cases decided by courts in a particular region or by a particular court; a compilation of decisions by an administrative agency, financial transactions of a company, or other such material; also called reports. See also *court reporter*.

repossess. V. For a lender to take possession of an item or property if the person who borrowed money to purchase it fails to make payments. N. *repossession*. See also *foreclose*.

represent. V. (1) To act or speak on someone's behalf. (2) To allege or claim that something is the case; to make a statement that allows the listener to form a judgment. N. *representation*. See also *misrepresent*.

representative. N. A person appointed to speak or act on someone else's behalf; an agent; a person who represents a group of people in a legislative body. ADJ. Typical of a type or class. See also *House of Representatives*, *personal representative*.

reprieve. N. The temporary postponement of a criminal sentence or other unpleasant event. V. *reprieve*.

reprimand. N. An official rebuke; formal censure of a person administered by his or her superior or by an organization. V. *reprimand*.

reprisal. N. Retaliation; an act done out of spite or to retaliate for some real or imagined wrong; seizure of people or goods belonging to a foreign nation done as retaliation for some wrong.

republic. N. A state or nation in which power is held by the people and their elected representatives, and in which supreme leaders are elected by the people instead of inheriting their positions. ADJ. *republican*.

republication. N. The reactivation by a testator of a will that he or she has revoked; the revival of a revoked will through a codicil.

repudiate. V. To deny an obligation or refuse to perform a duty, such as that required by a contract; to deny that something is valid; to refuse to accept something. N. *repudiation*.

repugnancy. N. Inconsistency between two statements, clauses, allegations, etc.

repugnant. ADJ. Inconsistent; incompatible; contrary.

reputation. N. The opinion about a person held by other people or by the community in general.

res. N. *(Latin)* Thing; a thing or object; the subject matter of a lawsuit.

rescind. V. To revoke or cancel a contract or agreement. N. *rescission*.

rescission. N. The revocation or cancellation of a contract or agreement; a cancellation of a contract that returns the parties to their condition before they entered into it. V. *rescind*.

rescript. N. A written court order providing directions on how to dispose of a case; a short judicial opinion by an appellate court providing reasons for its decision to be sent to the trial court that originally heard the case in question.

rescue. V. To save someone or something from danger or destruction. N. *rescue*.

rescue doctrine. N. (1) A doctrine that a person who endangers someone's life through negligence can also be held liable for injuries to anyone who tries to rescue the victim. (2) A doctrine that a person who tries to rescue a victim from danger caused by another's negligence cannot be charged with contributory negligence as a result of the rescue attempt, as long as the rescue is not reckless; also called humanitarian doctrine or good Samaritan doctrine.

reservation. N. (1) A clause in a deed or other instrument of conveyance that holds back a part of the estate being conveyed for the grantor. (2) A tract of land set aside for public use, such as a park or land for American Indians. (3) A court's setting aside a legal point for later consideration. (4) A doubt; a qualification in one's agreeing to something.

reserve. V. (1) To keep something back; to keep something for the future. (2) To delay judgment on a matter. N. Something held back or set aside for the future or for contingencies, such as money, troops, or land.

reservist. N. A member of the reserves.

res gestae. N. *(Latin)* Things done; a spontaneous remark or declaration made by a person just after an event but before he or she has had a chance to manufacture a falsehood, which is held to be inherently reliable. See also *spontaneous exclamation*.

reside. V. To live in a place; to dwell.

residence. N. The place where someone lives; a person's home or dwelling; the condition of living in a place. See also *domicile*.

resident. N. A person who lives in a place. ADJ. Living in a place.

resident alien. N. A person who is not a citizen of the country in which he or she resides but who has been granted permanent resident status by immigration authorities.

residue. N. The items and money that remain in an estate after all testamentary bequests have been made and all debts, taxes, and other costs have been paid; also called a residuary estate. ADJ. *residual, residuary*.

res ipsa loquitur. N. *(Latin)* The thing speaks for itself; a presumption that a defendant was negligent based on the fact that an accident occurred that ordinarily would not happen without negligence.

resist. V. To fight back; to oppose something.

resistance. N. Opposition; the use of force or arms to oppose or prevent something from happening.

resisting arrest. N. Using physical efforts to avoid being arrested by a police officer.

res judicata. N. *(Latin)* An adjudicated matter; a rule that a court's final judgment conclusively settles the rights of all parties involved.

resolution. N. A formal expression of the opinion or intended course of action of a legislative body or other group arrived at through a vote. V. *resolve*.

respite. N. A break; a reprieve; a temporary period of relief before something unpleasant happens, such as a punishment.

respond. V. To reply; to answer. N. *response*.

respondeat superior. N. *(Latin)* Let the superior respond; a doctrine holding that a master or employer is responsible for the actions of his or her servants or employees while they work within the scope of employment.

respondent. N. (1) The party against whom an appeal is brought; see also *appellant*. (2) The party against whom an equitable proceeding is brought.

responsible. ADJ. Obligated to do something; having care for or control over something or someone; answerable or accountable for or in charge of something; liable. N. *responsibility*.

responsive. ADJ. Answering.

responsive pleading. N. A pleading that responds to a prior pleading by the opposing party, such as an answer to a complaint.

rest. V. To conclude a case at trial, i.e., for a party to indicate that he or she has presented all testimony, evidence, and arguments, has nothing left to present, and is ready to submit the case to the jury or judge for consideration. N. That which is left over; see also *residue*.

restatement. N. One of a series of treatises on particular areas of law (such as contracts or torts) published by the American Law Institute, intended to show the current state of the law and likely developments in the future.

restitution. N. (1) A remedy in which a victim is restored to his or her original state or condition prior to the injury; the act of making good for some wrong; restoration of the status quo. (2) Paying money or other consideration as recompense for a loss or injury. (3) Restoration of stolen property to its owner.

rest period. N. A period of time during which an employee must rest and not perform work.

restrain. V. To hold back; to confine or limit; to prevent some action or restrict freedom. N. *restraint*.

restraining order. N. An order issued with an application for an injunction preventing the defendant from doing a particular act until the court decides whether to issue the injunction.

restraint of trade. N. Contracts or agreements between businesses that restrict free competition, control the market, and encourage monopolies; see also *Sherman Antitrust Act*.

restraint on alienation. N. A restriction on an owner's freedom to sell or give away a piece of property, usually unenforceable.

restrict. V. To limit, confine, or control; to limit freedom of motion or action. N. *restriction*.

restricted securities. N. Securities acquired from the issuer in a transaction not open to the public and not available to the general public to purchase.

restrictive covenant. N. (1) A provision in an agreement transferring property such as a deed, limiting the uses to which that property can be put. (2) A clause in an employment contract limiting an employee's work options if he or she leaves the employer.

retail. N. Sale of goods in small quantities to consumers, as opposed to selling in bulk for resale; see also *wholesale*. V. *retail*. ADJ. *retail*.

retailer. N. A person who sells goods to consumers, especially personal or household goods.

retail installment contract. N. A contract in which a buyer agrees to pay the seller for some item in installments, along with a finance charge or with the provision that the ultimate price will be higher than if the buyer paid the full price initially.

retain. V. To hold; to keep; to employ or hire; to pay someone, such as an attorney, an initial fee as a way of securing his or her services.

retainer. N. A fee paid to someone, such as an attorney, to secure his or her services for a particular matter or period of time.

retaliate. V. To strike back; to attack in response to a previous attack; to punish someone or take revenge for a real or imagined wrong. N. *retaliation*. ADJ. *retaliatory*.

retire. V. (1) To stop working and leave employment permanently, often after reaching the age when workers typically retire; to remove someone or something from active service. (2) To leave a place; for a jury to leave the courtroom to deliberate. N. *retirement*.

retirement plan. N. A financial package that is payable to an employee after retirement, such as a pension or 401(k) plan.

retract. V. To take back; to pull back; to withdraw a statement, offer, or promise. N. *retraction*.

retreat. V. To back up; to withdraw oneself from a difficult or dangerous situation. N. The act of backing up or withdrawing.

retreat, duty to. N. See *duty to retreat*.

retrial. N. A second or subsequent trial of the same matter.

retribution. N. (1) Appropriate and just punishment for a crime or misdeed. (2) Recompense; money or another consideration paid as restitution for wrongdoing.

retroactive. ADJ. Made effective as of a date in the past. N. *retroactivity*.

retroactive law. N. A law that applies to events that happened before it was passed. See also *ex post facto*, *retrospective law*.

retrospective. ADJ. Looking back to the past; concerned with the past; taking effect on a date in the past.

retrospective law. N. A law that affects events that happened or rights that accrued before it was passed. See also *ex post facto*, *retroactive law*.

return. V. To go back; to give something back to someone. N. (1) Profit made from an investment. (2) An official report, such as a census report or a report filed by a sheriff or other officer after serving process on someone; a report of the results of an election. (3) A document filed by a taxpayer with the Internal Revenue Service, summarizing a year's income, deductions, and taxes paid; also called a *tax return*.

revenue. N. Income; gross income of a business, individual, government, or any other entity that can earn money.

revenue bill. N. A legislative bill that increases or introduces taxes.

revenue ruling. N. An official interpretation of some point of tax law issued by the Internal Revenue Service.

reverse. V. For an appellate court to vacate or annul a decision made by a lower court. N. *reversal*.

reverse discrimination. N. Unfair treatment that results if efforts to rectify discrimination against a minority group inadvertently result in discrimination against a majority group, such as when a beneficiary of affirmative action takes a position that otherwise would have gone to a white male.

reversible. ADJ. Able to be reversed.

reversion. N. A right to property held by its original owner or his or her heirs to take it back when a current interest ends, such as at the end of a lease or on the death of the person who currently possesses it; also called reverter. V. *revert.*

reversionary interest. N. An interest held by someone who has the right to future enjoyment of property currently held by another person.

revert. V. To return to an earlier state; for a property to return to its former owner or his or her heirs. N. *reversion.*

revest. V. To return to a former owner or holder.

review. V. To examine and assess; for an appellate court to examine and reconsider a decision made by a lower court. N. *review.*

revise. ADJ. To examine a document and make changes and improvements. N. *revision.*

revised statutes. N. Statutes that have been amended and re-enacted.

revive. V. To bring back to life; to make effective again; to restore a will, contract, or law to validity. N. *revival.*

revoke. V. To cancel or withdraw a will or other instrument, or some power, authority, or privilege. N. *revocation.* ADJ. *revocable.*

revolt. N. A rebellion against established authority, intended to end it; refusal to obey authority. V. *revolt.*

revolution. N. The overthrow of a government.

revolving credit. N. A kind of consumer credit that is renewed automatically as the borrower pays off debts and allows the borrower continuous credit as long as he or she makes regular payments and does not exceed a set limit.

RIAA. ABBRV. Recording Industry Association of America.

RICO. ABBRV. Racketeer Influenced and Corrupt Organizations Act.

rider. N. An addendum or amendment to a document, such as an insurance policy or a legislative bill, written on a separate piece of paper and attached to the original.

right. ADJ. Correct; just or fair. N. A power or privilege; authority to do something; a legal, equitable, or moral entitlement to something; an individual liberty. See also *bill of rights*, *civil rights*, *privacy*.

right of first refusal. N. Entitlement to the first opportunity to do something before the opportunity is offered to others.

right of way. N. (1) The right of a person traveling on a road, in the air, or on a body of water to proceed ahead of others. (2) An easement that allows a person to pass through someone else's property, usually in order to reach his or her own property; a piece of land that is subject to a right of way.

right to die. N. A dying person's right to refuse medical treatment to extend his or her life when there is no hope of recovery, including the right to appoint a representative to speak on his or her behalf in the event of incapacity. See also *advance directive*, *living will*.

rigor mortis. N. The stiffness that overcomes a body after death.

riot. N. A violent uprising by a large group of people. V. *riot*.

riparian. ADJ. Having to do with the banks of rivers and streams.

riparian rights. N. The rights of those who own property on the banks of rivers and streams related to use of the water and the land bordering it.

ripe for judgment. N. Ready for a final decision by the court; the condition of a lawsuit in which all arguments have been made and evidence has been presented, and nothing is left but for the court to render a final judgment.

ripeness doctrine. N. The principle that federal courts will only hear cases involving actual controversies, not cases that are hypothetical, speculative, or otherwise not in need of immediate decision.

risk. N. Danger; peril; uncertainty; the possibility that something might be lost if a particular course of action is followed; the peril against which an insurer protects someone.

risk capital. N. Money directly invested in some business venture, usually in exchange for common stock in the company.

robbery. N. Theft involving the use of force; the felony of taking money or property from another person through the use of force or threats that make the victim afraid.

robbery, armed. N. Robbery committed by a defendant armed with a dangerous weapon; sometimes called aggravated robbery.

Roe v. Wade. n. The 1973 U.S. Supreme Court case that held that abortions are permissible for any reason up to the point of the fetus' viability.

rogatory letter. N. A letter sent from a judge to another judge in another state or country, asking that he or she question a witness who lives there.

rogue state. N. A nation that, due to its disregard of peremptory norms, authoritarian government, or support for terrorism, constitutes a threat to world peace.

roll. N. A register, list, or record; a record of court proceedings; a list of voters registered in a district.

roll over. V. To extend or renew a short-term loan; to transfer the contents of a retirement account to another retirement account without actually withdrawing the funds and thereby incurring a tax penalty.

Roman law. N. A body of law derived from ancient Rome; also used occasionally to refer to the system of civil law.

Roth IRA. N. An individual retirement account in which contributions are made from post-tax income and qualified withdrawals can be made tax-free. See also *individual retirement account.*

royalty. N. A percentage of the proceeds from the sale of a literary work, recording, or other intellectual property that is paid to the author, creator, or owner of the work by the person or company that is selling it.

rubric. N. A category; a statement of purpose; the heading of a document, such as a statute.

rule. N. A law, principle, regulation, or standard that prescribes suitable conduct in a given situation; a court order requiring someone to do something. V. (1) To control; to exercise power over someone or something. (2) To make a judgment in a lawsuit; to make an authoritative statement about the law.

rule against perpetuities. N. A rule in property holding that a contingent future interest in property must vest within twenty-one years of a life in being at the time the interest is created.

rule nisi. N. An ex parte order that will become final unless the affected party can show a reason why it should not.

rule of law. N. The belief that a court should make decisions by applying laws or legal and equitable principles to a matter without using discretion in their interpretation and application; also called supremacy of law.

ruling. N. A judge's or court's decision or authoritative statement about a question of law, the admissibility of evidence, etc.

run with the land. V. For a covenant affecting land to be transferred along with the property to which it is attached when the property is sold or given away, so that it continues to be binding on the new owner.

S

sabotage. V. To destroy or impede something deliberately, as part of war or a political or labor dispute. N. *sabotage*.

salable. ADJ. Able to be sold; fit for sale; merchantable.

salary. N. A regular fixed payment made by an employer to an employee as compensation for services rendered, generally set by the year or for another fixed period, as opposed to by the hour; see also *wage*.

sale. N. The act of exchanging a commodity for money; a contract between a buyer and a seller in which the seller transfers property to the buyer in exchange for money or the promise of money. V. *sell*.

sale, bulk. N. The sale of all of a merchant's stock, materials, merchandise, and equipment.

sale, cash. N. A sale in which the buyer pays the full purchase price at the time of sale.

sale, forced. N. A sale made without the owner's consent, ordered and administered by the court as part of a proceeding, such as foreclosure.

sale, judicial. N. A court-ordered sale of property administered by an officer of the court.

sale, tax. N. A court-ordered sale of a person's property to collect money for the owner's unpaid taxes. See also *auction, installment, retail, sheriff's sale*.

sale and leaseback. N. The sale of an item to a buyer who immediately leases it back to the seller, done to free up the seller's capital or to gain a tax deduction.

sale or exchange. N. A phrase used in tax to describe a sale or transfer of property that yields a taxable gain or loss.

sales tax. N. A tax paid on purchased goods, usually a percentage of the cost of an item, collected by the seller on behalf of the government.

salvage. N. The goods retrieved after the destruction or damage of a building or other property, or the value of those goods; the cargo retrieved from a wrecked ship or other vessel; the goods remaining after some destruction that are claimed by the insurer after it pays the owner for the loss; the act of rescuing goods from destruction. V. *salvage*.

salvage value. The value of an item after its useful life has ended; the value of a building scheduled to be moved or destroyed, as in condemnation.

same. ADJ. Identical; not different; equal or equivalent; unchanged; of the same type.

sample. N. An example or model; a specimen of some commodity offered as an example of the quality or design of the commodity as a whole.

sample, sale by. N. A sale in which the buyer examines only a sample of the item purchased, which creates an express warranty that all goods of that type are of the same quality and design as the sample.

sanction. N. (1) Official approval of some action. (2) A penalty or threatened penalty for disobeying a law or rule; penalties taken by one nation against another, such as trade restrictions, intended to force it to comply with some standard. V. *sanction*.

sane. ADJ. Of sound mind; in possession of one's mental faculties; not insane. N. *sanity*.

sanity hearing. N. A hearing in which the court determines whether a criminal defendant is mentally competent to stand trial.

Sarbanes-Oxley Act. N. A federal law passed in 2002 that increased auditing and reporting requirements for corporations. ABBRV. *Sarbox, SOX*.

satisfy. V. To fulfill an obligation or pay off a debt. N. *satisfaction*. ADJ. *satisfactory*. See also *accord and satisfaction*.

save. V. (1) To exempt; to reserve. (2) To rescue someone or something from danger; to keep safe. (3) To keep; to accumulate something such as money; to avoid expending or wasting something.

save harmless. V. To indemnify; to repay another party if a specific loss occurs. See also *hold harmless*.

saving clause. N. A clause inserted in a statute to make an exception to the statute's provisions, such as a grandfather clause; a clause that prevents the statute from affecting those who currently enjoy rights that the statute takes away.

savings. N. Money that is accumulated and held for the future.

savings account. N. A bank account in which money is held and accumulated, as opposed to being spent regularly as in a checking account.

savings and loan association. N. A mutually owned cooperative institution that exists primarily to make loans to members, particularly for the purchase of real estate, and to provide members with savings accounts, but that may offer other banking services.

scandal. N. (1) An event that is considered morally wrong and causes public outrage; the outrage provoked by a shocking event. (2) Malicious gossip about a shocking event that causes public outrage; defamation or slander based on such an event; damage to reputation that results from such malicious gossip. ADJ. *scandalous*.

schedule. N. (1) A plan for conducting events; a list of planned events that occur regularly. (2) An appendix attached to a document, such as a statute or tax return, describing in detail matters mentioned briefly in the document itself. V. To arrange for something to happen at a particular time.

school district. N. A government entity that oversees the operation of public schools in a defined area.

scienter. ADV. *(Latin)* Knowingly; used to describe situations where a defendant had guilty knowledge that a crime was being committed, such as knowledge that a misrepresentation he or she made was not true; often used as a noun to mean guilty knowledge or a mental state intending to deceive.

scintilla. N. *(Latin)* A spark; the tiniest particle; the merest trace of something.

scintilla of evidence. N. A very insignificant or small particle of evidence tending to support an issue, which is nevertheless enough to allow the matter to go to the jury.

scope. N. Range; boundaries; the area encompassed by some concept, activity, etc.

scope of authority. N. Authority that has been delegated to an agent to allow him or her to carry out the assigned task, including both powers actually authorized by the principal and those that are implied in the task.

scope of employment. N. The activities done by an employee as part of his or her employment; duties that are part of someone's job.

scrivener. N. A scribe, clerk, or notary; a person who prepares written instruments such as contracts and deeds for other people for a fee.

scrutiny. N. Close observation; critical and thorough examination. V. *scrutinize*.

seal. N. An impression in wax or another substance, or an impression on paper, placed on a document to verify that it has been legally executed. V. To place a seal on a document; to close a document and place a seal on it that must be broken for it to be read.

sealed and delivered. ADJ. Words used to describe a conveyance that has been properly executed, signed, witnessed, sealed, and delivered to the proper recipient.

sealed bid. N. A bid for a job submitted by a contractor in a sealed envelope; all sealed bids are opened at the same time and the job is awarded to the lowest bidder.

sealed instrument. N. An instrument signed and sealed by its maker.

sealed verdict. N. A verdict placed in a sealed envelope by a jury if the court is not in session when the jury reaches a decision, which it presents to the court when it reconvenes.

sealing of records. N. The sealing of a person's criminal records so that they can only be examined by court order, often done with juvenile criminal records to prevent their impeding the person in his or her efforts to become a productive adult.

search. V. To look for something; to explore hidden places in a person's house, vehicle, or other place in a quest for evidence of a crime. N. *search*.

search and seizure. N. A search in which the officers conducting the search take evidence of a crime if they find it.

search engine. N. A software application that allows users to search for the appearance of particular words or images on websites.

search warrant. N. A written order issued by a judge or judicial official in the state's name, authorizing a sheriff or other officer of the law to search a particular place for evidence of a crime and seize it if found.

seasonable. ADJ. At the appropriate time; within a reasonable time; at the time agreed upon.

seasonal. ADJ. Occurring during a particular season of the year.

seasonal employment. N. Employment that exists only at particular times of the year, such as harvest work.

SEC. ABBRV. Securities and Exchange Commission.

secede. V. To withdraw formally from a union, an alliance, or a political or religious group. N. *secession*.

secondary. ADJ. Coming after something; less important than something else; subsequent.

secondary distribution. N. A public sale of stock that has already been issued and sold once, as opposed to a new offering.

secondary party. N. A person who is responsible for paying a debt if the original debtor fails to; a person who has secondary liability for a debt.

second mortgage. N. A mortgage placed on property that already has a mortgage on it, which follows in priority behind the first mortgage.

secret. ADJ. Not known by others; hidden from view or concealed. N. *secret*.

secretary. N. (1) A clerk; an employee who handles correspondence, keeps records, types documents, and performs other administrative tasks; see also *legal secretary*. (2) An officer of an organization who handles correspondence, records, etc. (3) An official who heads a governmental department.

secretary general. N. The head of the United Nations.

secretary of state. N. (1) The head of the State Department of the United States, top-ranking officer in the Cabinet, responsible for advising the president on matters of foreign policy. (2) An officer in a state who supervises state business affairs and licenses corporations.

Secret Service. N. A government agency in the Treasury Department whose duties include protecting the president and investigating counterfeiting and credit fraud.

secure. V. To make something safe; to guarantee; to guarantee repayment of a loan by obtaining collateral. ADJ. Safe; backed by collateral.

secured debt. N. A debt that is guaranteed by certain items that the creditor may take if the debtor fails to pay back the loan.

secured transaction. N. A transaction that involves security, i.e., a transaction secured with collateral that can be taken by the creditor if the debtor defaults.

securities acts. N. Federal and state statutes that govern registration of and trade in corporate securities, including the Securities Act of 1933 and the Securities Exchange Act of 1934, administered by the Securities and Exchange Commission.

Securities and Exchange Commission. N. A federal agency that oversees the sale and issuing of corporate stocks and bonds and corporate takeovers. ABBRV. *SEC*.

Securities Investor Protection Corporation. N. An organization established by federal statute to help brokers and dealers in corporate securities who find themselves in financial difficulties.

security. N. (1) Safety; protection; the state of being protected from danger, loss, or threat. (2) Collateral; an item promised as a forfeit in case of default. (3) A stock, bond, debenture, or other interest that represents a share in ownership of a company or evidence of the company's indebtedness; an instrument that gives its owner the right to money or property; PL. *securities*. See also *stock, bond, Securities and Exchange Commission*.

Security Council. N. A group of fifteen United Nations member nations that work to prevent war and maintain peace throughout the world.

security deposit. N. Money or property given to a creditor by a debtor as a pledge of payment, usually returned to its owner if payment is completed satisfactorily; e.g., money given to a landlord by a tenant as a guarantee that the tenant will pay rent and observe other terms of the lease, to be forfeited if the tenant damages the property or otherwise breaks the bargain.

security interest. N. An interest in real or personal property that exists because the property has been offered as security for an obligation or debt.

sedition. N. Speech or actions intended to persuade the people to rise up against a government and, if possible, overthrow it; advocating treason. ADJ. *seditious*.

seduce. V. (1) To tempt or entice someone into sexual activity. (2) To tempt someone into doing something he or she knows is wrong or ill-advised. N. *seduction*.

segregate. V. To separate; to keep certain things or people away from one another; to separate people based on race, religion, sex, etc. N. *segregation*. See also *desegregate*.

seisin. N. Ownership of property; possession of a freehold estate in land.

seize. V. To take someone's property by force; for a police officer authorized by a search warrant to take the real or personal property of someone who has broken the law or who has been ordered to forfeit that property by the court; to take a person into physical custody. N. *seizure*. See also *search and seizure*.

Selective Service System. N. An agency of the executive branch of the U.S. government that administers the draft, requiring all males between the ages of 18 and 26 to register and inducting them into the armed services when necessary.

self-dealing. N. A fiduciary's use of property or funds entrusted to him or her for personal benefit, such as a trustee's using trust property for himself or herself.

self-defense. N. The act of defending oneself against threatened injury; the right to protect oneself or one's family from immediately threatened harm, which can serve as a defense in a criminal or tort action arising out of injuries caused by an act of self-defense.

self-employed. ADJ. Working for oneself, performing jobs for and receiving pay directly from clients instead of working for an employer for wages or a salary.

self-employment tax. N. The 15.3% tax that the self-employed must pay on their incomes to cover both employee and employer portions of Federal Insurance Contribution Act taxes.

self-executing. ADJ. Coming into effect automatically when specific criteria are met.

self-help. N. Handling some matter that could involve legal authorities without using the normal legal process, such as taking possession of collateral when a debtor defaults or evicting a tenant for nonpayment of rent without involving the police.

self-incrimination. N. The act of testifying against oneself or implicating oneself in a crime, which the Fifth Amendment forbids the government to require of anyone.

sell. V. To give someone property in exchange for money; to be in the business of selling something. N. *sale*.

seller. N. A person who sells something.

sell short. V. To sell shares of stock or other commodities borrowed from someone else, intending to buy them back at a lower price later so as to make a profit and still be able to return the shares or their value to their original owner. N. *short sale*. See also *hedge*.

semiautomatic weapon. N. A gun that fires only one bullet with each trigger pull and automatically loads a new bullet into the chamber with each shot, eliminating the need to cock or reload the gun after firing.

Senate. N. The upper chamber of the U.S. Congress; the upper chamber of a state legislature; a governing body of a nation, university, or other organization.

senator. N. A member of a senate.

seniority. N. The condition of having been in a job longer than someone else, which can result in preference for promotions and layoffs.

sentence. N. The punishment given by the court to a criminal defendant who has been found guilty of a crime. V. *sentence*.

sentence, concurrent. N. A sentence served simultaneously with another sentence.

sentence, custodial. N. A sentence that involves imprisonment.

sentence, death. See *death penalty*.

sentence, deferred. N. A sentence that is postponed to some future time and possibly never imposed if the defendant does not violate the terms of probation.

sentence, definite. N. A sentence set by law for a particular crime, not modifiable by the judge; also called determinate sentence or fixed sentence.

sentence, indefinite. N. A sentence that has a prescribed range of punishments set by law, for which the court and other officials have some discretion in sentencing and that may be ended early at the discretion of the parole board; also called indeterminate sentence.

sentence, interlocutory. N. A temporary sentence imposed on a defendant between conviction and final sentencing.

sentence, life. N. A sentence to prison for the rest of one's natural life.

sentence, mandatory. N. A sentence set by law for a particular offense, with no room for judicial discretion.

sentence, noncustodial. N. A sentence that does not involve imprisonment, such as a fine.

sentence, split. N. A sentence divided into a period of incarceration and a period of probation.

sentence, suspended. N. A sentence that is not imposed on the defendant on the condition that he or she does not violate terms specified at sentencing.

sentences, cumulative. N. Multiple sentences that are served one after another; also called consecutive sentences.

separable. ADJ. Able to be divided or separated. N. *separability*.

separable controversy. N. A cause of action brought as part of a larger suit that could be separated and could stand alone as its own lawsuit, which can serve as a basis for removing the entire lawsuit from state to federal court.

separate. ADJ. Not connected with something; distinct; forming an entity or unit by itself. V. (1) To divide; to move apart; to place a boundary between things. (2) For a judge to order witnesses at a trial to stay out of the courtroom except for when they are testifying. (3) For a husband and wife to move into different homes intending to no longer live together as a couple, often as a precursor to divorce; if the separation is ordered by a court, it is called a legal separation. N. *separation*.

separate but equal. ADJ. Describing a doctrine, now generally believed to be unconstitutional, that held that the races could be treated equally although segregated into different facilities.

separation agreement. N. A written agreement between a husband and wife who have separated and intend to divorce, arranging for division of property, custody of children, alimony, child support, and any other necessary matters.

separation of powers. N. The division of the U.S. government and many state governments into three branches—executive, legislative, and judicial—each of which wields a particular set of powers unique to it and not shared by the other branches, and that the other branches are not permitted to use.

SEP-IRA. ABBRV. Simplified Employee Pension Individual Retirement Account.

sequester. V. (1) To isolate; to separate or segregate; to hide away; to isolate a jury during a trial. (2) To seize property pending the outcome of litigation or to hold until a debt is paid; to impose spending restrictions on a government; to declare someone bankrupt. Also called sequestrate. N. *sequestration*.

servant. N. A person who works for someone else and is controlled by him or her; an employee; a person employed by a government, also called a civil servant. See also *civil service, independent contractor*.

serve. V. (1) To work for someone, especially as an employee; to hold a position in the armed forces. (2) To deliver a legal document such as a summons formally and in an official capacity.

service. N. The act of working for someone; the work that is performed by someone.

service, constructive. N. Any form of service other than personal service.

service, personal. N. Actual delivery of the document to the person named on it.

service, substituted. N. Service in which the document is presented to someone authorized to receive it on the named party's behalf.

service by mail. N. Delivery of a legal document through mail.

service by publication. N. Publication of a summons or other document as an advertisement in a newspaper named by the court, used in cases where the defendant cannot be found.

servicemember. N. A member of the military; a soldier in the armed forces.

service of process. N. The formal delivery to a defendant of the complaint, summons, or other legal document to notify him or her that a lawsuit has been brought.

servient estate. N. Land subject to an easement; land that the owner of a dominant estate is allowed to use for some specific purpose.

servitude. N. (1) The condition of being enslaved; the condition of a person who is bound to work for another person as a servant, either voluntarily or involuntarily; see also *indenture*. (2) An obligation or encumbrance on land that takes the form of a burden or restriction on the landowner, as opposed to an easement, which is a right or privilege enjoyed by the owner of the estate that claims it.

servitude, equitable. N. A servitude that is enforceable in equity.

session. N. A meeting of a court, legislature, or other body; the period when a court sits to hear cases.

session laws. N. A bound volume of the laws passed during a legislative session, compiled in the order of their enactment.

set aside. V. To vacate, annul, or reverse a judgment, order, or proceedings.

setback. N. A building's distance from a curb, building, property line, or other boundary.

set-off. N. A counterclaim brought by a defendant against a plaintiff that arises out of a different matter from that raised in the plaintiff's complaint, and that the defendant hopes to use to recover some amount from the plaintiff, thereby reducing or canceling the damages due to the plaintiff.

settle. V. (1) To resolve a matter; to conclude an estate; to finalize accounts; for the parties to a lawsuit to resolve their dispute on their own before a court reaches a final judgment on the matter after trial, thereby allowing the trial to be canceled and the lawsuit terminated. (2) To dispose of finally, such as after death; to give property to someone. N. *settlement*.

settlor. N. A person who creates a trust; a person who gives property to someone; see also *donor*.

sever. V. To cut; to divide or separate; to end a relationship; to separate causes of action or defendants that have been joined together to try them instead in individual lawsuits. N. *severance*.

severable. ADJ. Able to have portions removed without destruction of the whole; able to be divided. N. *severability*.

severable contract. N. A contract that contains two or more independent parts, one or more of which can potentially be breached without invalidating the entire contract.

severable statute. N. A statute that remains valid after portions of it are declared invalid and removed.

several. ADJ. (1) Three or more but not many. (2) Separate; regarded separately or individually. ADV. *severally*; see also *joint*.

several actions. N. Individual lawsuits brought against multiple defendants by the same plaintiff out of the same subject matter.

several liability. N. Liability for something held by every individual involved with some matter, which allows for a separate lawsuit to be brought against each party.

severalty. N. The ownership of property by one person, who does not share title with anyone else.

severance pay. N. A sum of money paid to a terminated employee as compensation for firing him or her.

severe. ADJ. Extreme; very bad; strict or harsh.

sex. N. (1) Sexual activity; sexual intercourse. (2) A physical category, either male or female, determined by reproductive organs; members of a group that have the same reproductive organs; the state of being a male or female; see also *gender*. ADJ. ***sexual***.

sex crime. N. A crime involving sex, either with a sexual motive or involving a sexual act, such as rape, sexual assault, or indecent exposure.

sex offender. N. A person who has been convicted of a sex crime.

sexual abuse. N. Illegal sexual contact between a minor and an adult.

sexual assault. N. Forcible sexual contact inflicted on an unwilling victim; see also *rape*.

sexual harassment. See *harassment, sexual*.

shall. V. A modal verb used to create a future tense; as used in statutes and legal documents, generally has an imperative sense, meaning "must," though it can also be used in a permissive sense, meaning "may." In traditional English usage, "shall" was the future modal verb for first person subjects (i.e., I and we) and "will" the verb used with second or third persons (i.e., you, he, she, and it) except in cases of obligation, strong determination, or an imperative meaning, where "will" was used for first person subjects and "shall" for second and third person subjects; in modern usage this distinction is seldom observed.

sham. N. Something that is false; a fake; a pretense. ADJ. False; not what it is purported to be.

sham pleading. N. A pleading that appears genuine but is not based on any real issue of material fact, and is so clearly false that it does not raise a bona fide issue.

sham transaction. N. A transaction that appears to be genuine but in fact is intended to deceive its creditors or the government.

share. V. To partake of a portion of something along with others, or to give a portion of something to another. N. A portion; a part of a larger thing; a unit of stock.

share and share alike. V. To divide something into equal portions for each person or entity that is entitled to a share.

shareholder. N. A person who owns shares of stock; synonymous with *stockholder*.

shareware. N. Software that a user may acquire and try free of charge, usually distributed with a request for voluntary payment. See also *open source*.

Sharia. N. Islamic law, based on interpretation of the Quran and other sources of Muslim doctrine.

sheriff. N. An officer elected by a county to keep the peace, enforce laws, serve process, execute judgments, and perform other such duties; the term is also sometimes used to refer to a deputy sheriff or sheriff's deputy.

sheriff's sale. N. A sale of property by a sheriff or court officer ordered by a court to satisfy a judgment, such as a foreclosure, often conducted as an auction.

Sherman Antitrust Act. N. A federal statute passed in 1890 to prevent monopolies and restrictions on free and open interstate and foreign commerce; see also *antitrust, Clayton Act.*

shield law. N. A law that prevents a court from requiring witnesses to reveal certain kinds of information, such as a law that prevents opposing counsel from questioning a victim of a sex crime about his or her past sexual behavior, or a law that allows journalists to refuse to disclose confidential information in a legal proceeding; see also *privilege.*

shift. V. To move something; to change position or emphasis; to transfer a burden of proof from one party to another.

shop. N. (1) A place of business where goods are sold. (2) A place where goods are manufactured; a factory, plant, or workshop.

shoplifting. N. Stealing merchandise from a store.

shop steward. N. A union official who is elected to represent his or her fellow workers in negotiations with management.

short. ADJ. (1) Covering a small distance or lasting a brief time; below the standard or required length. (2) Having sold borrowed shares or property in the expectation of being able to repurchase them at a lower price; see also *sell short.*

short-term. ADJ. For a short time; current; due within a short period of time, usually within a year.

show. V. To illustrate; to prove; to exhibit or display; to produce evidence of something.

show cause order. N. An order by the court made upon the motion of one party requiring the opposing party to appear before it and explain why the court should not take a particular action.

show-up. N. A face-to-face confrontation arranged by law enforcement officers between a suspect and a witness to or victim of a crime, usually done just after the crime has been committed and intended to allow the witness or victim to identify the person who has committed the crime.

shrink-wrap agreement. N. A contract or licensing agreement that is packaged inside a product and that cannot be read until the product is purchased and opened. See also *browse-wrap agreement, click-wrap agreement.*

sick. ADJ. Physically or mentally ill; can also include incapacity due to physical injury.

sick leave. N. A leave that an employee is allowed to take from work when either the employee or a close family member is sick or injured, either with or without pay but without loss of seniority or benefits.

sick pay. N. Compensation paid to an employee while on sick leave either temporarily or permanently, often as part of disability compensation.

side-bar. N. A place at the side of a judge's bench where the judge and attorneys can discuss matters privately, in the presence of the court reporter who records their conversation, but without the jury, parties, witnesses, or spectators hearing what they say.

sight draft. N. A negotiable instrument that is payable on sight, i.e., when presented; a draft that is payable on demand.

sign. V. To write one's name on a document to authenticate or execute it.

signatory. N. A party who signs his or her name to an agreement; a nation that signs on to an international treaty or other agreement.

signature. N. The act of signing one's name; one's name written by one's own hand, or affixed in some other way such as printing, engraving, stamping, allowing someone else to write one's name, a mark used instead of a name, etc., as long as the person whose name appears on the document intends it to be placed there to make the document effective.

signing statement. N. An official statement issued by a president when he or she signs a bill into law, explaining his or her reasons for signing and opinions about the new law.

silent. ADJ. Not speaking; knowing something but not saying anything or acting accordingly. N. *silence*.

silent partner. N. An investor in a business who contributes capital and shares profits and losses but does no active management.

similar. ADJ. Almost the same; resembling; alike in some ways.

similar sales. N. Sales of properties similar to the one in question, used to determine fair market value.

simple. ADJ. Pure; uncomplicated; used to describe a crime that is not aggravated or compounded. See also *aggravate*.

Simplified Employee Pension Individual Retirement Account. N. An individual retirement account in which an individual may contribute a set percentage of pre-tax income. ABBRV. *SEP-IRA*.

simulate. V. To imitate; to assume an appearance; to fabricate or counterfeit. N. *simulation*.

simulated fact. N. An invented fact; a lie.

simulated judgment. N. A judgment on a case of bad debt that appears valid but actually is meant to give unfair advantage to one of the parties or to perpetrate a fraud on third parties.

simultaneous death act. N. A law stating that in cases where distribution of property depends on the time that a person dies, and where two people die simultaneously or close enough together that it is impossible to determine who died first (such as when husband and wife perish together in an airplane crash), the law will presume that each died before the other and their property should be distributed accordingly.

sine qua non. N. *(Latin)* Without which not; something without which something else cannot happen; a requirement or necessity.

sinking fund. N. A fund used to accumulate money to replace equipment as it wears out, to repay debts as bonds mature, or for other long-term financial obligations.

sit. V. To hold a session of a court, a legislature, or other body.

situs. N. *(Latin)* Site, position; the location of a thing; the location of property for tax purposes; the place where a crime or other action takes place.

slander. N. Making a false and defamatory oral statement about someone that can injure his or her reputation; oral defamation. V. *slander*. See also *libel, defamation*.

slander of title. N. Criticizing a product in order to lower public opinion of it or to persuade a customer to purchase a different product.

SLAPP. ABBRV. Strategic Lawsuit Against Public Participation.

slave. N. A person owned by and forced to work for another person. See also *enslave*.

slip and fall. N. An accident in which a victim slips on something, such as liquid on the floor or a banana peel, and is injured, which serves as the basis for a lawsuit against the owner of the premises; a similar kind of accident is a trip and fall. See also *personal injury, plaintiff's attorney*.

small business. N. A business with a small number of employees, typically fewer than fifty or one hundred, or with low sales or profits.

small claims court. N. A court that handles matters involving small amounts of money in an informal, inexpensive, and usually fairly quick manner.

sober. ADJ. Not under the influence of drugs or alcohol. N. *sobriety*.

Social Security. N. A national program of social insurance in which employers and employees all contribute funds that are pooled and paid out to retired and disabled workers and to the surviving spouses of dead workers, administered by the Social Security Administration.

sodomy. N. Oral or anal sexual intercourse, or sexual intercourse with an animal; definition varies by state.

software. N. The programs a computer uses to perform particular tasks; applications. See also *hardware*.

solemn. ADJ. Formal; observing the proper form or ceremony.

solemnize. V. To make formal through an official ceremony; to perform a marriage in public before witnesses. N. *solemnization*.

sole proprietor. N. A person who owns a business alone, without co-owners or partners.

sole proprietorship. N. See *proprietorship*.

solicit. V. (1) To try to get something from someone; to ask for something; to request or entreat; to encourage someone to commit a crime. (2) To offer one's services as a prostitute. N. *solicitation*.

solicitor. N. (1) The head legal officer of a city, town, department, or other body. (2) In Britain, a lawyer who drafts wills, prepares conveyances, and handles all other legal matters aside from arguing cases in court, though in modern times solicitors do occasionally appear in court; see also *barrister*.

solicitor general. N. The attorney who ranks just below the attorney general of the United States and whose responsibilities include representing the U.S. government before the Supreme Court and other federal courts.

solitary confinement. N. Imprisoning someone alone in an isolated cell, without contact with fellow prisoners or without any human contact at all, even from prison employees.

solvent. ADJ. Able to pay debts; having enough money to cover one's expenses. N. *solvency*. See also *insolvent*.

sound. ADJ. In good condition; without defects; healthy. N. *soundness*.

sound and disposing mind and memory. N. Language often used in wills to mean the mental capacity necessary to create a will.

sound body. N. Healthy, without disease, injury, or physical impairment.

sound in. V. To aim at; to be connected with.

sound in contract. N. For a lawsuit to appear to be an action related to a contract, although it was brought as an action in tort.

sound in damages. N. For an action to be brought for damages only, not for recovery of property.

sound mind. N. Sane and mentally capable, with unimpaired faculties.

source. N. Origin; the place or person from which something comes; the person or thing that starts something.

sovereign. N. A ruler; a monarch or king; the supreme authority of a country. ADJ. *sovereign*.

sovereign immunity. N. A doctrine that prohibits lawsuits being brought against the government without its consent.

sovereign state. N. A state or nation that governs itself and is not subject to the authority of any other state or nation.

sovereignty. N. The power by which a government rules its state or nation.

spam. N. Unsolicited emails sent to large numbers of email addresses in the hope of enticing some readers to respond.

speaker. N. (1) The head of a legislative body. (2) A person who is speaking.

Speaker of the House. N. The chief officer of the House of Representatives.

special. ADJ. Unusual; better than or different from something else; meant for a particular purpose; belonging to a particular person or thing.

special counsel. N. An attorney who works for the attorney general on a particular matter.

special interest group. N. A group of people with a common interest who attempt to influence legislators to pass laws favorable to them.

special jurisdiction. N. A court's ability to hear only a limited category of cases.

special law. N. A law that affects only particular people and not the general public; a private law.

special use. N. A use of property that is not allowed under zoning laws but is permitted as an exception in a particular case.

specie. N. Money in the form of metal coins.

specie, in. ADJ. (1) In coins. (2) A contract performed exactly according to stipulated terms.

specific. ADJ. Clearly stated or identified; precisely defined; explicit. V. *specify.* N. *specification.*

specific performance. N. An equitable remedy in a case of breach of contract, in which the breaching party is required to perform the obligation under the contract. See also *bequest, intent.*

speculate. V. (1) To guess; to theorize or come to a conclusion about something without adequate evidence. (2) To engage in risky investments; to buy or sell stocks in the hopes that prices will rise or fall dramatically. N. *speculation.*

speech or debate clause. N. A clause in the Constitution that provides congresspeople with immunity from prosecution arising out of any speech or debate conducted during a legislative session, to ensure that legislators may speak freely without fear of reprisal.

speedy trial. N. A criminal trial conducted according to proper regulations and without unnecessary or arbitrary delays, a right guaranteed by the Sixth Amendment.

spendthrift. N. A person who spends a great deal of money quickly and without prudence; a person who wastes his or her estate through excessive spending, gambling, laziness, or other irresponsible behavior.

spendthrift trust. N. A trust set up to safeguard the funds of someone who would be expected to waste them by restricting the beneficiary's access to money and placing it out of the reach of creditors.

spirit of the law. N. The actual intention of a law; the meaning it is meant to convey, arrived at through interpretation and possibly consideration of the intentions of those who wrote it; see also *letter of the law*.

split. V. (1) To break into separate parts; to divide between two or more parties or entities. (2) To divide a single cause of action into several parts, each of which becomes the basis for its own action. ADJ. *split*.

spoliation. N. The act of destroying something; destruction of evidence that might prove unfavorable; destruction or modification of a document or instrument. V. *spoil*.

spontaneous. ADJ. Done on a sudden impulse without prior planning.

spontaneous exclamation. N. A statement made immediately after some exciting occurrence by someone who saw it or participated in it, before he or she has the chance to think about it; see also *res gestae*.

spouse. N. A husband or wife; a person who is married to another. ADJ. *spousal*.

spouse, surviving. N. A spouse who remains alive after his or her partner has died; see also *widow*.

spyware. N. Software that is secretly installed on a computer without the owner's knowledge or consent in order to collect personal information, to use the computer to send spam, to hijack the Web browser, or to conduct other illegal activities.

squatter. N. A person who sets up residence on property that does not belong to him or her. V. *squat*.

squeeze-out. N. Eliminating minority shareholders from a corporation by buying out minority shares or issuing many new shares that dilute the minority interest; also called a *freeze-out*.

stack. V. To apply multiple insurance policies to one loss.

stake. N. (1) An interest, such as in a business. (2) A wager; an amount of money or item of property placed by two people in the care of a third party who will give it to the party who becomes entitled to it based on the outcome of some event, such as the winner of a game or lawsuit.

stakeholder. N. (1) A person with an interest in a business or transaction. (2) A third party who holds property or money that is the subject of a contest between two other people, such as a lawsuit or a wager. See also *interpleader*.

stalk. V. To follow or watch a person with no legitimate purpose and in such a way that it alarms the person being followed. N. *stalking*.

stalker. N. A person who stalks another.

stand. (1) To appear in court when summoned to a trial. (2) To be in a particular state or condition; to remain in the same condition; for a law to remain in force. N. A position taken in an argument or fight.

standard. N. A norm; an established practice; a level, quality, or idea used as a benchmark for comparison. ADJ. Accepted; normal.

standard of care. N. The degree of care that an ordinary person of reasonable prudence would use in a specific situation.

standard of proof. N. The level of proof that must be offered to prove a case, such as "beyond a reasonable doubt" in criminal cases or a "preponderance of the evidence" in civil cases.

standing. N. (1) Position or status in a community; reputation. (2) Having a strong enough interest in a matter to be allowed to bring a lawsuit based on it; also called standing to sue. ADJ. Permanent; regular.

standing order. N. An order that is carried out as part of a regular routine, used to regulate procedures in a court or other body.

stand mute. V. For a criminal defendant to refuse to plead when charged.

stare decisis. N. (*Latin*) Stand by things decided; the principle that courts in common law will follow previously decided cases as much as possible and avoid upsetting precedents.

start-up. N. A newly created company.

state. V. To say; to express something in words, either spoken or written. N. (1) Condition. (2) An organized political unit with one government; one of the United States. (3) The government; the people who live in a state. (4) Ceremonies and pomp that accompany high governmental functions.

state action. N. A claim brought by a private citizen against the government, protesting governmental intrusion into his or her affairs and violation of his or her civil rights, usually brought under the due process clause of the Fourteenth Amendment and the Civil Rights Act.

state law. N. Laws passed by and enforced within a state, as opposed to federal law.

statement. N. A written or verbal expression of some fact or belief; an assertion or allegation made by a witness. See also *opening statement, prior inconsistent statement.*

state of mind. N. The mental condition at the time that some event occurs; a person's reasons for acting in a particular way.

state police. N. The police force hired by a state to keep the peace and enforce laws within a state.

status. N. (1) Social standing or rank; official classification. (2) Condition or state.

status crime. N. A crime based on a person's character or condition rather than on actually committing a wrongful act, such as the condition of being a drug addict; laws defining status crimes are generally held to be unconstitutional.

status quo. N. The usual state of things at a particular time.

status quo ante. N. The normal state of things before a particular event occurred.

status report. N. A report on the status of a business or endeavor as of a particular date or time.

statute. N. A formal written law passed by a legislature.

statute of frauds. N. A statute requiring that certain kinds of contracts be written in order to be enforced, common under English law and now codified in the Uniform Commercial Code.

statute of limitations. N. A statute that limits the time in which a lawsuit may be brought for an injury or a crime, after which the party with a grievance loses the right to sue; see also *laches*.

statutory. ADJ. Related to statutes; required by or governed by a statute.

statutory construction. N. Interpretation of a statute, often done by a judge when a statute is invoked during a lawsuit; see also *construe, construction*.

statutory rape. An act of sexual intercourse that involves consenting partners but is legally considered rape because one or both of the partners were below the legal age of consent.

stay. V. To stop; to put on hold. N. A judicial order that puts some action on hold temporarily.

stay of execution. N. A judicial order that prevents a judgment from being executed for a period of time.

steal. V. To take something that belongs to someone else without the owner's consent, intending to keep it or use it and never return it. ADJ. *stolen*. See also *larceny, theft*.

stealth. N. Cautious and secretive movement that is meant to go unnoticed. ADJ. *stealthy*.

step. PREFIX. A familial relationship through marriage, not blood.

stepchild. N. A natural child of one's spouse from a previous marriage or liaison.

stepparent. N. A person who is not a child's natural parent but who is married to the child's natural mother or father.

stipulate. V. To require or demand something as part of an agreement; for the parties or attorneys on opposing sides of a case to agree in writing on how to handle certain parts of the lawsuit in order to limit issues and speed up the proceedings. N. *stipulation*.

stock. N. (1) The capital of a business raised by selling shares in the business to people inside or outside the company; an ownership interest in a company or business; see also *security*. (2) Merchandise and goods for sale held by a business. (3) A person's ancestry. V. To keep merchandise available for sale.

stock, no-par. N. Stock issued with no face value, or with an extremely low face value.

stockbroker. N. A person employed by a customer to buy and sell securities on the customer's behalf.

stock certificate. N. A document that indicates that its holder has an ownership interest in a corporation.

stock exchange. N. A place or organization where shares of stock and other securities are bought and sold.

stockholder. N. A person who owns shares of stock; synonymous with *shareholder*.

stock market. N. A stock exchange; the entire marketplace of securities trading facilities; the economic concept of securities trading; also called the *market*.

stock option. N. The right to buy stock at a predetermined price, usually better than market price, during a specified period, offered as incentive or compensation to employees and managers of a company.

stock split. N. The splitting of single shares into two or more shares apiece, resulting in an increased total number of shares and in the shares held by individual shareholders. See also *broker, preferred stock, common stock, Securities and Exchange Commission, security.*

stolen. ADJ. Acquired through theft. V. *steal.*

stonewall. V. To refuse to answer questions or to give evasive answers in order to delay or block some action, particularly a political action.

stop. V. To prevent someone from moving; to restrain someone's liberty. N. ***stop.***

stop and frisk. N. The action by a police officer of stopping a person suspected to be armed and dangerous and running his or her hands over the outside of the suspect's clothing to locate any concealed weapons.

straddle. N. The securities trading practice of placing a contract to buy (put option) and a contract to sell (call option) on the same commodity or stock, hoping to profit from a large change in price in a volatile market. See also *hedge.*

Strategic Lawsuit Against Public Participation. N. A lawsuit filed by a large corporation against a much smaller adversary in order to silence the adversary by swamping it with legal burdens and costs. ABBRV. *SLAPP.*

straw man. N. (1) An argument placed in a brief or opinion solely for the purpose of refuting it. (2) A third party who acts as a nominal party to a property transaction, accepting a transfer of property and then immediately returning it to the transferor, in cases where it is necessary for the transferor to receive a new deed to the property; see also *dummy*.

streaming. ADJ. Constantly delivered over a telecommunications network.

street name. N. The name of a broker, rather than that of a customer; refers to securities that are held in a broker's name instead of in the name of the customer who owns them.

strict. ADJ. Rigid; adhering closely to rules without deviation, relaxation, or room for interpretation.

strict liability. N. (1) Tort liability imposed regardless of actual fault on a person or company that sells a product for injuries due to defective or dangerous products; see also *products liability*. (2) Criminal liability imposed regardless of criminal intent on a person who commits a certain type of criminal act, such as a parking violation.

strict scrutiny. N. A test that courts apply to determine the constitutionality of statutes that classify people by type (such as race or national origin) in ways that affect fundamental rights, in which the government has the burden of proving that there is a compelling state interest served by the classification and that the classification is the only way of achieving that purpose.

strike. N. A refusal to work by a group of employees, usually done to force management to grant some request made by the workers after negotiations have not produced the desired result; a refusal by a group of people to do some action that is expected of them as a way of forcing compliance with their demands. V. (1) To participate in a work stoppage. (2) To remove someone from a group; to eliminate a prospective juror.

strikebreaker. N. A person brought in to do the work of a striking employee; also called a scab.

strike off. V. (1) To remove a case from a court's docket due to lack of jurisdiction. (2) To finalize a sale at an auction by the auctioneer bringing down his or her hammer or otherwise announcing that the highest bidder is entitled to pay the amount of the bid and take the property.

sua sponte. ADV. *(Latin)* Of one's own volition; voluntarily; without prompting.

subcontractor. N. A person or business hired by a general contractor to perform a portion of a contracted project. See also *contractor*.

subdivide. V. To divide a part of something into smaller parts; to divide a plot of land into smaller parcels or lots. N. *subdivision*.

subject. N. (1) A topic; a person or thing that is being considered or discussed. (2) A citizen; a resident of a state or nation, excluding the monarch or ruler. V. To inflict; to make someone undergo something. ADJ. (1) Depending on. (2) Under some authority or control.

subject matter. N. A matter or topic presented for consideration or debate; the right or property that is the foundation of a dispute or lawsuit.

subject matter jurisdiction. N. A court's power to hear cases related to a particular kind of subject matter.

sub judice. ADJ. *(Latin)* Under a judge; under consideration by a court.

sublease. N. A lease of property to a third person by a person who is already leasing it; the original lessee remains responsible for the original lease. V. *sublet*.

submit. V. (1) To present something to someone else for consideration or decision; to present a proposal to the court for approval. (2) To yield to someone else's desires or authority; to obey.

subordinate. ADJ. Below someone or something else; of lower rank or importance. N. A person ranked below another. V. To rank something below something else; to give one debt or claim lower priority than another debt or claim. N. *subordination*.

suborn. V. To persuade someone to commit perjury through bribery or other inducement. N. *subornation*.

subpoena. N. An official court document ordering a person to appear in court or at a judicial proceeding at a specified time; also called subpoena ad testificandum.

subpoena duces tecum. N. A subpoena commanding a witness to bring certain documents and other relevant items to court or to a deposition.

subprime loan. N. A loan made to an individual who cannot obtain a loan from a traditional lender at market rates due to a low credit rating, typically made at a higher interest rate to offset the risks incurred by the lender.

subrogation. N. The substitution of one person for another with respect to an obligation, legal claim, or debt, with the substituted person assuming all duties of payment or performance and all rights that accompany the claim. V. *subrogate*.

subrogee. N. A person who is substituted for another.

subrogor. N. A person who substitutes another person for himself or herself.

sub rosa. *(Latin)* Under the rose; secret or confidential.

subscribe. V. (1) To write one's name on a document as a means of authenticating it or making it binding upon him or her; see also *sign.* (2) To agree to buy shares in a corporation. (3) To give money to a cause, such as a charity. (4) To pay a sum of money in order to receive something regularly, such as issues of a magazine. N. *subscription.*

subscriber. N. A person who subscribes.

subscription rights. N. The right of a person who already holds shares in a corporation to buy at a favorable price additional shares of the same type of stock.

subsidiary. ADJ. Under the control of another. N. A company controlled by another company that owns a majority of the shares of its stock; also called a subsidiary corporation.

subsidy. N. A grant of money from the government or a public body to assist an industry that provides services that are needed by the community. V. *subsidize.*

substance abuse. N. Using drugs or alcohol to the point that they detrimentally affect the life of the user and those around him or her.

substantial. ADJ. Important; large; considerable; valuable.

substantial evidence. N. Evidence adequate to support the proposition for which it is offered.

substantial performance. N. Performance that does not exactly meet the terms of an agreement but that does accomplish the intended purpose in a manner close enough to be considered as fulfilling the obligation; also called substantial compliance.

substantiate. V. To provide evidence to support a contention or prove a fact; to verify; to back up a story.

substantive. ADJ. (1) Related to actual rights or duties rather than rules or procedures. (2) Based in reality; having some real meaning.

substantive due process. N. The requirement found in the Fifth and Fourteenth Amendments that the substance and content of laws must be fair and reasonable and that they must not be applied arbitrarily or unreasonably.

substantive evidence. N. Evidence offered to prove a fact at issue in a trial, as opposed to character evidence about a witness.

substantive law. N. The part of law that defines rights and duties rather than procedural methods of enforcing those rights, i.e., the law of contract, tort, property, trusts and estates, etc., as opposed to civil procedure.

substitute. V. To replace one thing or person with another. N. A replacement.

subtenant. N. A person who leases property from someone who is already leasing himself or herself; a person who enters into a sublease.

subterfuge. N. A ploy to escape, evade, or conceal something; a deceitful means of accomplishing some goal.

subvert. V. To work to undermine established authority or overthrow the government. N. *subversion*. ADJ. *subversive*.

succeed. V. (1) To achieve a desired goal. N. *success*. ADJ. *successful*. (2) To take the place of someone or something in a position, elected office, or other situation; to follow and replace; to inherit a position or title. N. ***succession***; see also *successor*.

succession. N. (1) Several people or things of the same type following one after the other. (2) Inheriting a title or right to property through a will. (3) Following someone in a position, office, or other situation. See also *succeed*.

successor. N. A person or thing that takes the place of another in a position, elected office, or other situation.

successor in interest. N. The next person who would have title to or control over a property if the current owner were to lose it. See also *succeed*.

sue. V. To initiate and carry out legal proceedings against someone; to bring a lawsuit against someone. (2) To appeal to someone to grant something. N. *suit*.

suffer. V. (1) To experience pain or misery. (2) To tolerate.

sufferance. N. Tolerance; consent to some action implied by failing to object rather than explicitly approving.

suffering. N. Pain and misery.

sufficient. ADJ. Adequate; enough for the purpose for which it is required. N. ***sufficiency***.

sufficient evidence. N. Enough evidence to justify the legal action in question.

suffrage. N. The right to vote in a public election.

suffrage, women's. N. The right of women to vote in political elections, granted by the Nineteenth Amendment in 1920.

suicide. N. The act of killing oneself. V. ***commit suicide***.

sui generis. ADJ. *(Latin)* Of its own kind; unique; the only example of its type.

sui juris. ADJ. *(Latin)* Of one's own right; emancipated; of legal age; having the right to handle one's own affairs and not under the legal control of anyone else.

suit. N. (1) A lawsuit; a legal action in which a plaintiff appeals to a court to grant him or her a remedy for some injury. (2) An entreaty or appeal to an authority to grant some request.

suitor. N. (1) A person who applies or appeals to do something, such as a man who hopes to persuade a woman to marry him or a person who hopes to buy a business. (2) A person who brings a lawsuit; a plaintiff.

sum certain. N. A specified or fixed sum of money.

summary. N. A concise statement of the main points of a longer document. V. *summarize*. ADJ. (1) Concise. (2) Conducted without the usual formalities. (3) Done by a judge or magistrate without a jury.

summary judgment. N. A judgment that ends a lawsuit without trial in a case where a judge finds that there is no genuine issue of material fact and thus no need to send the matter to a jury.

summation. N. A last step in a jury trial before the jury begins deliberations, in which the attorneys for both sides sum up the evidence presented and call attention to the important points in their arguments; also called summing up.

summer associate. N. A law student who works at a law firm for the summer. See also *law, clerk*.

summon. V. To notify a defendant that he or she has been sued and must appear in court on a particular day.

summons. N. An order issued by a court informing a defendant that a lawsuit has been brought against him or her and summoning him or her to appear in court on a particular day to answer the complaint.

Sunday closing laws. N. Local or state laws that prohibit certain businesses from operating on Sunday; also called blue laws.

sunset clause. N. A clause in a statute stating that it will cease to be effective on a certain date unless it is renewed by the legislature.

sunshine laws. N. Laws requiring governmental agencies and departments to open their meetings to the public and make records of those meetings available to the public.

superior. ADJ. Above; better than; entitled to priority over something else.

superior court. N. A court of general jurisdiction, usually wider jurisdiction than an inferior court, though meaning varies by state.

supersede. V. To take the place of someone or something; to void one thing and replace it with something else.

superseding cause. N. Something that happens in between an action and an injury that interrupts the chain of causation and prevents the initial actor from being liable for the injury.

supervene. V. To occur after an event, in such a way as to change the circumstances.

supervening cause. N. Something that happens between an action and an injury that changes the circumstances enough that it becomes the cause of the injury.

supervisor. N. An employee who oversees the work of other employees.

supplement. N. Something added to something else to improve, enhance, or complete it. V. *supplement*. ADJ. *supplemental*, *supplementary*.

supplemental act. N. A legislative act that clarifies, extends, or completes an existing law.

supplemental jurisdiction. N. The discretionary jurisdiction of a federal court to hear and decide matters that are related to claims already within the court's original jurisdiction, such as claims that arise out of the same case or controversy as one already before the court or claims that add parties to the original parties.

supplemental pleading. N. An answer, complaint, or other pleading that adds new facts to an original pleading without changing it; see also *amend*.

supplemental proceeding. N. A proceeding done after a court has issued judgment against a debtor, to identify the debtor's property and use it to satisfy the judgment; also called supplementary proceeding.

support. V. (1) To provide someone with money, a home, and the necessities of life. (2) To encourage; to approve of; to defend; to aid. (3) To corroborate; to back up with evidence. (4) To hold something up; to bear the weight of something. N. *support*. See also *alimony, child support, maintain*.

suppress. V. To end something forcibly; to prevent information from being revealed; to control or restrain. N. *suppression*.

suppression of evidence. N. (1) A court's refusal to admit evidence acquired by unlawful means. (2) A party's refusal or failure to furnish opposing counsel with evidence that might prove unfavorable.

supra. ADV. *(Latin)* Above; used in a document to refer to something mentioned earlier in the document; see also *infra*.

supranational. ADJ. Transcending national boundaries, concerns, or governments.

Supremacy Clause. N. A clause in Article IV of the U.S. Constitution that makes the acts of the federal government the supreme law of the land, superior to all state laws and constitutions.

supreme. ADJ. The highest, most important, or most powerful; superior to all others. N. *supremacy*.

Supreme Court. N. The highest court in a state or in the United States; the court of last resort in many states and in the United States; also used as a name for a court of general jurisdiction in some states.

surcharge. N. (1) A charge added on top of a price or payment. (2) A financial penalty imposed on a fiduciary who fails to perform his or her duties properly. V. *surcharge*.

surety. N. A person who takes responsibility for someone else's debt, agreeing to pay it if the debtor fails to do so, usually bound by the same original instrument as the debtor and thus responsible for the debt from its inception. See also *guarantee*.

surgeon general. N. A federal officer who heads the U.S. Public Health Service; the head of a military medical service.

surplus. N. Excess; something left over after most of an asset or fund has been used for its designated purpose; a corporation's assets remaining after expenses and debts have been paid.

surplus, earned. N. Surplus earnings and profits retained by a corporation instead of being paid to shareholders as dividends.

surplus, paid-in. N. A corporation's surplus obtained by selling stock at a price above par value.

surprise. V. (1) To catch, capture, or discover someone unawares. (2) To astonish or amaze. N. (1) Coming upon someone unawares. (2) An unexpected event; a revelation or situation that a party to a trial has not expected and could not reasonably have prepared for, which potentially can be grounds for a new trial.

surrender. V. To give up; to yield; to hand something over to someone else; for a tenant to give up a lease before its term with the understanding that the landlord will terminate the lease. N. *surrender*.

surrender value. N. The amount that an insurer will pay a policy-holder if he or she gives up a life insurance policy, i.e., the policy's current value.

surrogate. N. (1) A substitute or deputy. (2) A judicial officer who handles matters such as probate, adoptions, and guardianships at the local level, such as within a county.

surrogate mother. N. A woman who bears a child for another couple, either by having her own egg fertilized with the husband's sperm or by having an embryo made from the couple's gametes implanted in her uterus, and after birth surrenders her parental rights to the couple.

surrogate parent. N. A person other than a child's parent who assumes parental responsibilities toward that child; an advocate appointed for a child by a juvenile court.

surtax. N. An additional tax imposed on something that has already been taxed.

surveillance. N. The monitoring or observation of a person or situation, especially done by police pursuing a suspected criminal or gathering evidence of a crime.

survival action. N. An action that survives the death of the party who brought it.

survival statute. N. A statute that allows the estate of a deceased person to maintain a cause of action for that person's pain and suffering up until the moment of death.

survive. V. To remain living; to live after someone else has died. N. *survival*. ADJ. *surviving*.

survivor. N. A person who remains alive after the death of someone else or after some event.

survivorship. N. Becoming entitled to property by outliving someone else who had an interest in it; the right of a joint tenant to take the entire property when his or her co-tenant dies.

suspect. N. A person who is believed to have committed a crime. V. To believe without proof that someone has committed a crime or misdeed; to have some slight idea that something is the case without having any proof. ADJ. Untrustworthy; unreliable; potentially dangerous.

suspect classification. N. A classification of people that seems to have no legitimate purpose, such as grouping people by race or sex when those traits could not be relevant to the matter at hand.

suspend. V. (1) To put on hold; to postpone. (2) To prevent someone from performing a job or attending school for a period of time as a punishment. N. *suspension*.

suspended sentence. N. A sentence for a criminal offense that is postponed indefinitely unless the convicted person commits another crime within a specified period.

suspicion. N. The act of suspecting; a belief that someone has committed a crime or misdeed. V. *suspect*. ADJ. *suspicious*.

sustain. V. (1) To support. (2) To uphold; to affirm the validity of something. (3) To suffer something unpleasant, such as an injury.

swear. V. To bind oneself or someone else with an oath.

swearing in. N. The act of administering an oath to a witness at a trial, to a public official, or to a person undergoing some other formal proceeding. ADJ. *sworn*.

sweepstakes. N. (1) A contest that awards prizes based on random drawings of entries, often used as a promotion of products. (2) A horse race or other gambling contest in which the winner or winners receive all the stakes placed on the race.

swindle. V. To use fraud to cheat someone out of money. N. *swindle*, *swindling*.

syllabus. N. A headnote at the beginning of a reported case, summarizing the key legal points contained within.

symbolic speech. N. Conduct or actions without words that express some sentiment or opinion, which may or may not be protected under the First Amendment.

syndicate. N. (1) A group of people or companies that form an alliance, permanent or temporary, to conduct some business or activity together. (2) An organization that supplies material to a large number of periodical publications. V. (1) To manage a syndicate; to be managed by a syndicate; to sell something to a syndicate.

(2) To publish or broadcast the same material in multiple publications at the same time.

syndication. N. The act of forming a syndicate; the condition of being owned or managed by a syndicate.

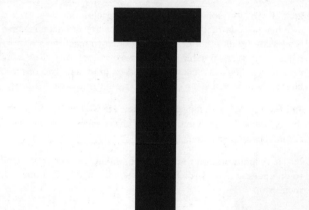

table 490

table. N. A list or chart that includes many items of information in a concise display. V. To postpone or suspend consideration of something, such as a proposed item of legislation.

table of cases. N. An alphabetical list of the cases mentioned in a legal book or document.

tacit. ADJ. Implied but not openly expressed; understood without being explicitly stated.

tack. V. To add something to something else, such as to add together periods of time in which a property is under adverse possession by different occupants in order to meet the statutory requirement for ownership, to combine coverage from two or more insurance policies in a claim for damages, or to unite two or more liens so as to increase the priority of one of them. N. *tacking*.

Taft-Hartley Act. N. A federal law enacted in 1947 as an addition to the National Labor Relations Act, giving employers increased rights in labor disputes.

tail. N. A limitation on the ownership of land, usually restricted to one person and his or her heirs. ADJ. Limited as to tenure or ownership.

tail, estate in. N. Inheritance that must be passed on to the recipient's children and grandchildren in a direct line. See also *fee tail*.

take. V. To grasp or lay hold of something; to seize a person or thing; to steal something; to assume ownership of something; to receive title to property.

take over. V. To acquire control over or management of a company. N. *takeover*.

take the fifth. V. To invoke the Fifth Amendment as justification for refusing to answer a question in a criminal prosecution.

taking. N. The act of taking something; a government's interference with or regulation of how a property owner can use his or her property in such a way that it substantially impairs the owner's property right. See also *condemn, eminent domain, larceny*.

tamper. V. To interfere with something so as to change it, especially in a destructive or unauthorized way; to attempt to influence a jury through bribery or other illegal means.

tangible. ADJ. Real; with a physical presence; perceptible to touch and sight. See also *intangible*.

tangible evidence. N. Evidence that can be seen or touched, as opposed to testimony.

tangible property. Physical things, such as land, buildings, and objects, that can be possessed.

tariff. N. A tax or duty imposed on imports and exports; see also *customs*.

tariff, protective. N. A fee imposed on imported goods of a certain type to protect producers and sellers of domestic goods of the same type.

tax. N. A charge imposed by the government on people and businesses on various activities and possessions, such as income, property, purchased goods, or inheritances, used by the government to fund itself and its programs. V. (1) To impose a tax. (2) To assess the costs of a legal action.

taxable. ADJ. Able to be taxed.

taxable estate. N. The amount of an estate that is subject to taxes, i.e., the gross estate minus any allowable deductions.

taxable gift. N. A gift that is subject to taxation.

taxable income. N. The amount of income subject to taxes, i.e., gross income minus credits and deductions.

taxable year. N. A twelve-month period used for calculating taxes; see also *fiscal year*.

taxation. N. The act of taxing; money paid as tax. See also *ad valorem tax, estate tax, gift tax, income tax, payroll tax, sales tax.*

tax benefit rule. N. A rule stating that an amount deducted in an earlier year but then recovered in a later year is to be included in the income of the later year.

tax bracket. N. A category of income that is subject to a particular tax rate.

tax court. N. A court that has jurisdiction over tax matters.

tax credit. N. An amount subtracted from a taxpayer's tax liability.

tax deduction. N. An amount subtracted from a taxpayer's taxable income.

tax evasion. N. The crime of paying less in taxes than the amount required by the government, such as by fraudulently reporting a lower income than what was in fact received.

tax exempt. ADJ. Not subject to taxation.

taxing power. N. The power granted to Congress by the Constitution to levy taxes.

taxpayer. N. A person or business that pays taxes; the person or entity subject to taxes on a particular transaction.

tax rate. N. The percentage of income or purchase price that must be paid in tax; see also *tax bracket*.

tax return. N. A document filed by a taxpayer with the Internal Revenue Service or state tax agency on which the taxpayer reports a taxable year's income, deductions, and credits, and calculates tax liability.

tax shelter. N. A fund, transaction, business arrangement, or other method used by a taxpayer to reduce taxable income or tax liability.

telecommunication. N. Using signals to transmit information over a distance, such as over a telephone or over a computer network.

telecommute. V. To perform one's job at some location other than the traditional workplace, such as at home, and using information technology to communicate with the workplace.

teleworker. N. An employee who performs his or her job at some location other than the traditional workplace, using information technology to communicate with the workplace.

temporary. ADJ. Not permanent; provisional; lasting for a limited time.

temporary disability. N. Disability due to illness or injury that prevents a person from working for a period of time but that is expected to end when the person recovers.

temporary restraining order. N. An order issued by a court forbidding a party to take some action as a temporary measure to protect a plaintiff until a formal hearing on an injunction can take place. ABBRV. *TRO*.

tenancy. N. The condition of being a tenant; an interest in land held by a tenant.

tenant. N. (1) A person who rents property from a landlord. (2) A person who owns or possesses property.

tenant, life. N. A person who holds an interest in property until the end of a life, either the tenant's or someone else's.

tenants, joint. N. Two or more people who share an interest in property, each of them owning the whole interest; when a joint tenant dies, his or her interest in the property ends.

tenants by the entirety. N. A husband and wife who hold property as joint tenants, with one spouse taking the whole title when the other dies.

tenants in common. N. Two or more tenants who hold an undivided interest in property but who each have a separate title to a proportional share; when a tenant in common dies, his or her share of the property goes into his or her estate.

tender. V. To offer or present something to someone; to present someone with money as payment; to offer to perform some service for a price. N. *tender*.

tender, legal. N. Valid money; money that a creditor must accept as payment of a debt.

tender of delivery. N. A seller's actual delivery of goods to a buyer; a seller's placing goods at the buyer's disposal and notifying the buyer of that fact.

tender offer. N. An offer to purchase shares of stock, often above market price, in a company made by a person or business that wished to acquire control of the company.

tenement. N. A building, house, dwelling, or other structure affixed to land; a building divided into separate residences that are rented; a dilapidated or run-down apartment building.

tenure. N. (1) A right to hold property; the condition of holding property. (2) The time that a person spends in a position or an office. (3) A state of guaranteed permanent employment awarded to professors, teachers, and a few other employees who have worked for an institution a specified period of time.

term. N. (1) A word or expression for something. (2) The duration of something; a fixed period of time; a period of time in which a court is in session. (3) A condition or requirement in a contract or agreement, usually used in the plural, i.e., *terms*. V. To give a name to something.

terminable. ADJ. Able to be terminated.

terminable interest. N. An interest in property that ends when a particular event occurs or does not occur.

terminate. V. To end; to expire; to fire an employee. N. *termination*.

terms of use. N. The rules presented by the creator or producer of a work such as a software application to its users, explaining the rights and obligations that accompany use of the work.

territorial court. N. A court in a U.S. territory that functions as both a state and a federal court.

territorial integrity. N. The principle that a state's borders are sacrosanct; the idea in international law that one state or nation should not aid actions that could reform the borders of another state or nation.

territorial jurisdiction. N. A court's or government's power over a specified territory or region.

territorial sea. N. The waters that are considered the territory of the state off which coast they lie; a band of waters parallel to the coast that can be no more than twelve nautical miles wide. See also *Law of the Sea*.

territorial waters. N. All waters contained within a state or country and all ocean waters within a three-mile border around its coast.

territory. N. A defined area of land; an area or region under the control of one government or ruler; the area in which a judge has jurisdiction; a region that is organized and governed according to the terms of a particular nation but has not yet been admitted to statehood in that nation. ADJ. *territorial*.

terror. N. Extreme fear or dread, which can lead to intimidation; the fear typical of someone who is afraid of being hurt or killed.

terrorism. N. The use of violence to achieve political ends in order to intimidate citizens and governments into acquiescing to the demands of the terrorists.

terrorist. N. A person who engages in terrorism. ADJ. *terroristic*.

terrorize. V. To frighten someone terribly; to use violence or threats to fill someone with dread and alarm.

testament. N. A will; the part of a last will and testament that disposes of someone's personal property.

testamentary. ADJ. Related to or given by a will.

testamentary capacity. N. The mental ability required to compose and execute a valid will, i.e., the ability to understand who one is, what one owns, and what the will will do.

testamentary disposition. N. A gift of property from a deceased person to a living one, done through a will.

testamentary intent. N. A testator's true intention in writing a will or naming a recipient of property.

testator. N. A person who writes and executes a will; a deceased person whose property is disposed of according to the terms of his or her will. FEM. *testatrix*.

test case. N. A lawsuit that serves as a test of the validity of a law, principle, or cause of action; one lawsuit chosen out of many similar ones brought at the same time to be heard by the court and decided as a test of the right of all the similar cases; also called a test action.

testify. V. To speak under oath; to give evidence as a witness in a deposition or lawsuit; to serve as proof of something.

testimony. N. The spoken evidence given by a witness under oath in court or at a deposition, or written evidence provided by a witness under oath through an affidavit.

theft. N. The act of taking something that belongs to someone else, without the owner's permission and with no intention of returning it; stealing; see also *larceny, steal*.

theorize. V. To create a theory; to generate a possible explanation for some situation.

theory. N. A set of principles or ideas that serve as the basis or explanation for some action or situation; a generally accepted body of principles based on known facts that explains some circumstance; an idea or premise about something; a legal or factual principle that serves as the basis for a case. See also *hypothesis*.

thief. N. Someone who steals.

third degree. N. Thorough and prolonged questioning administered to a criminal suspect by the police with the intention of getting the person to confess to a crime. ADJ. A category of crime less serious than first degree or second degree.

third party. N. A person who is not directly involved in a transaction; someone who is not a party to an agreement.

third party beneficiary. N. A person who is not a party to a contract but who will benefit from it and has rights under it.

third party complaint. N. A complaint filed by a defendant in an existing lawsuit against someone who is alleged by the defendant to be liable for damages to the plaintiff.

threat. N. A statement of an intention to harm someone or damage his or her property; a person or thing that seems likely to cause damage or danger; a menace. V. *threaten*.

thrift institution. N. A savings and loan or savings bank; also called a *thrift*.

time. N. (1) Duration; how long it takes to do something. (2) A specific moment.

time-and-a-half. N. An hourly pay rate commonly paid for overtime work, calculated by adding 50% of the usual hourly rate to the usual hourly rate.

time deposit. N. A certificate of deposit; an account from which a depositor must wait a specific period of time before withdrawing.

time is of the essence. N. A phrase used in contracts in which performance by one of the parties at or by a specific time is an essential term. See also *reasonable time*.

timeshare. N. A property, often a vacation home, that is owned by several parties, each of whom is entitled to use it for a specified period of time every year.

tithe. N. A tenth of one's income contributed to something such as a charity or church; in feudal times, the tenth of a farm and other productions that was required to be donated to the church. V. *tithe*.

title. N. (1) A right or claim of ownership of property. (2) The official name of a job or position; the formal address given to a person in a position or job or of particular social status. (3) The name of a book, article, artwork, or other creation. (4) The name of a legislative bill or legal action. V. To name a book or other composition or creation.

Title IX. N. Title IX of the Education Amendments of 1972, a federal law banning sex discrimination in schools and universities, both academic and athletic.

Title VII. N. Title VII of the Civil Rights Act of 1964, a federal law that prohibits employment discrimination on the basis of sex, race, religion, or national origin.

title company. N. A company that checks titles to property in order to find defects and encumbrances, and that also issues title insurance.

title insurance. N. Insurance issued by a title company that has investigated the title to a property, guaranteeing that it has no known defects and insuring against claims based on a defective title.

title of record. N. The official title to a property, found through a title search. See also *bad title, cloud on title, good title*.

title search. N. An investigation done by a title company in which it examines the history of a title in the registry of deeds and then prepares an abstract summarizing the transfers of the title and the absence of defects on it.

Tobacco Master Settlement Agreement. N. A civil settlement in which several major tobacco companies agreed to pay money to the states to pay the health care costs of people injured by smoking and to limit the advertising of tobacco products.

to have and to hold. N. A phrase used in a conveyance expressing the fact that the transferor intends for the transferee to receive the property; also used in many marriage ceremonies to convey the parties' intention to be joined to one another.

toll. N. A payment for the right to use something once, such as the right to drive across a bridge. V. To suspend; to deny or take away.

tombstone ad. N. An advertisement in a newspaper announcing that a corporation is going to put up for sale an offering of stock.

tonnage. N. Capacity of a ship; the amount of cargo a ship can carry; the amount of cargo a ship is carrying.

tonnage duty. N. A tax imposed on ships according to tonnage, assessed when they enter a country.

tort. N. A private injury or wrong; a violation of a socially recognized duty owed to a plaintiff that results in injury to the plaintiff; torts can be caused intentionally, through negligence, or under strict liability. ADJ. *tortious*.

Tort Claims Act. N. A federal law that makes the U.S. government liable for damages in tort, waiving sovereign immunity except in specific cases; many states also have tort claims acts.

tortfeasor. N. A person who commits a tort against another.

torture. N. The infliction of severe mental or physical pain on a person in order to intimidate or punish the victim or to elicit information. V. *torture*.

total disability. N. A person's inability, due to physical or mental affliction, to perform any work that he or she is qualified to do and that is available in the community.

totality of the circumstances test. N. A test that examines all the circumstances surrounding an event to determine whether a person's constitutional rights have been violated by a search and seizure.

total loss. N. Complete destruction of property, such that it can no longer be used at all and retains little or no value.

to wit. ADV. *(Middle English)* To know; namely; that is to say.

tract. N. A parcel of land.

trade. N. (1) Buying and selling goods or services. (2) An exchange; a one-to-one transfer. (3) A skilled job, especially one that involves manual work. (4) A particular kind of business; the people who work in a particular kind of business or profession. V. To buy and sell, to exchange. See also *commerce.*

trade agreement. N. An agreement made by two nations regulating trade between them.

trade dress. N. The appearance and image associated with a particular product, including labels, colors, size, shape, and advertising techniques unique to the product.

trade fixture. See *fixture.*

trademark. N. A name, word, symbol, or device used by the manufacturer of a product to identify that product and distinguish it from other similar ones produced by competitors, which can be registered with the U.S. Patent and Trademark Office; also called a mark. See also *copyright, patent, trade name.*

trademark, arbitrary. N. A name for a product that is in no way descriptive or suggestive of the product, such as "Apple" computers, that is easily registered but difficult to educate consumers about.

trademark, descriptive. N. A name for a product that is descriptive of what it is or does, which cannot be registered unless it has taken on a distinctive meaning over time.

trademark, fanciful. N. A name invented for a particular product, such as "Exxon," that is easily registered but difficult to educate consumers about.

trademark, generic. N. A name for a product that has become synonymous with the product itself, such as "aspirin," which cannot be registered for trademark protection.

trademark, strong. N. A trademark that is inherently distinctive, such as an arbitrary or fanciful one, which is entitled to greater protection than a weaker one, such as a generic or descriptive mark.

trademark, suggestive. N. A name for a product that evokes characteristics of the product, and that is considered inherently distinctive and thus allowed to be registered.

trade name. N. A name used by a business to identify itself, which stands for the business's reputation and goodwill.

trade secret. N. A secret formula, pattern, plan, process, machine, or method of compiling information known and used exclusively by one business that could give competitors an advantage if they acquired it.

trade usage. N. A practice or custom accepted by the practitioners of a particular trade that they have every reason to expect to be followed by other practitioners of that trade in a particular transaction; the accepted meaning of a particular word or phrase within a trade. See also *course of dealing.*

traffic. N. Trade in some commodity; buying, selling, or trading of goods and services, often used regarding trade in illegal commodities such as drugs. V. *traffic.*

transact. V. To conduct business; to carry on some activity.

transaction. N. One instance of conducting business, such as buying or selling an item; an agreement or act involving at least two people that alters their legal rights in relation to one another.

transaction or occurrence test. N. A test used to determine whether a cause of action arises out of the same transaction or event that is the subject matter of an existing claim brought by the opposing party, in which case it must be brought as a counterclaim or forever be barred from litigation.

transcribe. V. To record spoken words in writing.

transcript. N. An official, certified, written record of a trial or other proceeding prepared by a court reporter.

transfer. V. To move a person or thing from one place to another; to move an object from the possession of one person to the possession of another; to change the title of property from one owner to another; to convey. N. *transfer.*

transferable. ADJ. Able to be transferred.

transfer agent. N. A person or company that oversees the sale of shares of publicly traded corporations and keeps records on shareholders.

transferee. N. A person who receives something that is transferred.

transferee liability. N. Tax liability imposed by the Internal Revenue Service on a person who has received transferred property in cases where it cannot find the transferor who actually owes the taxes.

transferor. N. A person who transfers something to someone else.

transfer pricing. N. The practice of transferring goods, services, loans, intellectual property, or other commodities to other jurisdictions or countries in order to set prices at local levels and gain tax advantages.

Transfers to Minors Act. See *Uniform Transfers to Minors Act.*

Transportation Security Administration. N. A federal agency within the Department of Homeland Security created in 2001 to oversee security of transportation systems within the United States. ABBRV. *TSA.*

treason. N. The act of betraying one's country, such as by aiding an enemy of the state or plotting to overthrow the government. ADJ. *treasonous.*

treasure trove. N. Treasure found; a cache of money, precious metals, or other valuable items with no known owner found buried in the earth or in a hidden place; the person who finds a treasure trove is entitled to it before anyone except the true owner.

treasury. N. A place where wealth is stored, especially public funds; the branch of the government responsible for saving and distributing revenue.

treasury bill. N. A promissory note issued by the U.S. Treasury with a maturity period of one year or less, which yields no interest but is sold at a discount and paid in full on maturity.

treasury bond. N. (1) A bond issued by the U.S. Treasury that matures in a term greater than five years. (2) A bond issued and then bought back by the same corporation.

treasury note. N. A note issued by the U.S. Treasury for an intermediate term, i.e., maturing in one to five years, which pays interest by coupon.

treasury stock. N. Stock issued and then later repurchased by a corporation.

treaty. N. A formal agreement between two or more nations concerning some matter of public welfare.

treaty clause. N. A clause in the Constitution that gives the president the power to make treaties with other nations and the Senate the right to approve them.

treble. ADJ. Triple. V. To triple; to multiply by three.

treble damages. N. An award of damages that is tripled as further punishment for the wrongdoer.

trespass. V. To enter or disturb property owned by someone else without the owner's permission. N. *trespass*.

trespass, continuing. N. A permanent state of trespass, as when someone builds a house on his or her own land that encroaches onto the property of someone else.

trespass, criminal. N. Trespassing on property that has been posted with signs warning away trespassers, or remaining on someone else's property after being ordered to leave.

trespasser. N. A person who trespasses.

trespass on the case. N. A common law action that allowed someone to recover for injury that resulted indirectly from a defendant's actions; also called case.

trial. N. A formal judicial proceeding in which a judge and sometimes a jury hear the evidence in a case and decide the rights of the parties in a civil case or the guilt or innocence of the defendant in a criminal case. See also *bench trial, jury trial*.

trial court. N. The court in which a case is first presented, as opposed to an appellate court.

tribunal. N. A judicial court; a judge's seat or bench; a judge or group of judges with jurisdiction in an area.

TRO. ABBRV. Temporary restraining order.

truancy. N. Refusal to attend school by a minor required to attend, without permission or justification.

truant. N. A student who refuses to attend school.

true. ADJ. Accurate; reliable; in agreement with the facts; genuine; loyal. N. *truth*.

true bill. N. An indictment; the endorsement of an indictment by the grand jury who has made it.

true copy. N. A copy of a document that is not necessarily an exact duplicate of the original but is close enough to be clearly understood and recognized.

true value. N. The fair market value of property.

trust. N. (1) Confidence that someone will act in a particular way; firm belief in someone's reliability. (2) A legal arrangement in which one person or company (the trustee) holds title to property that is intended to benefit someone else (the beneficiary); the trustee has a fiduciary obligation to administer the trust's assets and distribute its income to benefit the beneficiary or beneficiaries. (3) An organization managed by a trustee. (4) A company or group of companies that attempts to control a market or create a monopoly. v. To believe in someone's or something's reliability, ability, or honesty.

trust, active. N. A trust that must be actively managed by the trustee.

trust, charitable. N. A trust created to benefit a class or the public for educational, charitable, scientific, or religious purposes.

trust, passive. N. A trust that does not require any action by the trustee.

trust, resulting. N. A trust that has not been explicitly created but that arises when it seems that a person transferring property to another must have wanted the person who receives title to the property to use it to benefit someone else. See also *cestui que*.

trust company. N. A company that acts as a trustee for people who want to create trusts.

trustee. N. The person who holds the property of a trust and administers it in a fiduciary capacity for the benefit of the beneficiaries.

trustee in bankruptcy. N. A person who handles the administration of bankruptcies, managing the financial affairs of the bankrupt person or company and paying creditors.

trust fund. N. Property or money held in a trust, administered by a trustee and intended to benefit someone who does not own it.

trust indenture. N. A document containing the terms and conditions governing a trust.

trustor. N. A person who creates a trust; a settlor.

trusty. N. An inmate in a correctional institution who, due to good behavior, is allowed a degree of freedom and responsibility denied to other prisoners.

truth-in-lending act. N. A federal law requiring lenders to reveal to consumers applying for commercial credit the true cost of that credit, in order to enable consumers to shop around for the most favorable credit terms.

try. V. To examine a case in a judicial trial; to subject a criminal suspect to a trial.

TSA. ABBRV. Transportation Security Administration.

turn-key contract. N. A building contract in which the contractor assumes all risks and performs all work, leaving the owner of the project nothing to do toward its construction but "turn the key" to open the door once it is finished.

turnover. N. The rate of replacement of goods, funds, or personnel; in a company, the rate at which employees leave and are replaced by others.

turntable doctrine. N. Another term for "attractive nuisance," so-called because railroad turntables are known to attract children who can be harmed by playing on them.

turpitude. See *moral turpitude*.

tying arrangement. N. A seller's refusal to sell a buyer a desired item unless the buyer also purchases a specific other item, whether the buyer wants the additional item or not.

tyranny. N. Rule by a tyrant.

tyrant. N. A single absolute ruler; a ruler who holds absolute power over the state; a despot.

UCC. ABBRV. Uniform Commercial Code.

UCCC. ABBRV. Uniform Consumer Credit Code.

UGMA. ABBRV. Uniform Gifts to Minors Act. See *Uniform Transfers to Minors Act*.

UIT. ABBRV. Unit investment trust.

ultimate facts. N. The facts that ultimately form the basis of the decision in a case.

ultrahazardous. ADJ. Extremely dangerous; involving a serious risk of harm to people or property that cannot be avoided no matter how careful one is.

ultrahazardous activity. N. An activity that is so abnormally dangerous that no amount of care can prevent risk of harm, and that therefore gives rise to strict liability.

ultra vires. ADJ. *(Latin)* Beyond the powers; outside one's official authority; used especially to describe actions by a corporation that exceed the powers granted to it by its charter or by state law.

UN. ABBRV. United Nations.

unanimous. ADJ. Agreed to by all concerned parties without a negative vote or opinion. N. *unanimity*.

unauthorized. ADJ. Done without official authorization or permission.

unauthorized use. N. Using an automobile without permission of the owner.

unavoidable. ADJ. Impossible to avoid or prevent.

unavoidable accident. N. An accident that could not have been prevented by the parties involved in it, no matter what steps they took to avoid it, and not caused by their negligence or lack of skill or care.

unborn. ADJ. Not yet born; can refer to a fetus in the womb or a child who has not yet been conceived.

unclean hands. N. The equitable doctrine that a plaintiff's own fault must be considered when determining the remedy he or she should receive from a defendant. See also *clean hands doctrine*.

unconscionable. ADJ. Unreasonably detrimental; grossly one-sided; so unfair or oppressive to the interests of a party to a contract as to render the contract unenforceable. N. *unconscionability*.

unconstitutional. ADJ. Conflicting with the Constitution of the United States or another constitution.

uncontestable. ADJ. Not able to be challenged or contested.

uncontestable clause. N. A clause in a life insurance policy that says the insurer may not contest a claim after the policy has been in force for a specified period of time.

under control. ADJ. Of a vehicle, able to be stopped quickly when necessary.

under protest. ADV. Unwillingly; done under compulsion while making one's unwillingness known; used to describe an action done unwillingly and with objection.

under the influence. ADJ. Intoxicated; suffering from mental and physical impairment due to consumption of alcohol or drugs.

underwrite. V. (1) To insure; to accept the liability for something. (2) To agree to buy all unsold shares from an issue of stocks or bonds. (3) To provide financial support for some enterprise. N. *underwriting*.

underwriter. N. A person, bank, insurance company, or other institution that underwrites something.

undivided. ADJ. Not divided or broken up into portions.

undivided interest. N. An interest in property held by tenants in common, joint tenants, or tenants by the entirety, each of whom has a right to use the entire property; also called an undivided right; see also *tenant*.

undue. ADJ. Improper; unwarranted; exceeding what is necessary.

undue influence. N. Excessive or improper influence exerted on a person writing a will or giving away property by someone who wants to take away the person's free will and dominate the action; influence that interferes with someone's free will or judgment and subjugates it to someone else's wishes.

unearned. ADJ. Not earned.

unearned interest. N. Interest paid to someone by a financial institution before it is actually earned.

unearned surplus. N. All surplus that is not earned, including surplus from the revaluation of assets, surplus from contributions by shareholders or others, and paid-in surplus. See also *income, unearned*.

unemployment insurance. N. Insurance that pays benefits to temporarily unemployed workers; in the United States, an insurance program that federal law requires each state to fund and administer.

unethical. ADJ. Not ethical; not according to morals or the ethical standards of a profession.

unfair competition. N. The tort of fraudulently trying to pass off one's goods as those of another company, or to use the reputation of another company to sell one's own product, as through misleading advertising or packaging.

unfair labor practices. N. Acts forbidden to both employers and employees under the National Labor Relations Act, including for a union to coerce employees and employers, or to refuse to bargain, or for an employer to interfere with the employees' attempts to exercise their rights.

unfit. ADJ. Not suitable for a particular purpose; not qualified; incompetent.

uniform. ADJ. Conforming everywhere to the same standard; remaining the same everywhere; applying equally to everyone concerned.

Uniform Code of Military Justice. N. A compilation of laws governing the conduct of military personnel.

Uniform Commercial Code. N. A compilation of laws governing commercial transactions, including the sale of goods, commercial paper, banking, and secured transactions. ABBRV. *UCC*.

Uniform Consumer Credit Code. N. A law adopted by some states that regulates consumer credit. ABBRV. *UCCC*.

Uniform Gifts to Minors Act. See *Uniform Transfers to Minors Act*. ABBRV. *UGMA*.

uniform laws. N. Compilations of laws that address various subject areas and attempt to make the law in those areas uniform, such as the Uniform Commercial Code, Uniform Consumer Credit Code, and Uniform Transfers to Minors Act; also called uniform acts.

Uniform Resource Identifier. N. A commonly used synonym for Uniform Resource Locator. ABBRV. *URI*.

Uniform Resource Locator. N. The series of characters that will retrieve a particular web page when typed into the address bar in a Web browser; a domain name or IP address plus other information that specifies a particular page. ABBRV. *URL*.

Uniform System of Citation. N. A guide to legal citation published by the Harvard Law Review Association and accepted as the standard guide to citation; synonymous with *Blue Book*.

Uniform Transfers to Minors Act. N. An act governing transfers of property to a trust managed by a custodian for the benefit of named minors; an act called the *Uniform Gifts to Minors Act* was the original law of this type, but the Uniform Transfers to Minors Act has replaced it in most states. ABBRV. *UTMA*.

unilateral. ADJ. One-sided; performed by one party in a situation without the participation or agreement of other parties; affecting only one party or group in a particular situation. See also *contract, unilateral*.

uninsured. ADJ. Without insurance coverage.

uninsured motorist coverage. N. Insurance that covers the insured for injury or damage caused by a driver who does not have liability insurance.

union. N. (1) A group of states or nations with a central government. (2) The act of joining together; a state of togetherness or harmony. (3) A labor organization that exists to negotiate with employers on behalf of workers in matters such as wages, hours, and workplace safety.

unionize. V. To become a member of a labor union or persuade others to join it. ADJ. *unionized*.

United Nations. N. An international organization founded in 1945 to help nations cooperate in matters of human rights, economics, security, and international law. ABBRV. *UN*.

United Nations Framework Convention on Climate Change. N. A nonbinding international treaty passed in 1992 that states the desirability of reducing greenhouse gas emissions and slowing climate change. See also *Kyoto Protocol*.

United States Attorney. N. An attorney appointed by the president to represent the U.S. government in civil lawsuits and other matters in a judicial district; see also *district attorney*.

United States Citizenship and Immigration Services. N. A bureau in the Department of Homeland Security that oversees immigration, naturalization, visa applications, and petitions for asylum. See also *Immigration and Naturalization Services*. ABBRV. *USCIS*.

United States Code. N. A compilation of federal statutes, updated every six years and supplemented in between. ABBRV. *USC*.

United States Code Annotated. N. The annotated version of the USC, supplemented with case notes, cross-references, and historical references. ABBRV. *USCA*.

United States Constitution. N. The principles according to which the federal government of the United States is organized, enacted in 1787 and modified by twenty-seven amendments.

United States Court of Federal Claims. N. The federal court that hears claims against the U.S. government; this court replaced the Court of Claims in 1982. Synonymous with *Claims Court, U.S.*

United States Customs Service. N. The government service that collects customs duties, seizes contraband, processes people and goods coming in and out of the United States, and enforces applicable trade statutes.

United States Department of Treasury. N. The department of the federal government that handles financial policy, collects taxes, issues currency, manages public debt, and oversees several bureaus including the Bureau of Alcohol, Tobacco, Firearms and Explosives, the Secret Service, and the Internal Revenue Service.

United States Department of Veterans Affairs. N. A federal agency that provides benefits and services to military veterans. ABBRV. *VA.*

United States Marshal. N. An officer appointed by the president for a judicial district who executes all writs and orders issued by federal courts.

United States Tax Court. N. An administrative agency that functions as a court to hear disputes over amounts of income, estate, and gift taxes between taxpayers and the Internal Revenue Service.

unities, four. N. The four conditions that must exist in order to create a joint tenancy under common law, including unity of interest, unity of time, unity of possession, and unity of title.

unit investment trust. N. A registered trust that purchases fixed-income securities and holds them to maturity, sold to investors in units (typically of $1,000 each). ABBRV. *UIT.*

unity. N. The state of forming a united whole; agreement or harmony between people.

unity of interest. N. Sharing an interest in the same property.

unity of possession. N. Holding equal rights to use and possess the same property.

unity of time. N. Sharing an interest in property simultaneously.

unity of title. N. Receiving an interest in property through the same conveyance or instrument.

unjust. ADJ. Not just; unfair.

unjust enrichment. N. Knowingly receiving and accepting a benefit without paying for it or a benefit that rightfully belongs to someone else.

unlawful. ADJ. Against the law; illegal.

unlawful assembly. N. The gathering of three or more people with the intention of disturbing the peace or committing some unlawful act; definition varies by state.

unlawful detainer. N. The act of keeping possession of a property by someone who once had a right to it but no longer does, such as a tenant whose lease has ended but who refuses to leave.

unlawful entry. N. Entering property without the owner's consent through the use of force or fraud.

unlisted security. N. A security that is not listed on a stock exchange and can only be traded over the counter.

unnatural act. N. Sexual acts that were historically considered unnatural or wrong, including sodomy or buggery; see also *crime against nature*.

unnecessary hardship. N. A condition found when the physical characteristics of a piece of property prevent it from being used for purposes permitted by zoning laws, or when it would be prohibitively expensive to use it in the permitted ways, so zoning laws are therefore found to impose unreasonable difficulties on the property owner and a variance is warranted.

unrealized. ADJ. Not achieved; not converted into money.

unrealized profit or loss. N. Profit or loss that has not yet been converted into actual money, existing only in principle or "on paper," such as a rise or loss in stock prices.

unreasonable. ADJ. Arbitrary; excessive; unfair; irrational.

unreasonable search and seizure. See *search and seizure*.

unsolicited. ADJ. Unasked-for; not requested or sought after.

URI. ABBRV. Uniform Resource Identifier.

URL. ABBRV. Uniform Resource Locator.

usage. N. A practice that is usual within a particular business; the typical way of doing an activity or interpreting a word or phrase within a profession or kind of business. See also *custom*, *trade usage*.

USA PATRIOT Act. N. Uniting and Strengthening America by Providing Appropriate Tools Required to Intercept and Obstruct Terrorism Act of 2001; a law passed shortly after September 11, 2001, that strengthened U.S. law enforcement agencies for the purpose of preventing future terrorist attacks.

USC. ABBRV. United States Code.

USCA. ABBRV. United States Code Annotated.

USCIS. ABBRV. United States Citizenship and Immigration Services.

use. V. To employ someone or something; to put into action; to enjoy the benefits of real or personal property. N. The act of using; the fact of being used; the right to enjoy the benefits of property.

useful. ADJ. Able to be put to some beneficial use.

useful life. N. For tax purposes, the period during which an asset is expected to be useful to its owner before wearing out or otherwise becoming useless.

user. N. A person who uses something.

usufruct. N. The civil law right to use property that belongs to someone else.

usurer. N. A person who lends money at unreasonably high interest.

usurp. V. To take over; to supplant; to take over a position of power by force. N. *usurpation*.

usurper. N. A person who usurps a position.

usury. N. Lending money at excessively high interest rates. ADJ. *usurious*.

U.S. v. Microsoft. N. An antitrust lawsuit brought by the U.S. Department of Justice against Microsoft Corporation in 1998, in which the United States alleged that Microsoft had violated antimonopoly laws by bundling its operating system and Web browser software, thus unfairly preventing rivals from competing for customers.

UTMA. ABBRV. Uniform Transfers to Minors Act.

utmost. N. The greatest amount or extent possible. ADJ. *utmost*.

utmost care. N. Highest care; the care that a very cautious and competent person would use.

utmost resistance. N. The highest degree of resistance a person is capable of, historically required of a victim of rape in order to charge the offender with rape.

utter. V. (1) To say something out loud. N. *utterance*. (2) To offer forged money as valid; to introduce forged money into circulation. N. *uttering*. ADJ. Complete; total; absolute.

V

v. ABBRV. Versus.

VA. ABBRV. United States Department of Veterans Affairs.

vacate. V. (1) To leave; to make empty. (2) To make void; to annul.

vacation. N. A break from work; leave from work to be used for any purpose, particularly recreation.

vagrancy. N. The act of living as a vagrant.

vagrant. N. A person with no regular job or home who wanders from place to place and supports himself or herself by begging.

vague. ADJ. Uncertain; unclear; not clearly defined or stated. N. *vagueness*.

valid. ADJ. Properly executed and legally binding; legitimate; acceptable. N. *validity*. See also *void*.

validate. V. To make valid.

valuable. ADJ. Worth money; important.

valuable consideration. N. Something of value given in exchange for a performance or a promise, which entitles the recipient of the promise to enforce a claim against a promisor who fails to perform.

value. N. (1) Worth; cost or price in money; the price a seller would give a buyer in a bona fide transaction in an open market. (2) Importance; utility. (3) A moral principle. V. (1) To estimate the worth of something. (2) To consider important.

vandal. N. A person who willfully destroys or damages property.

vandalism. N. The act of willfully destroying or damaging property. V. *vandalize*.

variance. N. (1) A discrepancy. (2) A disagreement between the allegations in a pleading and the evidence offered to prove them. (3) Permission to use property in a way not allowed under applicable zoning ordinances; see also *unnecessary hardship*.

vehicle identification number. N. A unique seventeen-digit number that identifies any given motor vehicle. ABBRV. *VIN*.

vehicular. ADJ. Of or related to motor vehicles, such as automobiles and motorcycles. See also *homicide, vehicular*.

vend. V. To sell.

vendee. N. A buyer.

vendor. N. A seller.

venire. N. *(Latin)* To come; the writ that summons potential jurors to court; the group of potential jurors for a case.

venture. N. A risky undertaking; a business enterprise that involves some risk. V. To dare to do something; to undertake some enterprise that involves risk of loss.

venture capital. N. Funding for a new business that involves risk but has potential for great profits. See also *joint venture*.

venue. N. The place where something happens; a court that has jurisdiction over a matter; a court in which cases from a particular location may be brought; the district in which a federal lawsuit is brought.

veracity. N. Truth; honesty; accuracy.

verbal. ADJ. Expressed in words; oral; spoken rather than written.

verdict. N. A jury's or judge's finding on a question of fact, to be used by the court in determining its final judgment.

verdict, general. N. A verdict that announces which party prevails; the ordinary kind of verdict.

verdict, partial. N. A verdict that finds a criminal defendant guilty of one or more charges and innocent of the others.

verdict, special. N. A jury's determination on a particular question of fact alleged in the pleadings. See also *directed verdict*.

verify. V. To confirm the truth, accuracy, or authenticity of something; to attest to the truth of something in an affidavit or other sworn statement. N. *verification*.

versus. ADV. *(Latin)* Against; used in the title of a lawsuit to indicate which party is against which. ABBRV. *v.* or vs.

vest. V. To accrue; to take effect; to bestow on someone; to give someone authority, power, or a right; to gain a legal right to something; to come into possession of something.

vested. ADJ. Fixed; settled; secure in someone's possession; having the right to present or future enjoyment; established or protected by law or contract.

vested estate. N. A property interest currently in someone's possession or that will certainly come into his or her possession in the future, and therefore can be given away or sold by him or her.

vested gift. N. A gift given at present, or a gift that will certainly take effect in the future and that is not contingent on some condition.

vested interest. N. An interest that is recognized as belonging to someone who has the right to give it away; a personal stake in some matter.

vested pension. N. A pension to which an employee is unconditionally entitled because he or she has completed the required period of employment, whether or not he or she is working for that particular employer at the time of retirement.

vested right. N. In constitutional law, a right that is so firmly attached to a person that it cannot be taken away by someone else.

vesting. N. An employee's acquisition of an unconditional right to receive retirement benefits after working for an employer for the required period.

veteran. N. A person who has served in the armed forces and been honorably discharged.

veto. N. The act of rejecting a law or decision that has been passed by a legislature, usually done by a president or governor who must sign it in order for it to become valid.

veto, line-item. N. The power to reject some portions of a law without rejecting the whole thing. See also *pocket veto*.

vexatious. ADJ. Troublesome; annoying; worrisome.

vexatious litigation. N. A lawsuit brought without probable cause, out of malice toward the opposing party.

viable. ADJ. (1) Feasible; able to work. (2) Of a fetus, capable of living outside its mother's womb, with or without artificial life support. N. *viability*.

vicarious. ADJ. Experienced or done through another person.

vicarious liability. N. Liability imposed on one person for the actions of another based on a relationship between them, such as that between a principal and an agent or a parent and child.

vice. N. Immorality; bad behavior; a bad habit. PREFIX. Next in rank; a deputy for someone else, such as a vice president.

vice crime. N. A crime involving immorality, such as drug use or prostitution.

Vienna Convention on the Law of Treaties. N. An international treaty effective in 1980 that codified and clarified accepted international law on the creation of treaties.

VIN. ABBRV. Vehicle identification number.

violent. ADJ. Using physical force, especially unwarranted force used to intimidate or physically defeat someone else, often accompanied by anger or strong emotions. N. *violence*.

violent crime. N. A crime involving physical force, such as assault or murder.

violent death. N. Death caused by a violent external force, such as another person.

virtual. ADJ. Almost but not quite as described or intended; effective for all practical purposes, though not officially acknowledged.

virtual representation. N. The condition of being represented in a lawsuit without being named as a party by a party who shares the same interest, with the nonparty agreeing to be bound by the judgment.

virus. N. A computer program that can copy itself and install itself onto a computer without help from or the knowledge of the computer's owner or user.

visa. N. A document or stamp issued by a country to a foreign national, giving the holder the right to enter the country for a specified period and for specified purposes.

visitation. N. A formally organized meeting with someone, especially the time that a divorced spouse is allowed to spend with the children from his or her marriage.

visitation rights. N. Rights granted to divorced parents without custody to visit their children, and occasionally granted to grandparents as well.

vitiate. V. To ruin something; to void or annul; to impair something's effectiveness.

viz. ABBRV. *(Latin)* Videlicet, meaning obviously, namely, or of course; in other words; used to explain or rephrase preceding words in order to clarify them.

voice exemplar. N. A recording of someone's voice made during a criminal investigation, to be used as a basis for comparison against recorded evidence.

void. ADJ. Invalid; not legally binding; ineffective; empty. See also *valid.* V. To declare something legally invalid.

void ab initio. ADJ. Never having had legal validity; void from the beginning.

voidable. ADJ. Able to be annulled or voided due to some irregularity or problem, but valid until that happens.

voidable contract. N. A contract that may be legally voided by one or both parties, but that is valid until voided.

void for vagueness. ADJ. Describes a statute so obscure, difficult to understand, or unclear that it is impossible for ordinarily intelligent people to agree on a meaning, and so it must be void.

void on its face. ADJ. Describes a statute or instrument that has such obvious errors or imperfections that it must be invalid, especially excessively broad legislation that does not address a particular crime specifically enough and inadvertently impairs many legal rights.

voir dire. N. *(French)* To say the truth. (1) The preliminary examination of potential jurors by the judge and attorneys to decide whether they are qualified for jury service and whether any conflicts exist. (2) A hearing done during a trial outside the hearing of the jury in order to determine some point that the court must rule on without the jury.

voluntary. ADJ. Done willingly, without the influence of or pressure from someone else.

vote. N. An indication of a choice for candidates in an election; an individual ballot or other means of indicating such choice submitted by a voter; the right to vote.

voter. N. A person who votes; a person who has the right to vote.

Voting Rights Act. N. A federal law passed in 1965 that guarantees all citizens the right to vote without discrimination by forbidding districts to require people to meet conditions such as literacy tests or educational requirements.

voting trust. N. A device in which corporate shareholders transfer their voting rights to a trustee who votes for them in corporate elections in order to pool their votes and control corporate affairs.

vouch. V. To verify; to confirm that a person is of good character or qualified for a position; to assert that something is true, based on personal experience.

voucher. N. A small printed document that entitles its holder to some good or service; a receipt; a document that authorizes the payment of cash.

voyeur. N. A person who receives sexual gratification from watching other people engaged in sex acts or seeing other people naked, or from watching others in pain.

voyeurism. N. The act or condition of being a voyeur.

W-4. N. A form filled out by an employee informing the employer how many tax deductions the employee may take and thus how much the employer should withhold.

wage. N. Compensation for work performed, particularly pay by the hour or by production paid weekly or daily to a manual or skilled worker; often called wages. See also *salary*. V. To carry on some enterprise, particularly a war.

wage, living. N. Compensation sufficient to support a family above poverty conditions.

wage, minimum. N. The lowest hourly wage an employer is allowed to pay workers in most jobs, set by statute.

wager. N. A bet; an agreement made by two parties that one of them will pay the other a specific sum if a certain condition occurs. V. *wager*.

waiting period. N. A period of time that must elapse before a person can take some action or enforce some legal right.

waive. V. To voluntarily give up a legal right or claim.

waiver. N. The act of intentionally and voluntarily surrendering a right or claim; a document that records a person's surrender of a right or claim.

wanton. ADJ. (1) Reckless; malicious; deliberate, unprovoked, and in disregard of the safety of others. (2) Immodest; sexually promiscuous.

war crime. N. During wartime, a violation of the laws of war. See also *Geneva Conventions*.

ward. N. (1) A territorial division in a town or city. (2) An area of a hospital or prison. (3) A person, especially a child, under the care and supervision of a guardian.

ward of the court. N. A person who is under the care of the court, or for whom the court has appointed a guardian.

warehouse. N. A building used to store goods. V. (1) To store goods in a warehouse. (2) For a mortgage broker to retain a mortgage until the mortgage resale market improves. (3) For a corporation to notify certain investors of a tender offer before it is made public, allowing those investors to purchase stock at a low price.

warehouse receipt. N. A document issued by a person who runs a warehouse, indicating that the goods have been deposited into his or her care, which serves as a document of title for its holder.

warrant. N. A written order issued by some authority directing someone to do a certain act, particularly an order issued by the state directing a law enforcement officer to arrest someone. V. (1) To justify; to make necessary. (2) To guarantee or confirm; to affirm that a title is good; to confirm that something is as it is represented. See also *search warrant*.

warrant, death. N. A warrant issued by a governor or other high officer ordering a law enforcement officer to execute a convicted criminal who has been sentenced to death.

warrant, stock. N. A certificate entitling its holder to buy a certain number of shares of stock for a specified price.

warrantee. N. A person who receives a warrant.

warrantless arrest. N. An arrest made without a warrant, occasionally justifiable if the arresting officer has sufficient probable cause.

warrantor. N. A person who makes a warranty.

warranty. N. A promise or assurance that something is true, of a certain quality, or useful for a particular purpose; an assurance by one party to a contract that a certain fact is true, given to save the other party the trouble of confirming it, which is in effect a promise to cover any losses suffered by the other party if the fact turns out not to be true.

warranty, express. N. A promise included with the terms of a sale agreement, assuring the purchaser that the goods are of a particular quality and promising to fix or replace them if they are not as promised.

warranty, implied. N. A warranty implied by the seller's actions or words.

warranty deed. N. A deed that contains a warranty of good title.

warranty of fitness for a particular purpose. N. A promise by the seller, expressed or implied, that the purchased item will be suitable for the use to which the buyer wishes to put it.

warranty of habitability. N. An assurance, expressed or implied, given by a landlord to a new tenant that the premises are suitable for human habitation.

warranty of merchantability. N. An implied assurance by a seller that the goods he or she sells are fit for the general purpose for which they are sold.

Warsaw Convention. N. An international convention that regulates international air transport of people and goods.

wash sale. N. (1) A sale of stock followed by a purchase of the same stock within a short period of time, usually thirty days; losses on such a sale and repurchase may not be recognized for tax purposes. (2) Simultaneous buying and selling of a stock issue to generate interest in the stock, forbidden by the Securities and Exchange Commission.

wash trade. N. The sale of a security at a loss and the repurchase of the same security within thirty days before or after the sale, which does not result in a capital loss for tax purposes; a wash sale.

waste. N. (1) The act of using something carelessly for no good reason. (2) The things left over from producing something, which have no value and must be disposed of. (3) Damage to or neglect of property by a life tenant that reduces the property's value. V. *waste*.

wasting asset. N. A natural resource that is depleted as it is used and that eventually will cease to be useful, such as a coal mine; also called wasting property.

watered stock. N. Stock issued by a corporation whose total worth is less than its capital investment; stock issued for less than adequate consideration, as a bonus or as part of compensation, which means that its true value is actually less than its stated market value.

watermark. N. (1) A transparent mark on a piece of paper that can be seen when the paper is held to a light, used as a sign of genuineness. (2) A mark on the bank of a body of water that indicates the highest or lowest point to which the water has risen or dropped.

way. N. A road, path, or passage. See also *right of way*.

ways and means. N. Raising money for governmental purposes.

weapon. N. An object designed or used to hurt or kill, either offensively or defensively.

weapon of mass destruction. N. A weapon that can kill or injure a very large number of people simultaneously and destroy an enormous range of territory, usually without the aggressor having to come near its area of effectiveness.

Web. N. See *World Wide Web*.

webmaster. N. The individual responsible for administering and maintaining a website.

website. N. A collection of documents, images, and other forms of digital information on one computer that broadcasts them on the Internet.

Web traffic. N. The visits a website receives from users.

weight of evidence. N. The preponderance of the evidence; the side of the case that has more evidence supporting it.

welfare. N. (1) Well-being, quality of life. (2) Financial aid paid by the government to the needy.

wellness. N. General physical and mental well-being.

Westlaw. N. A privately owned online legal research system that provides access to reported decisions, federal and state statutes, law review articles, and many other materials; see also *LexisNexis*.

wetland. N. An area of land on the edge of a body of water, where aquatic and terrestrial life forms intersect.

when issued. ADV. Shortened form of phrase "when, as, and if issued," used to describe a security that has not yet been authorized for issue, or that has been authorized but does not in fact exist yet, which can be purchased in a conditional transaction that becomes complete when the stock is officially issued.

whereas. CONJ. (1) Considering that something is the case; used in legal documents to begin an introductory statement. (2) In comparison to; in contrast with.

whistleblower. N. An employee who reports wrongdoing by his or her employer or coworkers.

whistleblower acts. N. Federal and state laws that prevent employers from retaliating against employees who report wrongdoing in the workplace.

WHO. ABBRV. World Health Organization.

wholesale. N. The selling of goods, usually in large quantities, to retailers who will in turn sell them to consumers.

wholesaler. N. A person or company who buys large quantities of goods from manufacturers or suppliers, and then sells them to retailers.

widow. N. A wife who remains alive after her husband dies.

widow's allowance. N. Property and money that a widow can claim from her husband's estate for her own support.

widow's election. N. See *election by spouse*.

wiki. N. A website that can be edited by any user.

wildcat strike. N. A strike not authorized or organized by a labor union, usually illegal.

will. N. (1) Desire; intention; choice. (2) A document in which a person describes how to distribute his or her property after death. V. To leave property to someone through a will. See also *holograph, last will and testament, living will, testament*.

willful. ADJ. Deliberate; intentional; premeditated.

willful and wanton misconduct. N. Conduct that displays an intentional disregard of one's legal duties or of the safety of others.

willful, deliberate, and premeditated. N. A description of the mental state necessary for some crimes, such as first-degree murder. See also *wanton*.

will, joint. N. A will disposing of joint property or property that is owned individually but is treated as common property, signed by all parties who hold the property.

will, mutual. N. A will in which two people make mutual provisions for one another; also called a reciprocal will.

winding up. N. Concluding the affairs of a corporation or partnership that is being liquidated, including paying off debts and distributing the remaining assets.

WIPO. ABBRV. World Intellectual Property Organization.

wiretapping. N. Using an electronic device to eavesdrop on telephone conversations or other communications; see also *eavesdrop, pen register*.

withdraw. V. To retreat; to remove or take away; to take money out of an account. N. *withdrawal*.

withhold. N. To hold something back; to keep something that is desired by someone else; to deduct income tax from an employee's pay and send it to the Internal Revenue Service on the employee's behalf. N. *withholding*.

with prejudice. ADV. Describes a claim or action that has been dismissed and that may not be brought again as a new action.

without prejudice. ADV. With no legal rights affected; describes a claim or action that may be brought as a new action after dismissal.

without recourse. ADJ. (1) Having no further rights or possible remedies. (2) Nonrecourse.

witness. N. A person who has seen or experienced some event; a person who testifies under oath about seeing or experiencing some event, or about the character of someone involved in a lawsuit. See also *character witness, material witness.*

Witness Protection Act. N. A federal statute that provides for the protection of witnesses in cases involving organized crime.

word of art. N. A word that has a particular meaning when used in a particular field, such as law or medicine, and that has a different meaning or no meaning when used in ordinary speech; also called term of art.

workers' compensation. N. A system of benefits provided by employers to employees who are injured on the job.

Workers' Compensation Acts. N. Federal and state laws that regulate the awards given by employers to employees injured on the job, generally holding that an employer is strictly liable for all injuries regardless of the employee's fault, and preventing employees who receive workers' compensation from filing civil lawsuits in an attempt to win damages.

work/life. N. A person's combined work and nonwork activities.

work made for hire. N. A copyrightable work prepared either by an employee in the course of employment, or by someone commissioned to do the work, on the condition that the person who prepares the material is paid for the job and does not retain any rights to it, including copyright. The employer or commissioner of the work is considered the author for copyright purposes.

work product. N. Documents, notes, memoranda, and other materials prepared by an attorney as part of representing a client, especially in anticipation of litigation on a particular matter.

work product rule. N. A rule protecting work product from discovery.

work release program. N. A program that allows an inmate in a correctional institution to go out to work during the day and return to the institution at night.

World Bank. N. A financial institution that exists to reduce global poverty by providing loans to help poor nations develop.

World Health Organization. N. An agency of the United Nations that works to promote international public health. ABBRV. *WHO.*

World Intellectual Property Organization. N. An agency of the United Nations that promotes creative activity and the protection of intellectual property. ABBRV. *WIPO.*

World Trade Organization. N. An international organization that regulates trade among nations. ABBRV. *WTO.*

World Wide Web. N. The body of interlinked documents on websites, accessible through the Internet by using a Web browser. Synonymous with *Web.*

worth. N. Monetary value; the quality of something. See also *net worth.*

wraparound mortgage. N. A second mortgage combined with an older mortgage with a lower interest rate than the current one, which results in a new interest rate between the old and current mortgages; the borrower makes payments to the new lender, who in turn makes payments to the lender that provided the original mortgage.

writ. N. A written command issued by a court or other authority ordering someone to do a particular act.

writing. N. The act of writing; a written document or instrument.

writ of assistance. N. An equitable remedy that transfers title to property that has been determined by the court to belong to the recipient.

writ of attachment. N. A court order to seize a debtor's property; see also *attach*.

writ of certiorari. See *certiorari*.

writ of error. N. A writ issued by an appellate court to a lower court ordering it to send the appellate court the record of a case tried in the lower court so that the appellate court can review it for errors in application of the law.

writ of execution. N. A writ ordering a law enforcement officer to enforce a judgment by the court.

writ of prohibition. N. An order issued by a higher court to a lower one preventing it from exceeding its jurisdiction.

written instrument. N. Something set down in writing; see also *instrument*.

wrong. ADJ. (1) Incorrect; false. (2) Immoral; dishonest; violating the rights of another. N. An immoral, unjust, or injurious act; a violation of someone's legal rights that results in harm; a breach of one's legal duty that results in harm to someone else.

wrongdoer. N. A person who violates someone's rights or injures someone else.

wrongful. ADJ. Causing injury; infringing on someone's rights; reckless; unfair.

wrongful act. N. An act that infringes on someone's rights and injures him or her.

wrongful death. N. A statutory offense or tort for death caused by a wrongful act or negligence for which an action can be brought on behalf of the dead person's beneficiaries.

wrongful life. N. A medical malpractice claim that can be brought on behalf of a child injured at birth, born with birth defects, or other situations in which the parents allege that the child is the victim of bad medical practice or advice.

WTO. ABBRV. World Trade Organization.

x. N. A mark used as a signature by someone who cannot write.

Y

year-and-a-day rule. N. A common law rule, discarded by some jurisdictions, requiring that death occur within one year and one day of some wrongful act for that act to be considered murder.

yellow dog contract. N. An employment contract that threatens to fire an employee if he or she joins a labor union, prohibited under most laws and unenforceable in court.

yield. V. (1) To produce; to deliver. (2) To surrender; to give up. N. That which is produced by something; the money produced from an investment.

yield, current. N. Current return on an investment measured as a percentage of its current price.

yield to maturity. N. The return that an investor will receive from a bond held until it matures.

youthful offender. N. A criminal who is older than a juvenile but still young, usually between the ages of 18 and 25, who might receive special consideration at sentencing to maximize chances of rehabilitation.

Z

zone. N. An area with a particular characteristic or assigned use. V. To divide a town or city into geographical areas with different building requirements and land use restrictions.

zoning. The act or condition of dividing a town or city into zones.

zoning, aesthetic. N. Zoning designed to encourage the preservation of beauty or aesthetic features in an area.

zoning, cluster. N. Zoning that permits small lot sizes and closely spaced homes along with large areas of public green space such as parks.

zoning, density. N. Zoning that emphasizes clustered housing and aims for a particular population density. See also *variance*.

APPENDIX

List of Common Abbreviations

1L. A first-year law student.

2L. A second-year law student.

3L. A third-year law student.

ABA. American Bar Association.

ABM. Anti-ballistic missile.

ACLU. American Civil Liberties Union.

ACRS. Accelerated cost recovery system.

ADA. Americans with Disabilities Act.

ADEA. Age Discrimination in Employment Act.

ARM. Adjustable rate mortgage.

BATFE. Bureau of Alcohol, Tobacco, Firearms and Explosives.

BLS. Bureau of Labor Statistics.

CDA. Communications Decency Act.

CDC. Centers for Disease Control and Prevention.

CFAA. Computer Fraud and Abuse Act.

C.I.F. Cost, insurance, and freight.

CIPA. Children's Internet Protection Act.

COBRA. Consolidated Omnibus Budget Reconciliation Act of 1985.

CPA. Certified public accountant.

CTBT. Comprehensive Test Ban Treaty.

DHS. Department of Homeland Security.

DMZ. Demilitarized zone.

DNI. Distributable net income.

DNS. Domain Name System.

DRM. Digital rights management.

EPA. Environmental Protection Agency.

ERA. Equal Rights Amendment.

ERISA. Employment Retirement Income Security Act of 1974.

ESOP. Employee stock ownership plan.

EU. European Union.

FAA. Federal Aviation Administration.

FBI. Federal Bureau of Investigation.

FCC. Federal Communications Commission.

FDA. Food and Drug Administration.

FDIC. Federal Deposit Insurance Corporation.

FEMA. Federal Emergency Management Agency.

FFL. Federal Firearms License.

FICA. Federal Insurance Contribution Act.

FOIA. Freedom of Information Act.

FSA. Flexible spending account.

List of Common Abbreviations

FTC. Federal Trade Commission.

FUD. Fear, uncertainty, and doubt.

GATT. General Agreement on Tariffs and Trade.

HIPAA. Health Insurance Portability and Accountability Act.

HMO. Health maintenance organization.

HSA. Health savings account.

ICANN. Internet Corporation for Assigned Names and Numbers.

INS. Immigration and Naturalization Services.

IPO. Initial public offering.

IRA. Individual retirement account.

IRS. Internal Revenue Service.

MPAA. Motion Picture Association of America.

NAFTA. North American Free Trade Agreement.

NASDAQ. National Association of Securities Dealers Automated Quotations.

NLRB. National Labor Relations Board.

NPT. Nuclear Nonproliferation Treaty.

NRA. National Rifle Association.

NRC. Nuclear Regulatory Commission.

OSHA. Occupational Safety and Health Act.

RIAA. Recording Industry Association of America.

RICO. Racketeer Influenced and Corrupt Organizations Act.

SEC. Securities and Exchange Commission.

SEP-IRA. Simplified Employee Pension Individual Retirement Account.

SLAPP. Strategic Lawsuit Against Public Participation.

TSA. Transportation Security Administration.

UCC. Uniform Commercial Code.

UCCC. Uniform Consumer Credit Code.

UGMA. Uniform Gifts to Minors Act.

UN. United Nations.

USA PATRIOT Act. Uniting and Strengthening America by Providing Appropriate Tools Required to Intercept and Obstruct Terrorism Act of 2001.

USCIS. United States Citizenship and Immigration Services.

UTMA. Uniform Transfers to Minors Act.

VA. United States Department of Veterans Affairs.

WHO. World Health Organization.

WIPO. World Intellectual Property Organization.

WTO. World Trade Organization.

ABOUT THE AUTHOR

Amy Hackney Blackwell received her AB from Duke University, her MA in history from Vanderbilt University, and her JD from the University of Virginia School of Law. She is an attorney and practiced law for several years. Besides writing and practicing law, she has also taught LSAT preparation classes and paralegal courses, as well as spending several years as a researcher in the University of Virginia Law Library.